THE DEVIL'S MOUSETRAP

Robert Campin
(d. 1444), *Triptych
of the Annunciation:*
right wing, *Joseph
in His Workshop.*
The Metropolitan
Museum of Art,
The Cloisters
Collection, 1956.
(56.70) All rights
reserved, The
Metropolitan
Museum of Art

The

DEVIL'S MOUSETRAP

Redemption
and
Colonial American
Literature

LINDA MUNK

New York   *Oxford*   •   Oxford University Press   1997

Oxford University Press

Oxford   New York
Athens   Auckland   Bangkok   Bogota   Bombay   Buenos Aires
Calcutta   Cape Town   Dar es Salaam   Delhi   Florence   Hong Kong
Istanbul   Karachi   Kuala Lumpur   Madras   Madrid   Melbourne
Mexico City   Nairobi   Paris   Singapore   Taipei   Tokyo   Toronto   Warsaw

and associated companies in
Berlin   Ibadan

PS
186
- M86
1997

Published by Oxford University Press, Inc.
198 Madison Avenue, New York, New York 10016

Oxford is a registered trademark of Oxford University Press

Library of Congress Cataloging-in-Publication Data
Munk, Linda.
The devil's mousetrap : redemption and colonial American
literature / Linda Munk.
p.   cm.
Includes bibliographical references and index.
ISBN 0-19-511494-9
1. American literature—Colonial period, ca. 1600–1775—History
and criticism.   2. Christian literature, American—Puritan authors—
History and criticism.   3. American literature—New England—
History and criticism.   4. Edwards, Jonathan, 1703–1758—Criticism
and interpretation.   5. Taylor, Edward, 1642–1729—Criticism and
interpretation.   6. Mather, Increase, 1639–1723—Literary art.
7. Puritan movements in literature.   8. Redemption in literature.
9. Puritans in literature.   I. Title.
PS186.M86   1997
810.9'382—DC20   96–41397

9 8 7 6 5 4 3 2 1

Printed in the United States of America
on acid-free paper

For
Cheyne, Marc-David, Natalie, Nina, Anthony

Preface

Religion stands on tip-toe in our land,
Readie to passe to the *American* strand.
                    George Herbert, "The Church Militant"

I write the Wonders of the CHRISTIAN RELIGION, flying from the Depra-
vations of Europe, to the American Strand.
                    Cotton Mather, *Magnalia Christi Americana*

Perry Miller wrote in 1939, "Recent writers on New England History have
tended to minimize the importance of abstract theology and of the pulpit, to
point out that whatever the theology, Puritan conduct can be explained without it. This conclusion has the advantage of appealing to an age that has no
relish for theology, and of making the task of writing about New England appreciably simpler."[1] All subjects connected with one another in the Puritan
mind; they were not departmentalized into literature, theology, and history.

What links the following chapters, essays in intellectual history, is the fact
of three colonial New England divines, Increase Mather, Jonathan Edwards,
and Edward Taylor, whose theology, however mediated, is set in models of
thought taken over from Judaism, biblical and postbiblical, and from the early
Church Fathers. Those are backgrounds of thought on which they drew. That
Saint Augustine's mousetrap is set at the start of the book is deliberate: it introduces and informs the close readings of Edwards, Mather, and Taylor that
follow. The idea of redemption as it developed in Judaism and in the early
Church had somehow to be drawn out; Puritan conduct cannot be explained
without it, and a mousetrap may catch him who a sermon flies. As well, the
mousetrap serves as a device to suggest how biblical exegesis was approached
by the early Fathers, whose perceptions of the relation between Old and New
Testaments, between type and antitype, are sometimes misrepresented to students of American literature. Used by the Fathers rhetorically to prove the

truth of Christian revelation, a typological reading of the two-part Bible is inseparable from the history of Christian apologetics.

Readers with no relish for theology who would like the Bible, the Fathers, the Rabbis, and Puritan millennialism to be reduced and boiled down to paraphrase, like jam, may dismiss this book. Even the most rigorously pruned catena of excerpts and proof-texts is hard going. If language used in the pulpit by Edwards, Mather, and Taylor is accurate and plain, it is also full of allusions to the Bible and the Apocrypha, to Puritan treatises, and to postbiblical exegesis, Jewish and Christian; and those allusions depend on a library of knowledge shared by the reader and the author. That library, alas, we no longer share.

As the spirit moved me, I take up the terms Old Testament, Hebrew Bible, Talmud, Pentateuch, New Testament, Scripture, Gospel, Christ, B.C., A.D., C.E., and B.C.E.; these are signs and proper names, not totems. Nor like a museum guide do I keep announcing to readers what they are looking at, where they have been, where they are headed, and why they should bother to keep on reading. There are pleasures in merely circulating, as Wallace Stevens knew. References given in the notes to primary sources may be inconsistent and uncoordinated: Church Fathers are cited from here and there, depending on where a reasonable English translation turned up. References to Migne's *Patrologia* are provided when I have them. Works by seventeenth-century Puritan Hebraists—Joseph Mede, Henry Ainsworth, and Thomas Brightman, for example—may be cited from more than one edition, depending on the library I was in at the time. This book was written in three countries using the holdings of six different libraries. Other inconsistencies there are too, but in a study of New England culture, they are authorized by Emerson: "A foolish consistency is the hobgoblin of little minds, adored by little statesmen and philosophers and divines."[2]

"I need hardly add that to demonstrate is not the same as to endorse"; Sacvan Bercovitch added that to an essay about New England Puritanism published in the late 1970s.[3] Confusing methodology and claim makes the task of reading and of writing about one's reading appreciably simpler. But this book makes no claims, promotes no ideology, stands on no pulpit, takes no metaphysical or doctrinal position, rarely draws conclusions, and does not argue. The reader can draw his or her own conclusions. Nor by virtue of practice or training should I be writing about religion: beside the theologian's, my learning is inadequate. I have no Hebrew to speak of, my Greek and Latin are poor, and my knowledge of Jewish and Christian biblical exegesis is fragmentary. Still, outsiders may notice things.

Experiments in methodology, not a methodological project, this book tries to make sense of early American texts against their conventions and against the theological certainties of their authors. I proceed inductively. "My personal way has been from the observed detail to ever broadening units which rest, to an increasing degree, on speculation" (Leo Spitzer). Each of the chapters is independent; each one is intended to gloss the others; they are best read in order, cumulatively. The cohesive principle is cross-reference and allusion. Expediency determines the form. To cite Marianne Moore's remarks about Hebrew poetry: "Ecstasy affords / the occasion and expediency determines the form."

Acknowledgments

Without the generosity of other scholars, theologians especially, this book could not have been written. On Saint Augustine, I have consulted Carol Harrison, who directed me to treatises and sermons I could not have found on my own. Robert Hayward, the angel of great counsel, untangled for me the matter of the angel of the Lord, the subject of chapter 2. He also translated for me the Aramaic Targums I needed, took me through the rabbinic texts cited in chapters 2 and 4, and translated from the Greek text Gregory of Nyssa's sermon on the nativity. On the preexistent logos and its rhetorical use in early Christian apologetics, Andrew Louth directed me to apposite texts by Justin Martyr, Tertullian, and Irenaeus. Sheridan Gilley and Alan Ford have shared their understanding of millennialism and Calvinism; the smallest clue can set a chapter right, or can at least save it from some of the errors made by its author, who is thankful for small mercies. The support of two distinguished Americanists, Charles W. Mignon and Emory Elliott, has been invaluable. Eleanor Cook first taught me about American poetry and prose. If I did not abandon this book, it is because these scholars did not abandon me.

Two colleagues at the University of Toronto have been gracious about the timing of study leave: Catherine Rubincam, Dean of Humanities at Erindale College, and Brian Corman, Acting Chairman of the Department of English (1994–95). This project took rough shape in 1993 at the University of Durham, England. Chapter 2 on Jonathan Edwards was written and rewritten in Bern, Switzerland. The project was more or less completed during the academic year 1995–96, when I was in residence at Wolfson College, University of Oxford. Sections of chapter 4 on Edward Taylor were given as short papers at the University of Durham and in Oxford at the Twelfth Annual Patristics Conference (1995).

I should like to acknowledge the courtesies extended to me by librarians and keepers of rare books in Canada and in England, especially the staff of Palace Green Library, University of Durham; Knox College and Trinity College Libraries, University of Toronto; the Theology Faculty Library, University of Oxford; and, at the Bodleian Library, by the well-tempered staff in Duke Humphrey's.

Toronto/Bern   L. M.
September 1996

Contents

THE DEVIL'S MOUSETRAP

CHAPTER ONE

The Devil's Mousetrap

But if there were not a strong power of Satan in us, how comes it that the blood of Christ must be shed, to destroy him that had the power of death, *that is the Devil*.

John Cotton (1585–1652)[1]

And what did our Redeemer do to him who held us captive? For our ransom He held out His Cross as a trap [*muscipula*]; he placed in It as bait His Blood.

Saint Augustine

Saint Augustine's phrase "Muscipula Diaboli" (the Devil's mousetrap) is cited by the distinguished art historian Meyer Schapiro in an essay published in 1945: "'Muscipula Diaboli,' The Symbolism of the Mérode Altarpiece." In the right wing of the triptych (by the Master of Flémalle, Robert Campin), Joseph, the husband of Mary, is portrayed as an artisan who fashions intricate wooden mousetraps. "Not only is the presence of Joseph in the context of the *Annunciation* exceptional in Christian art," Schapiro writes, "we are surprised also that his craft of carpentry should be applied to something so piquant and marginal in métier."[2]

But the mousetrap is not marginal, nor from a theological point of view is it insignificant: "this detail of the mousetrap is more than a whimsical invention of the artist suggested by Joseph's occupation." Its context, we are told, is informed by Saint Augustine, who in his sermons employs the figure of the mousetrap "to explain the necessity of the incarnation":

> The devil exulted when Christ died [writes Augustine], but by this very death of Christ the devil was vanquished, as if he had swallowed the bait in the mousetrap. He rejoiced in Christ's death, like a bailiff of death. What he rejoiced in was then his own undoing. The cross of the Lord was the devil's mousetrap [*muscipula diaboli*]; the bait by which he was caught was the Lord's death.[3]

Exsultavit diabolus quando mortuus est Christus, et in ipsa morte Christi est diabolus victus: tamquam in muscipula escam accepit. Gaudebat ad mortem quasi praepositus mortis. Ad quod gaudebat, inde illi tensum est. Muscipula diaboli, crux Domini: esca qua caperetur, mors Domini.

Looking closely at the small mousetrap in the Mérode Altarpiece, one can indeed make out the figure of a wooden cross. Other instruments of the Passion appear on Joseph's work bench: nails, pliers, hammer, a spearlike knife, a small bowl. The metaphor of the mousetrap "appealed to St. Augustine as an especially happy figure of the Redemption; it occurs no less than three times in his writings."[4] Here, in another of Augustine's sermons, the mousetrap is again metonymy for the cross, and thus for the crucifixion:

> We fell into the hands of the prince of this world, who seduced Adam, and made him his servant, and began to possess us as his slaves. But the Redeemer came, and the seducer was overcome. And what did our Redeemer do to him who held us captive? For our ransom He held out His Cross as a trap; he placed in It as bait His Blood.[5]

> Et quid fecit Redemptor noster captivatori nostro? Ad pretium nostrum tetendit muscipulum crucem sua: posuit ibi quasi escam sanguinem suum.

Within its narrow compass, Augustine's "fable" contains a précis of the history of redemption as it was understood in the early Church from the time of Irenaeus (ca. 130–ca. 200), Bishop of Lyons, who (according to some theologians) "introduced the theory that the death of Christ was a ransom paid to the Devil."[6] At the Fall, Satan, "the prince of this world," seduced Adam, who, along with his descendants, became a slave to sin and to death. In order to release us from captivity, thus from bondage to death, sin and the Devil, Jesus Christ, the second Adam, offered Satan a ransom; that ransom was the Redeemer's blood, his death on the cross. For the first thousand years or so of Christian history, until it was gradually displaced by Anselm of Canterbury's unfortunate theory of "satisfaction," the ransom theory of the atonement was "the dominant orthodox theory on the subject."[7] The present chapter, an extended, wandering gloss on Augustine's mousetrap, begins by focusing on the meaning of redemption, word and event, as it moves through the Hebrew Bible and into the New Testament, often by way of the Septuagint (LXX)— the ancient Jewish translation of the Hebrew Bible into Greek.

❖   ❖   ❖

Two Hebrew terms for "redeem" are ga'al and padha. Used almost interchangeably in the Hebrew Bible, according to David Daube, ga'al "primarily signifies 'to recover a man or thing that had once belonged to you and your

family but had got lost.'" The other term, *padha*, used by the Deuteronomist
to characterize God's acts at the time of the Exodus, means "the deliverance
of men or things from their doom." The notion of *ga'al* "is central to the social
legislation of Old Testament times—regarding the recovery of a relative enslaved, of family property alienated, of the blood of a murdered relative," and
so on.[8] If one of your relatives had sold himself into slavery, Daube tells us, "it
was your right and duty to 'recover,' *ga'al*, the enslaved relative." The bond of
kinship which commits God to the duty of redemption is not, of course, the
law of blood, but the law of election.[9]

In the Book of Exodus, the children of Israel are enslaved in Egypt by
Pharaoh; "God acts as a father demanding back his son from the tyrant who
has enslaved him." ("Thus saith the Lord, Israel is my son, even my firstborn:
And I say unto thee, Let my son go, that he may serve me" [Exod. 4:22–23].)
In Augustine's parable of the mousetrap, it is the Devil from whom mankind
is ransomed or redeemed by Christ:

> O Good Merchant [Augustine pleads], buy us. Why should I say buy us, when
> we ought to give thee thanks that Thou hast bought us? . . . Any one can buy
> his servant, create him he cannot; but the Lord both created and redeemed His
> servants; created them that they might be; redeemed them that they might not
> be captives ever. . . . And what did our Redeemer to him who held us cap-
> tive? For our ransom He held out His Cross as a trap [*muscipula*]; he placed in It
> as bait his own Blood.[10]

Both *ga'al* and *padha* (and their word groups) are given in the English Bible
as "to ransom" and "to redeem": "But because the Lord loved you . . . hath
the Lord . . . redeemed [*padha*; LXX *lutron*] you out of the house of bond-
men, from the hand of Pharaoh king of Egypt" (Deut. 7:8). "For the Lord has
redeemed [*padha*] Jacob, and ransomed [*ga'al*] him from the hand of him that
was stronger than they" (Jer. 31:11). "And the ransomed [*padha*] of the Lord
shall return, and come to Zion with songs and everlasting joy upon their
heads" (Isa. 35:11). "I will ransom [*padha*] them from the power of the grave; I
will redeem [*ga'al*] them from death" (Hos. 13:14). "Wherefore say unto the
children of Israel, I am the Lord, and I will bring you out from under the bur-
dens of the Egyptians, and I will rid you out of their bondage, and I will redeem [*ga'al*] you with a stretched out arm . . ." (Exod. 6:6). "Let Israel hope
in the Lord: for with the Lord there is mercy, and with him is plenteous redemption. And he shall redeem [*padha*] Israel from all his iniquities" (Ps.
130:7–8). Personified, those iniquities may be called "Satan" and his
metonymic eqivalents, which include Leviathan, Rahab, Behemoth, and
other sea monsters.

In a broad sense, the Hebrew words *padha* and *ga'al* mean "to free," sometimes by repayment that may be literal or figurative. Moses, for example, is instructed to "redeem" [*padha*; LXX *lutron*] "every firstling of an ass"; "the first born of man"; "the first born of thy sons" (Exod. 13:13–15; 34:20). In Second Isaiah, the Lord says to a personified Jerusalem, the "captive daughter of Zion": "Ye have sold yourselves for nought; and ye shall be redeemed [*ga'al*; LXX *lutron*] without money" (Isa. 52:3). Earlier in Isaiah the Hebrew word *kopher*, usually given as "atonement" in the AV, is translated as "ransom": "For I am the Lord thy God, the Holy One of Israel, thy Saviour: I gave Egypt for thy ransom [*kopher*; LXX *lutron*]" (Isa. 43:1–3). We still speak about "covering" someone's debt. To cite Daube, in Judaism, as in Christianity, "God would, in fact, he must, 'recover' those who were his property, his children, friends or slaves."[11]

The Hebrew term for "redeemer" (*gô'el*; cognate with *ga'al*) appears in a well-known verse from Job: "For I know that my redeemer liveth and that he shall stand at the latter day upon the earth" (19:25). Compare Psalm 78, wherein the redeemer, the *gô'el*, is compared to a rock: "And they remembered that God was their rock, and the high God their redeemer"(78:35). "Redeemer" appears at least a dozen times in Isaiah: "As for our redeemer, the Lord of Hosts is his name, the Holy one of Israel" (47:4); "And the Redeemer shall come to Zion, and unto them that turn from transgression in Jacob, saith the Lord" (59:20). Below, the prophet rehearses events of the Exodus, Israel's redemption from bondage:

> In all their affliction he was afflicted, and the angel of his presence saved them: in his love and in his pity he redeemed [*ga'al*; LXX *lutron*] them; and he bare them, and carried them all the days of old. But they rebelled and vexed his holy Spirit: therefore he was turned to be their enemy, and he fought against them. Then he remembered the days of old, Moses and his people, saying, Where is he that brought them up out of the sea with the shepherd of his flock? where is he that put his holy Spirit within him? That led them by the right hand of Moses with his glorious arm, dividing the waters before them, to make himself an everlasting name? . . . thou, O Lord art our father, our redeemer [*gô 'el*]; thy name is from everlasting. (Isa. 63:9–16)

Israel is "redeemed" [*ga'al*] and "purchased" from Egypt, "the house of bondage" (Exod. 13:3), where Pharaoh (portrayed as the Devil in the thirteenth-century *Bible Moralisée*)[12] once held Israel, his slave or his servant (Heb. *ebed*), captive: "Thou in thy mercy hast led forth the people which thou hath redeemed [*ga'al*]. . . . Fear and dread shall fall upon them . . . till thy people pass over, O Lord, till the people pass over which thou hast purchased" (Exod. 15:13, 16). Throughout Scripture, God's purchase or redemption of Israel from slavery in Egypt is recalled and recited: "Art thou not it that hath cut Rahab, and wounded the dragon? Art thou not it which has dried the sea, the waters of the great deep; that hath made the depths of the sea a way for the ransomed [*ga'al*] to pass over?" (Isa. 51:10–11). The Children of Israel are pursued by Pharaoh and his great army as far as the Red Sea when, like a giant trap or snare, it closes over them. "He rebuked the Red sea also, and it was dried up: so he led them through the depths, as through the wilderness. And he saved them from the hand of him that hated them, and redeemed [*ga'al*] them from the hand of the enemy" (Ps. 106:9–11).

We shall explore briefly the idea of redemption as it moves into the New Testament. One word translated as "redeem" in the English Bible is the Greek *agorazo* and its cognates, literally "to buy" or "to purchase." In Galatians, Paul writes: "Christ hath redeemed [*exagorasen*] us from the curse of the law, being made a curse for us . . ." (3:13). "But when the fulness of the time was come, God sent forth his Son, made of a woman, made under the law, To redeem [*exagorase*] them that were under the law . . ." (4:4–5). Paul's model of chiasmus is noteworthy: those "under the law" are redeemed from "the curse of the law" by Christ, who on their behalf is "made a curse [*katara*]." If the children of Israel were once in bondage to Pharaoh, they are now, according to Paul, in bondage to the Law (*nomos*): observing "days, and months, and times, and years," they "desire again to be in bondage" (Gal. 4:9–10). In Paul's drama of redemption, the Jewish Law, the "ministration of death" (2 Cor. 3:7), is no more than an instrument of bondage; at the same time, it is metonymy for the hostile forces of "this present evil world" (Gal. 1:4).[13]

For Augustine, before the Devil was captured by the cross—before Christ offered his blood as bait, as a ransom paid to free mankind from bondage—we were slaves to sin and death (terms interchangeable with the Devil or Satan, the Evil One). The economy of the crucifixion is reiterated in the Epistle to the Hebrews: Christ took on flesh and blood "that through death he might destroy him that had the power of death, that is, the devil; And deliver them who through fear of death were all their lifetime subject to bondage [or to slavery]" (2:14–15). All these tropes of victory over demonic tyrants that held or hold us captive—sin, death, the Devil, Pharaoh, the "elements of the world" (Gal. 4:3), Satan, the Law, Antichrist, or, for the Reformers, the Vicar of Rome, the Whore of Babylon—resonate with the prototype of bondage, captivity, and redemption: the Exodus of Israel from Egypt. "Remember thy congregation, which thou hast purchased of old: the rod of thy inheritance which thou hast redeemed [*ga'al*; LXX *lutron*]; this mount Zion, wherein thou hast dwelt" (Ps. 74:2). The Lord who spoke to Moses from the burning bush and gave the Decalogue on Sinai is the Lord of his son Israel's redemption from Pharaoh: "I am the Lord thy God, which have brought thee out of the land of Egypt, out of the house of bondage" (Exod. 20:2).

Another word translated as "redeem" and as "ransom" in the New Testament (the King James Version, or AV, is cited throughout) is the Greek *lutroo* with its derivatives, whose root meaning is to undo, to loosen, to dissolve:[14] "Even as the Son of man came not to be ministered unto, but to minister, and to give his life a ransom [*lutron*] for many" (Matt. 20:28); "Who gave himself a ransom [*antilutron*] for all, to be testified in due time" (1 Tim. 2:6). (Thus a question posed by several early Fathers: "To whom was the ransom paid"?) Augustine's mousetrap is metonymy for the cross and for the blood shed on the cross. In turn, the cross is metonymy for redemption "by means of death," to follow Hebrews 9:15, a text wherein the blood of Christ is compared to the expiatory sacrifice or sin offering made by the high priest on the Day of Atonement. Here the yearly offering made by the high priest (who enters through the temple veil into the Holy of Holies) is said by the author of Hebrews to be a "figure" or parable (*parabole*) of the blood shed on the cross: "Neither by the blood of goats and calves, but by his own blood he entered in once into the holy place, having obtained eternal redemption [*lutron*] for us" (9:12). As priest and as sacrifice, Christ "offered himself without spot to God" (9:14); that offering was made "for the redemption of the transgressions that were under the first testament" (9:15).

The first epistle of Peter includes the phrase "a lamb without blemish": "Forasmuch as ye know that ye were not redeemed [*lutron*] with corruptible things, as silver and gold . . . But with the precious blood of Christ, as of a lamb without blemish and without spot" (1 Pet. 1:18–19). The phrase "lamb without blemish" evokes its prototype, the sacrificial "lamb without blemish" of Hebrew Scripture, an image evoked by the author of Revelation, wherein redemption is depicted as a blood offering: "in the midst of the throne and of the four beasts, and in the midst of the elders stood a Lamb as it had been slain"; falling down before the Lamb, the beasts and the elders sing: "for thou wast slain, and hast redeemed [*agorazo*] us to God by thy blood" (5:6, 9). Further on in Revelation, we read that someone called "the accuser [*kategor*] of the brethren is cast down," overcome "by the blood of the lamb" (Rev. 12:10–11). Again, the *kategor* or accuser is another name for Satan. The slain lamb of Revelation is the "Lamb of God [*amnos tou theou*], which taketh away the sin [*hamartia*] of the world" (John 1:29).[15]

According to Cyril of Alexandria (fifth century), the slain lamb of the crucifixion was "foreshadowed" in the Old Testament: "Now the Lamb, foreshadowed of old in types, is led to the slaughter as a spotless sacrifice for all in order to do away with the sin of the world, to overthrow the destroyer of mankind, to annihilate death by dying for all, to rid us of the curse which lay upon us. . . . For when we were guilty of many sins, and for that reason were liable to death and corruption, the Father gave His Son as a ransom [*antilutron*], one for all."[16]

One sacrificial lamb in particular should be introduced: the young lamb or kid [Heb. *seh*] of the Passover. In his first letter to the Corinthians, Paul explicitly refers to Christ as the "passover": "For even Christ our passover [*pascha*] is sacrificed for us" (5:7), an allusion to Exodus 12, in which Moses and Aaron are instructed by God to

> Speak ye unto all the congregation of Israel, saying, In the tenth day of this month they shall take to them every man a lamb [*seh*]. . . . Your lamb shall be without blemish, a male of the first year: ye shall take it out from the sheep or from the goats: And ye shall keep it up until the fourteenth day of the same month: and the whole assembly of the congregation of Israel shall kill it in the evening. And they shall take of the blood, and strike it on the two side posts and on the upper door post of the houses, wherein they shall eat it. (12:3–8)

The saving blood of the paschal lamb (or kid), later conflated by Christian exegetes with the saving blood of Christ, is said to be the Lord's "token" or sign (Heb. *oth*) (12:22, 13). (The same word is used to signify the mark [*oth*] set upon Cain [Gen. 4:15].) Below the mysterious angel of destruction appears; Moses says to the elders: "For the Lord will pass through to smite the Egyptians; and when he seeth the blood upon the lintel, and on the two side posts, the Lord will pass over the door, and will not suffer the destroyer [Heb. *mashit*] to come into your houses to smite you" (Exod. 12:23). Like the saving blood sprinkled on the lintels and doorposts on the night of the first Passover, the circumcision of Abraham is said to be "a token [*oth*] of the covenant" (Gen. 17:11). A midrash on Exodus 12:8 connects the two events—the blood marked on the doors and the blood of circumcision: "Why did God protect them [the Israelites] through blood? So that He should remember in their favour the blood of Abraham's circumcision. On account of two kinds of blood were Israel redeemed from Egypt—the blood of the Passover and the blood of the circumcision."[17] Another midrash, cited in Geza Vermes's remarkable essay on Genesis 22 (the binding of Isaac), links that crucial event to the Exodus: "And when I see the blood [on the doors], I will pass over you (Ex. xii.13)—I see the blood of the Binding of Isaac."[18] (Jon Levenson speaks about the "apotropaic effect of the blood of the paschal lamb."[19]) Hence, in a detail we return to later, the Rabbis have conflated midrashically the saving blood of the paschal lamb and the Akedah.

Most compelling about the blood marked on the doors in Egypt is its adaptation into Christian iconography as a commentary on and foreshadowing of the crucifixion (which Paul explicates in terms of the Passover). In the Epistle to the Hebrews "the law" (*nomos*) is said to be a "shadow [*skia*] of good things to come, and not the very image of the things [*eikona ton pragmaton*]" (10:1). The comparison between the shadowy, typical ritual of the Exodus event and the thing itself, between figure and fulfillment, informs the iconography of an early twelfth-century altar crucifix, with its scenes from the Passover story. In one scene, a man writes on the lintel of a tall house the Hebrew letter *tav*, a sign of the Israelites' redemption from bondage and the precursor of the cross as talisman.[20] In another scene, Aaron the high priest marks the letter *tav* on the people's foreheads, an episode that does not figure in the Exodus story at all but evokes a passage from Ezekiel that is itself a midrash or commentary on the lamb's blood marked on the doors at the Passover: "Go through the midst of the city, through the midst of Jerusalem, and set a mark [*tav*] upon the foreheads of the men that sigh and that cry for all the abominations that be done in the midst therof" (Ezek. 9:4). Those with marked foreheads will be saved; those without the Lord's *tav* or mark will be slain. The theme of the marking of foreheads as a sign of salvation, Cain's included, modulates into John's vision in Revelation: "Hurt not the earth, neither the sea, nor the trees, till we have sealed the servants of our God in their foreheads" with the "seal [*sphragida*] of the living God" (7:3, 2).[21]

In terms of the narrative pattern of the Hebrew Bible, what is especially notable about the event of the Lord's passing over or turning away from doors marked with the "apotropaic" blood of the paschal lamb (or the Destroying Angel's turning away from those doors) is its function as a fixed sign of redemption from bondage. Moses is instructed to "observe this thing for an ordinance to thee"; the ordinance "is the sacrifice of the Lord's passover, who passed over the houses of the children of Israel in Egypt, when he smote the Egyptians, and delivered our houses" (Exod. 12:27). Then, because of a divine and supernatural trick, Pharaoh (or bondage) is destroyed by the waters of the Red Sea, and God's praises are sung by the Israelites in a well-known ode of triumph: "Thou in thy mercy hast led forth the people which thou hast redeemed [*ga'al*]. . . . Fear and dread shall fall upon them . . . till thy people pass over, O Lord, till the people pass over, which thou hast purchased" (15:13, 16). Redemption from Egypt is a sign of God's mercy to his people, Israel; Psalm 77 includes:

> I will remember the works of the Lord: surely I will remember thy wonders of old. . . . Thou art the God that doest wonders: thou hast declared thy strength among the people. Thou hast with thine arm redeemed [*ga'al*] thy people. . . . The waters saw thee, O God, the waters saw thee; they were afraid: the depths also were troubled. . . . Thou leddest thy people like a flock by the hand of Moses and Aaron. (11–20)

Psalm 78 rehearses in catalogue the Exodus, admonishing the backsliding Israelites, who in their pride have forgotten God's mercy to them: the Lord "divided the sea"; "led them with a cloud"; "clave the rocks in the wilderness"; "brought streams also out of the rock"; "rained down manna." In short, the Lord redeemed them from bondage and "delivered [*padha*] them from the enemy," the hated Egyptians, their taskmasters. The Lord "made his own people to go forth like sheep, and guided them in the wilderness like a flock"; "He chose David also his servant, and took him from the sheepfolds . . . to feed Jacob his people and Israel his inheritance." These saving events of the Exodus are adduced in the New Testament as proof-texts: the author of Hebrews, for instance, who evokes an extended series of redemptive acts (including the binding of Isaac), says of Moses, "Through faith he kept the passover, and the sprinkling of blood, lest he that destroyed the firstborn should touch them. By faith they passed through the Red sea as by dry land: which the Egyptians assaying to do were drowned" (Heb. 11:28–29).

❖   ❖   ❖

We shall now focus on the Christian typology of the Exodus. For Paul, the miraculous rock in the wilderness "was Christ"; we were "baptized" in the pillar of cloud and in the Red Sea, and the backsliding Israelites were warning examples, types (*tupoi*) of ourselves:

> Moreover, brethren, I would not that ye should be ignorant, how that all our fathers were under the cloud, and all passed through the sea; And all were baptized unto Moses in the cloud and in the sea; And all did eat the same spiritual meat; And all did drink the same spiritual drink: for they drank of that spiritual Rock that followed them: and that Rock was Christ. But with many of them God was not well pleased: for they were overthrown in the wilderness. Now these things were our examples [*tupoi*], to the intent we should not lust after evil things, as they also lusted. (1 Cor. 10:1–6)

Augustine, identifying Pharaoh with the Devil and the Red Sea with the waters of baptism, transforms the pursuing Egyptians into personified sins, "blotted out" at the Red Sea: "we have been brought out of Egypt where we were in bondage to the devil, as unto Pharaoh, where we were busied with works of clay in earthly desires and therein had sore labour. . . . Brought out hence we were made to pass through Baptism, as the Red Sea (red, because hallowed by the blood of Christ) with all our enemies dead that followed after us, that is, all our sins blotted out."[22] In the same vein, Theodoret (ca. 393–ca. 466), one of the Antiochene Fathers, constructs an ingenious set of parallels for the Exodus events: "The Red Sea is a type of the baptismal font; the cloud, of the Holy Spirit; Moses, of the Saviour Christ; his rod, of the Cross; Pharaoh, of the devil; the Egyptians, of the demons; manna, of the eucharist food; and the water which sprang from the rock, of the saving blood of Christ."[23] To read as a type or figure of Christ's blood the water "that came out abundantly" from the rock in the wilderness (Num. 20:11) is to take for granted, as Paul does, that the rock is Christ, that the wound in Christ's side corresponds to the cleft in the rock; it is also to conflate the rock, the cleft in the rock, and the water that sprang from the rock (when Moses smote it twice with his rod) with the water of baptism *and* with the apotropaic blood of the first paschal lamb, marked on the lintels and doorposts of the Israelites' houses to save their firstborn sons from the wrath of the Destroying Angel.[24]

Paul refers to Christ as the "passover," just as he refers to Christ as the miraculous rock: "For even Christ our passover [*pascha*] is sacrificed for us." The Fourth Gospel presents the story of the Passion in terms of what A. M. Ramsey calls "the sacrificial victim who expiates sin and brings communion between God and man, slain as he is at the passover time . . . and slain as a peace offering without the breaking of a bone."[25]

> But when they [the soldiers] came to Jesus, and saw that he was dead already, they brake not his legs: But one of the soldiers with a spear pierced his side, and forthwith there came out blood and water. . . . For these things were done, that the scripture [*graphe*] should be fulfilled [*plerothe*], A bone of him shall not be broken. (John 19:33–34, 36)

Thus in the Fourth Gospel the slaying of the paschal lamb is said to be "fulfilled" in the crucifixion (although in Judaism the paschal lamb was not considered an expiatory sacrifice). In Exodus 12, as we have seen, Moses and Aaron are instructed to keep the unblemished paschal lamb "until the fourteenth day of the same month: and the whole assembly of Israel shall kill it in the evening. And they shall take of the blood, and strike it on the two side posts and on the upper door post of the houses, wherein they shall eat it" (12:3–8). The manner in which the lamb shall be eaten is also specified in Exodus 12: "In one house shall it be eaten; thou shalt not carry forth ought of the flesh abroad out of the house; neither shall ye break a bone thereof" (12:46). Alluding directly to Exodus 12, Psalm 34 reads: "He [the righteous] keepeth all his bones: not one of them is broken" (34:20).

Parallels drawn between the blood of the paschal lamb "sprinkled" on the doors of the Israelites and the blood of Christ are commonplace in apologetic writings of the early Church. Following Paul and John, Justin Martyr (ca. 100–ca. 165), in his dialogue with Trypho, an educated Jew, connects the death of the paschal lamb to the crucifixion, the blood of the lamb to the blood of Christ, and those who slayed the paschal lamb to the Jews, redeemed "from death" through the blood of Christ just as their fathers were redeemed from Egypt:

> And the blood of the passover, sprinkled on each man's door-posts and lintel, delivered those who were saved in Egypt. . . . For the passover was Christ,

who was afterwards sacrificed, as also Isaiah said, "He was led as a sheep to the slaughter" [Isa. 53:7]. And it is written, that on the day of the passover you seized Him, and that also during the passover you crucified Him. And as the blood of the passover saved those who were in Egypt, so also the blood of Christ will deliver from death those who have believed. Would God, then, have been deceived if this sign had not been above the doors? I do not say that; but I affirm that He announced beforehand the future salvation for the human race through the blood of Christ.[26]

The alignment of the saving blood marked on the doors and the saving blood of Christ is found in the thirteenth-century *Bible Moralisée*, in which a roundel depicting the slaying of the paschal lamb is placed directly above the roundel of the cross. The blood flowing down from the lamb into a bowl alludes to the blood flowing from Christ's side, just as the knife used to slay the lamb alludes to Longinus's spear. Off to one side, the text reads: "The sacrifice of this lamb signifies the sacrifice of Jesus Christ on the Cross."[27] Similarly, and again glossing its referent, the event of the cross, the paschal lamb is shown on several twelfth-century altar crosses reproduced in Gertrud Schiller's study of Christian iconography. In one picture, the slaughtered lamb is placed over the threshold of the house, its blood flowing into a chalice; in another, Aaron the high priest marks a tall house with the Hebrew letter *tav*, his bowl or ink pot presumably filled with the blood of the lamb lying in the doorway. Another, less familiar version of Christ as paschal lamb is found on the Klosterneuburg Altar, where the bringing in of the lamb, identified as "Agnus Paschalis," is coordinated with Christ's entry into Jerusalem.[28]

For some early Church Fathers, the efficacy of the saving blood marked on the lintels and doorposts in Egypt (the "event") *depended* in a mysterious way on its fulfillment or completion or "afterlife"—the blood shed on the cross.[29] According to Melito, second-century Bishop of Sardis, "the mystery of the Lord [was] enacted in the sheep, the life of the Lord in the sacrifice of the sheep, the type of the Lord in the death of the sheep." That the Destroying Angel did not "smite Israel," Melito contends, is *because* the blood of the paschal lamb was a figure or type of the blood of Christ. For Melito, then, figures or types are by no means empty signs, shadows without substance. Types partake of the *logos* they are presumed to signify; the *logos* is implicit in the type, is coincident with the type. Thus Melito questions the Destroying Angel: "Tell me, angel, what stayed thy hand, the sacrifice of the sheep or the life of the Lord? The death of the sheep, or the type of the Lord?"[30] A midrash cited earlier in the present chapter attributes the efficacy of the blood marked on the doors in Egypt to Isaac's sacrifice in Genesis 22: "And when I see the blood, I will pass over you (Ex. xii.13)—I see the blood of the Binding of Isaac."[31]

John Chrysostom (ca. 347–407) echoes Melito, insisting "that the blood sprinkled on the lintels of Jewish homes at the first Passover was effective *because it was a type of the blood of Christ.*"[32] Henri de Lubac refers to "l'exégèse spirituelle des Pères"; both Melito and John Chrysostom focus on what they perceive to be the spiritual sense of the Exodus, its *hyponoia.*[33] Implicit in the blood sprinkled on the lintels and doorposts of the Israelites' houses is its spiritual sense—the blood of Christ on the cross. When the mysterious *mashit* of Exodus 12 passed over the houses of the Israelites, he saw on their lintels and doorposts the blood of the binding of Jesus Christ.

❖   ❖   ❖

The "lamb [*seh*] without blemish," the paschal lamb of Exodus, may be either a young sheep or a young goat, a kid ("The lamb shall be without blemish, a male of the first year: ye shall take it out from the sheep or from the goats"). In Genesis 22, the Akedah or binding of Isaac, the same Hebrew word, *seh,* is used to signify the absent lamb: "Behold the fire and the wood," Isaac remarks to his father, "but where is the lamb [*seh*] for a burnt offering?" (22:7). Abraham replies: "My son, God will provide himself a lamb for a burnt offering."

> And they came to the place which God had told him of; and Abraham built an altar there, and laid the wood in order, and bound Isaac his son, and laid him on the altar upon the wood. And Abraham stretched forth his hand, and took the knife to slay his son. And the angel of the Lord called unto him out of heaven, and said, Abraham, Abraham: and he said, Here am I. (22:9–11)

When Abraham looks up, he sees a ram "caught in a thicket by his horns: and Abraham went and took the ram, and offered him up for a burnt offering in the stead of his son" (22:13). Rabbinic exegesis emphasizes the voluntariness of Isaac's sacrifice, and it is Isaac's willingness to suffer death that Vermes focuses on in his study of the relation between the crucifixion and the Akedah.[34] In Christian exegesis, as a typological sacrifice *ante legem,* the event was sometimes understood not only as a type of the crucifixion but also as "a prefiguration of the sacrifice of Christ in the Eucharist."[35]

That Isaac carrying the wood for his own sacrifice is a type or figure of Christ carrying the cross is a standard topos of early Christian expositors, as is the link between the thicket in which the ram was caught by its horns and the crown of thorns. But again, what for me is most remarkable about Chrysostom's reading of the Akedah is the relation between the two events, which for him somehow coexist. At the sacrifice of Isaac, Chrysostom writes, the matter (*pragma*) was hidden or concealed, whereas at the sacrifice of Christ the matter "came out" and was made plain. The *pragma* was common to both events, but "in a different degree of revelation" (to cite K. J. Woollcombe).[36] Often obscured or ignored by twentieth-century scholars, the patristic approach to typology ("l'exégèse spirituelle des Péres"), whereby the divine *pragma* is inherent and therefore present in the type, informs Melito's and Chrysostom's passages on the efficacy of the saving blood marked on the lintels, cited above. Type and antitype are by all means historical: the blood marked on the doors in Egypt to avert the *mashit*, the Destroying Angel of Exodus 12, is real, as is the blood shed on the cross to redeem mankind from the Devil, sin, and death. Likewise the binding of Isaac and the crucifixion are within the stream of historical time. But for the Church Fathers (as for the first-century Jewish philosopher Philo of Alexandria), "historical" events of the Old Testament included a concealed, privileged sense, and could be read allegorically.[37] To recite Augustine's well-known model of concealment and revelation: "The New Testament lies hidden in the Old; the Old Testament is revealed in the New": *In Vetere Novum lateat, et in Novo Vetis pateat.*[38]

Connections drawn by Christian expositors between the binding of Isaac and the crucifixion are familiar even to those unaware of biblical exegesis in its written form: one of the typological windows in Canterbury Cathedral, for example, depicts Isaac bound and lying on the cross-shaped, chiastic faggots of the altar, a conflation of the binding of Isaac with Christ on his way to and fixed onto the cross.[39] Isaac's cross-shaped pieces of wood are depicted also in windows at Bourges and at Chartres.[40] The figural relation between Isaac and Christ is explicated in the *Biblia Pauperum*, a late-medieval compendium of types wherein eighty events or types of the Old Testament are shown flanking their New Testament antitypes, in a way of organizing pictorial space that suggests the christocentric model informing a figural reading of the Christian two-part Bible. Two plates in the series include Isaac: Christ bearing the wooden cross, and the crucifixion.[41] In the first, Christ is flanked by two scenes: Abraham and Isaac on their way to Mount Moriah, and the widow woman of Zeraphath (1 Kings 17:8–12), whose two sticks of wood, held in the form of an X, are said to be "mystical symbols of the cross." In the rendering of Abraham and Isaac, the father leads, helped along by a walking stick and carrying with him a long knife and the fire for the sacrifice; the son follows him, carrying a bundle of faggots on his shoulder, in a visual parallel to the cross shouldered by Christ. In the background the ram appears, as does the altar. The text written beneath the scenes reads: "The boy carrying the pieces of wood prefigures you O Christ."

Proof-texts are then assembled: a shorthand allusion to Jeremiah, another to Ezekiel, another to the well-known verse from Isaiah 53, "He is brought as a lamb to the slaughter" (AV)—a lamb intended by the compilers of the *Biblia Pauperum* to signify both Isaac and Christ; just as in the passage cited above from Justin Martyr, the same verse from Isaiah is used to link Christ with the slain paschal lamb of Exodus 12, whose blood was daubed on the houses of the Israelites. Although in this case Isaiah's lamb acts as a linking reference between the sacrifice of Isaac and the crucifixion, it also establishes a link between the suffering servant of Isaiah 53 and Christ, who, as lamb and as servant, gave his life as "a ransom [*lutron*] for many" (Matt. 20:28). Similarly, the lamblike servant of Isaiah "was wounded for our transgressions, he was bruised for our iniquities . . . and with his stripes we are healed. . . . He was oppressed, and he was afflicted, yet he opened not his mouth: he is brought as a lamb [*seh*] to the slaughter, and as a sheep before her shearers is dumb, so he openeth not his mouth" (Isa. 53:5, 7). In its Septuagint version, the passage from Isaiah moves entire into the New Testament as proof-text, in which at the conversion of the Ethiopian eunuch by Philip the mute lamb is identified as Christ (Acts 8:32).

We have yet to look at another plate in the *Biblia Pauperum*—the crucifixion, flanked on the left by Abraham's sacrifice of Isaac (who kneels on the altar, praying, while the angel stays Abraham's hand) and on the right by Moses, who lifts up the serpent in the wilderness. First the story of Moses, cited here from the *Biblia Pauperum*:

> According to Numbers xxi 4–8, when the Lord wanted to free from serpents the people whom the serpents had bitten he instructed Moses to make a brass serpent and hang it upon a stake so that whoever looked at it would be rid of serpents. The serpent hung up and stared at by the people signifies Christ on the cross, whom every believing person who wants to be rid of the serpent (that is, the devil) should gaze upon.[42]

There are are two kinds of serpents in the biblical story: the poisonous "fiery serpents" that "bit the people; and much people of Israel died" (Num. 21:6), and their antidote, the "serpent of brass": "And Moses made a serpent of brass, and put it upon a pole, and it came to pass, that if a serpent had bitten any man, when he beheld the serpent of brass, he lived" (21:9). A version of homeopathy appears to be involved here, whereby like cures like.

In the New Testament, the healing serpent, the remedy that, according to the gloss in the *Biblia Pauperum*, got rid of the Devil, is identified with the cross and also with the "eternal life" promised by Christ: speaking to Nicodemus, Jesus says, "And as Moses lifted up [*hypsosen*] the serpent in the wilderness, even so must the Son of man be lifted up: that whosoever believeth in him should not perish, but have eternal life" (John 3:14–15). Augustine glosses the verse in chiasmus: "The serpent's bite brings death, the death of the Lord bringeth life." Christ "took death upon Him, and hung up Death upon the cross; and from Death itself mortal men are delivered."[43] (To hang up death on the cross is, from Augustine's perspective, to catch the Devil with a mousetrap.) A. M. Ramsey overhears in the phrase "lifted up," just cited, another passage in John ("now shall the prince of the world be cast out. And I, if I be lifted [*hypsotho*] up from the earth, will draw all men unto me"

[12:31–32]); he also overhears a passage from Isaiah, which describes the suffering servant lifted up in a figurative sense: "Behold, my servant . . . shall
be exalted and extolled, and be very high" (52:13). That servant, we recall,
has already been linked to the slain paschal lamb. The cast-out "prince of the
world" is, of course, Satan.

◈   ◈   ◈

At this juncture, the *Biblia Pauperum* will direct us back to Augustine's
mousetrap by way of an involved metonymic chain. As everyone knows, the
subtle serpent who seduced our parents Adam and Eve may be conflated with
Satan (the adversary or accuser) or the Devil, who is also conflated with the
great sea serpent Leviathan. One text beneath the crucifixion plate in the
Biblia Pauperum is taken from from God's challenge to Job: *Numquid capies
leviathan hamo?* ("Can you capture Leviathan with a hook?") The Authorized
Version reads: "Canst thou draw out leviathan with an hook? or his tongue
with a cord which thou lettest down? Canst thou put an hook into his nose?"
(41:1–2). However displaced and disguised, that "hook" (*hamo*) is surely the
key to fables about mousetraps baited to catch the Devil, whose principal in-
dustry is setting traps. Here several cords should be drawn together. First,
"leviathan" is a transliteration of a Hebrew word that appears once in Job,
twice in the Psalms (74 and 104), and twice in a verse of Isaiah's: "In that day
the Lord with his sore and great and strong sword shall punish leviathan the
piercing serpent, even leviathan that crooked serpent; and he shall slay the
dragon that is in the sea. In that day sing ye unto her, A vineyard of red wine"
(27:1–2).

Then there is a connection to be made between Leviathan, translated as
drakon in the Septuagint, and Pharaoh, who, as we know, is deeply involved
in the redemption of the Israelites from Egypt, the house of bondage. "Art
thou not it that hath cut Rahab, and wounded the dragon? Art thou not it
which hath dried the sea, the waters of the great deep; that hath made the
depths of the sea a way for the ransomed [*ga'al*] to pass over?" (Isa. 51:10–11).
Since Leviathan appears in Psalm 74 "in the middle of an allusion to the
miracles connected with the Exodus of the Israelites," the beast "is to be understood as the crocodile, the emblem of 'Pharaoh, the king of Egypt, the
great dragon (*tannîm*) that lieth in the midst of his rivers'" (Ezek. 29:3).[44] To
extend the passage from Ezekiel: "But I will put hooks in thy jaws, and I will
cause the fish of thy rivers to stick unto thy scales, and I will bring thee up out
of the midst of thy rivers, and all the fish of thy rivers shall stick unto thy
scales" (29:4). What the *Biblia Pauperum* implies in its allusion to Job 41 is
that Satan, the prince or god of this world, cannot or else will not be caught
with an ordinary fishhook and bait; he can only be caught by means of the
cross, or, in other words, with the flesh and blood of Christ.

✦   ✦   ✦

Apparently Gregory, Bishop of Nyssa (ca. 330–ca. 395) was the first to em-
ploy the simile of the divine fishhook by which the Devil was deceived and
caught. The "Enemy," he writes, "chose Christ as a ransom [*lutron*] in exchange for those who were shut up in death's prison. But it was beyond his
power to look upon the unveiled appearance of God; he would only see in
Christ a part of the fleshly nature. . . . That was the reason why the Godhead was veiled in flesh, that Satan should observe what was familiar and
congenial and thus have no fear in approaching the transcendent power."[45]

> God therefore concealed Himself beneath the veil of our nature; the devil, like
> a voracious fish, gobbling up the bait swallowed the hook of the Godhead . . .
> and was caught.[46]

Expounding the passage from Gregory of Nyssa, Pope Gregory the Great
revises the metaphor of hook and bait: "Who can be ignorant that on a hook
the bait is shown, the point is concealed? For the bait tempts that the point
may wound. Our Lord, then, when coming for the redemption of mankind,
made as it were a kind of hook of Himself for the death of the devil."[47] Likewise the desert hermit St. Anthony (recorded by Athanasius): "The devil
may vaunt his power, but he lies; in his words there is no truth. For, in spite of
all his boastings, it is none the less true that like a dragon he was hooked by
the Saviour. He was harnessed like a beast of burden, like a fugitive slave he
had his nose pierced by a ring and his lips by a bracelet."[48] In Augustine's
fable, we recall, Christ's "mortal Flesh" was the Devil's "mousetrap" (*muscipula*).[49] As late as the thirteenth century, the trope of the divine hook and
bait is still current: "Jesu Christ hath hid the hook of his divinity under the
meat of our humanity, and the fiend would take the meat of the flesh and was
taken with the hook of the Godhead. . . . He laid out his bait to our deceiver and adversary; he hath set forth his cross."[50]

Jean Gerson (1363–1429) takes up the trope of hook and bait to prove that
those in hell were redeemed at the incarnation. His imagery recalls medieval
illustrations of the Harrowing of Hell, often depicted as the gaping mouth of a
grotesque water beast: "But the hook of divinity that was concealed within
and joined to the flesh, tore open the devil's jaws and liberated the prey,
which you would imagine he held and devoured."[51] We recall Ezekiel 29:4:
"But I will put hooks in thy jaws, and I will cause the fish of thy rivers to stick
unto thy scales"; Martin Luther, whose gastrointestinal tract was not perfect,
embellishes the trope. Unable to digest the flesh of Christ (which has stuck in
his gills), the Devil vomits him out and chokes to death. "For Christ sticks in
his gills, and he must spue Him out again, as the whale the prophet Jonah,
and even as he chews Him the devil chokes himself and is slain, and is taken

captive by Christ."[52] Thus for Luther the words of Hosea are fulfilled: "I will ransom [*padah*] them from the power of the grave; I will redeem [*ga'al*] them from death . . ." (Hos. 13:14). The emetic quality of Christ's flesh may have been suggested to Luther by Cyril of Jerusalem (ca. 315–386): "The Lord was to suffer for us [Cyril writes], but had the devil known Him, he would never have approached Him. . . . God, therefore, took a body to offer it to the devil as a bait. But instead of feasting on it, as he had intended, Satan was forced to vomit all those that he had already devoured."[53]

◨   ◈   ◨

Finally we return to the figure of Augustine's mousetrap, "muscipula diaboli," whose meaning, like the meaning of all fables or parables, is more or less concealed. The figure of chiasmus or reversal determines the passage from Augustine recited below: the death of Adam, "the first man" caught in the Devil's "snare" of lies and deception and false pride, is undone by the death of Christ, the second Adam ("the figure [*tupos*] of him that was to come" [Rom. 5:14]), who traps the Devil by means of the cross. The Devil's mousetrap (set by the Devil for Adam) has been turned retributively into the Devil's mousetrap (set for the Devil by Christ). Like the ransom theory itself and like the root sense of the Greek *lutron* (undoing, loosening), the rhetorical figure of chiasmus is an undoing by means of a crossing or *chi*. In a balance created by inversion, the order of words in one of two parallel phrases or clauses is somehow reversed in the other: the Devil traps Adam; Christ, the second Adam, traps the Devil. Phrased by Irenaeus, the Devil "who had led man captive, was justly captured in his turn by God; but man, who had been led captive, was loosed from the bonds of condemnation."[54] Augustine's story of the mousetrap depends on an inversion of terms, a rhetorical undoing and reversal, whereby the subject (the Devil), imagining he had triumphed over Christ, becomes the object of his own deadly game.

> If Christ had not been put to death, death would not have died. The devil was conquered by his own trophy of victory. The devil jumped for joy, when he seduced the first man and cast him down to death. By seducing the first man, he slew him: by slaying the last man, he lost the first from his snare. . . . The devil jumped for joy when Christ died; and by the very death of Christ the devil was overcome: he took, as it were, the bait in the mousetrap. He rejoiced at the death, thinking himself death's commander. But that which caused him joy dangled the bait before him. The Lord's cross was the devil's mousetrap: the bait which caught him was the death of the Lord [*Muscipula diaboli, crux Domini: esca qua caperetur, mors Domini*].[55]

Having evoked the Devil's mousetrap, with its fleshy bait, we return to the figure of Joseph, who in the Mérode Altarpiece is depicted as an artisan who fashions intricate wooden mousetraps: metonymy for the trap or hook or snare or net of the cross, thus for redemption from sin and death. Any kind of trap involves deception; in its figurative sense, the Latin word for mouse-catcher, *muscipulator*, refers to "a deceiver" (Lewis and Short). To go about tempting prey, the mouse-catcher (or fisherman or hunter) places an attractive morsel of food in a trap or on a hook; as soon as the prey seizes the morsel, it is caught. ("Who can be ignorant that on a hook the bait is shown, the point is concealed?" writes Gregory the Great.[56]) To continue the homily: trapping mice depends on fraud, on disguise of some kind, on representation that is misrepresentation, on concealment and on seduction. Catching mice depends on a trick. If in Augustine's fable the bait held out to the Devil is the blood or flesh of Christ, what was concealed? What was the Devil's undoing? How was Satan deceived? Without that key, the fable is a worn-out figure of speech, and Augustine insisted on the thingness of signs. What is the point?

In part, the key is given by Gregory of Nyssa in the excerpt cited above: "God therefore concealed Himself beneath the veil of our nature." Not only does Gregory allude to the double nature of Christ, the God-man, he also revises the trope of "the deception of the Devil," the deceiver deceived, that is expounded in the works of Irenaeus, Origen, Ambrose, Leo the Great, Gregory the Great, and Augustine, whose predecessor Ambrose (who could read silently, without moving his lips) calls the transaction with the Devil a "pious fraud."[57] Gregory of Nyssa anticipates our objections, perhaps: "It will be objected that we ascribe a lie to God, For He approached the devil not under the form of His Godhead but under that of humanity that He might not be known by him; in other words He made use of false pretenses."[58]

When, in his immense pride, the Devil rejoices in Christ's death on the Cross, it is because he is blind to Christ's divinity, which, like a hook or snare, is concealed within or beneath the humanity. Seeing only the too-familiar, delectable flesh, the Devil made "a grave miscalculation" (in the words of one scholar).[59] His "seeming victory was turned to defeat when the Saviour rose from the grave" (in the words of another).[60] The Godhead is the concealed hook; the human nature is the bait. To cite H. E. W. Turner on the fabulous transaction with the Devil: "The devil gulps down the bait represented by the humanity of our Lord and is left caught and hanging on the hook with the Divine *Logos* playing the line."[61] (The lurid detail of the "hanging" Devil transfixed on the hook of Christ's divinity was added by John of Damascus, apparently: "Death crept towards the Saviour; He swallowed the bait of His body, but he was caught on the hook of His Godhead.")[62]

At least one crucial matter remains unexplored: Where does the idea of the Devil's deception, the deceiver deceived, come from? Paul refers to a mystery:

"the hidden wisdom . . . Which none of the princes [leaders] of this world
knew: for had they known it, they would not have crucified the Lord of glory"
(1 Cor. 2:7–8). Of the apostolic Fathers, it was Ignatius (ca. 35–ca. 107) who
first suggested that the mystery of the incarnation had been deliberately kept
from the Devil: "Now the virginity of Mary was hidden from the prince of this
world, as was also her offspring, and the death of the Lord; three mysteries of
renown which were wrought in silence by God."[63] More centrally, in the writings of Origen, the great Alexandrine Father (ca. 185–ca. 254), there is a passage "which for the first time contains *in extenso* the idea of the deceit of the
devil."[64] Hastings Rashdall puns on Origen's name: "I am afraid it is impossible to deny that the notion of a trick on the part of God, by which the devil
was lured into compassing his own ruin, does find its origin in certain passages
of Origen."[65] Glossing Matthew 20:28, "the Son of man came . . . to give
his life [*psyche*] a ransom [*lutron*] for many," Origen wonders:

> But to whom did He give His soul [*psyche*] as a ransom [*lutron*] for many? Surely
> not to God. Could it be then to the evil one? For he had us in his power, until
> the ransom for us should be given to him, even the life [or soul] of Jesus, since
> he (the evil one) had been deceived, and led to suppose that he was capable of
> mastering that soul, and he did not see that to hold Him involved a trial of
> strength greater than he was equal to. Therefore also death, though he thought
> he had prevailed against Him, no longer lords it over Him, He (Christ) having
> become free among the dead, and stronger than the power of death. . . .[66]

Origen is followed closely by Gregory of Nyssa:

> It was by means of a certain amount of *deceit* that God carried out this scheme
> on our behalf. For that not by pure Deity alone, but by Deity veiled in human
> nature, God, without the knowledge of His enemy, got within the lines of him
> who had man in his power, is in some manner a *fraud* and a *surprise*. . . .
> Whereas he, the enemy, effected his deception for the ruin of our nature, He
> who is at once the just, and good, and wise one, used His device of deception
> for the salvation of him who had perished, and thus not only conferred benefit
> on the lost one, but on him, too, who had wrought our ruin.[67]

Even the marriage of Mary and Joseph is thought to be part of the plan to
deceive our malicious enemy: Ambrose suggests "that the marriage of the Virgin was part of the trickery by which the Devil was deceived, as also our
Lord's silence as to His own divine nature."[68] The widely held belief that the
incarnation was concealed from the prince of this world informs and underwrites Augustine's metaphor of the Devil's mousetrap, the device of deception
and of redemption, which in the Mérode Altarpiece is fashioned by the Virgin's "bourgeois husband to catch the devil and overcome the passions."[69] By
the late Middle Ages, Schapiro tells us, Joseph was regarded as "the guardian

of the mystery of the incarnation and one of the main figures in the divine plot to deceive the devil."[70]

◈   ◈   ◈

As soon as the crucifixion is said to be the ransom paid for mankind's redemption, a question arises: To whom was the payment made? From whom were we recovered [ga'al] with the bait of Christ's blood? Whose slaves were we? (To recite Origen: "But to whom did He give His soul as a ransom [lutron] for many? Surely not to God. Could it be then to the evil one?") Origen concludes we were ransomed from the Devil:

> If therefore we were bought with a price, . . . we were bought doubtless from some one whose slaves we were, and who demanded such a price as he pleased for the release of those whom he held. It was the devil, however, who held us, to whom we had been allotted (or into whose power we had been dragged) by our sins. He therefore demanded as our price the blood of Christ.[71]

In Augustine's version of the purchase, the blood of Christ, the ransom price, was placed in a mousetrap: *In muscipula posita est esca vitae huius*.[72] What might have inspired that *muscipula* (*mus-capio*, or mouse-trap)? For if the ransom theory with its fishhooks and bait and other paraphernalia is found generally in the early Fathers, the mousetrap is not; it is peculiar to Augustine ("Tandis que la métaphore de la rançon est banale chez les Pères, celle de la souricière est propre à saint Augustin").[73] To follow Jean Rivière's generous documentation (his monograph on Augustine appeared in 1933), Augustine found the mousetrap in the recension of the Latin Bible used in the Africa of his day. (Augustine was ignorant of Hebrew, Gerald Bonner confirms, and had "a limited working knowledge of biblical Greek."[74]) So the mousetrap is not so far-fetched after all; used in the context of redemption, *muscipula* (sometimes *muscipulum*) comes with the high authority of the Old and New Testaments. (Jerome's Vulgate replaced *muscipula* with *laqueus*, a term used both literally and figuratively for a noose or snare.)[75]

In particular, Rivière concludes, the term *muscipula* was used in the African psalter (about twenty times) to approximate the Greek *pagis*, used in the Septuagint for a snare, or net, or trap, or gin.[76] Thus, "Our soul is escaped as a bird out of the snare of the fowlers: the snare is broken, and we are escaped" (Ps. 124:7); the African psalter had the poor soul caught in a *muscipula*; the Vulgate reads: *anima nostra quasi avis erepta est de laqueo venantium*. Another example: "Keep me from the snares which they have laid for me, and the gins of the workers of iniquity" (Ps. 141:9). As far as Augustine was concerned, those snares or engines were mousetraps; the Vulgate reads, *custodi me de manibus laquei quod posuerunt mihi*.

Crucially, in Augustine's Latin version of the Gospels, the image of the mousetrap is attributed to Jesus himself: the day of our redemption draws terribly near; we are warned in Luke 21 that "the kingdom of God is nigh at hand"; the day will come upon us "unawares. For as a snare shall it come upon all them that dwell on the face of the whole earth" (21:31, 34–35). In the African redaction of Luke 21, that "snare" (Gr. *pagis*) was a mousetrap—*muscipula*. Fascinated, I shall move cautiously toward one last snare. According to a marginal note in the Vulgate, the words of Luke 21:35—"For as a snare shall it come upon all them that dwell on the face of the whole earth"—allude to Isaiah 24, which reads: "Fear, and the pit, and the snare [Heb. *pach*; LXX *pagis*], are upon thee, O inhabitant of the earth" (24:17). When the earth is made empty and waste and is turned upside down (to paraphrase Isaiah), when like a drunkard the foundations of the earth "reel to and fro" and the earth is "clean dissolved," the workers of iniquity shall be caught in a vast snare. Whether in the African version of Isaiah 24 known to Augustine that snare was a mousetrap is not known.

Augustine did not just retain the image of the mousetrap; he caressed it, with obvious pleasure ("On a vu d'ailleurs que l'image de la *muscipula* est par lui, non seulement retenue, mais caressée avec un visible plaisir . . ."[77]), as I have done.

CHAPTER TWO

Jonathan Edwards and the Angel of the Lord

A History of the Work of Redemption

"A heathen asked Rabbi Joshua b. Karha: Why did God speak to Moses from the thorn bush? Rabbi Joshua replied: If he had spoken from a carob tree or from a sycamore, you would have asked me the same question. But so as not to dismiss you without an answer, God spoke from the thorn bush to teach you that there is no place where the Shekinah is not, not even a thorn bush."[1]

According to Jonathan Edwards, *Christ* spoke to Moses from the burning thorn bush. The "redemption of the children of Israel out of Egypt," he declares in the Redemption Discourse, "was by Jesus Christ as is evident, for it was wrought by him that appeared to Moses in the bush; for that was the person that sent Moses to redeem the people but that was Christ, as is evident because he is called the angel of the Lord, Ex. 3:2–3." Edwards's interpretation continues thus:

> The bush represented the human nature of Christ that is called the branch. The bush grew on Mount Sinai, or Horeb, which is a word that signifies a dry place, as the human nature of Christ was a root out of a dry ground. The bush burning with fire represented the sufferings of Christ in the fire of God's wrath. It burned and was not consumed, so Christ though he suffered extremely yet perished not, but overcame at last and rose from his suffering. Because this great mystery of the incarnation and suffering of Christ was here represented, therefore Moses says, I will turn aside and behold this great sight. A great sight he might well call it when there was to be seen represented God manifested in the flesh, and suffering a dreadful death, and rising from the dead.[2]

Before examining Edwards's reading of Moses and the burning bush, let us recall the relevant passage from Exodus:

Now Moses kept the flock of Jethro his father in law, the priest of Midian: and he led the flock to the backside of the desert, and came to the mountain of God, even to Horeb. And the angel of the Lord appeared unto him in a flame of fire out of the midst of a bush: and he looked, and, behold, the bush burned with fire, and the bush was not consumed. . . . And when the Lord saw that he turned aside to see, God called unto him out of the midst of the bush, and said, Moses, Moses. And he said, Here am I. And he said, Draw not nigh hither: put off thy shoes from off thy feet, for the place whereon thou standest is holy ground. (Exod. 3:1–2, 4–5)

In Edwards's revision, "the angel of the Lord"—*mal'ak* YHWH, in the Hebrew Bible—has apparently been conflated with the Word, the Logos that was "in the beginning" (John 1:1). The present chapter is an attempt to place Edwards's radical christology in its theoretical and historical context.[3]

❖   ❖   ❖

Excerpted from *A History of the Work of Redemption,* a series of thirty sermons preached in 1739, the extended passage cited above is informed by this one from Edwards's "Types of the Messiah," a treatise on biblical typology composed between 1744 and 1749:

The things that are said of the burning bush do wonderfully agree with the Old Testament representations of the Messiah. It was not a high tree, but a bush, as the Messiah is called "the low tree" (Ezek. 17:24), and elsewhere "the twig" and "the tender plant" [Ezek. 17:22; Is. 53:2]. This bush was a root out of a dry ground, for it was a bush that grew in Mt. Horeb, which was so called for the remarkable dryness of the place. The word signifies "dryness"; there was no spring about the mountain till Moses there fetched water of the dry rock. . . .

That bush was the growth of the earth, as the human nature of Christ in the Old Testament is represented to be. Yet it had the divine nature of Christ in it, *for this angel of the Lord that is said to appear in the bush has been proved to be the same with the Messiah* from the Old Testament in my discourse on "the Prophecies of the Messiah." This angel is said to dwell in this bush (Deut. 33:16), the more to represent the divine nature of the Messiah dwelling in the human nature. (emphasis added)

Drawing parallels between the thorn bush that burned but was not consumed and the Messiah's resurrection from the dead, Edwards identifies the angel in the bush as the Messiah: "The angel that dwelt out of that bush, who was the Messiah, comes out of the fire and appears in the bush, and [is] delivered alive from the flames to work redemption for his people."[4] Edwards's allusion to "The Prophecies of the Messiah," his unpublished commentary on Deuteronomy 18, directs us to a passage wherein "the angel that appeared to Moses in the bush" is called by three names: "the Messiah," "the angel of his Presence," and "the angel of the covenant."[5]

Nor are these isolated examples of Edwards's pronounced tendency to read back the presence of the discarnate, preexistent Christ into the Old Testament and to identify him with the angel of the Lord, the *mal'ak* YHWH of the Hebrew Bible. After the children of Israel were redeemed from Egypt, Edwards informs us, "The people went out with a high hand and Christ went before 'em in a pillar of cloud and fire. . . . And when Pharaoh and his hosts, and Satan by them, pursued the people, Christ overthrew their enemies in the Red Sea. . . . Thus *Christ the angel of God's presence* in his love and in his pity redeemed his people and carried [them] in the days of old as on eagles' wings, so that none of their proud and spiteful enemies, neither Egyptians nor devils, could touch 'em" (176; emphasis added).[6] Indeed, we learn, "Christ wrote the ten commandments on tables of stone with his own finger" (183). At the battle of Jericho, "Christ fought as the captain of their host and cast down great hailstones" (193). Nor in the Old Testament could Satan, our adversary and accuser, have been resisted without Christ's management:

> When Satan the grand enemy had conquered and overthrown man, the business of resisting and conquering him was committed to Jesus Christ. He thenceforward undertook to manage that subtile, powerful adversary. He was thus appointed the captain of the Lord's hosts and captain of their salvation, and always acted as such thenceforward, and so he appeared from time to time and he will continue to act as such to the end of the world. (131)

Similarly, in the passage from the Redemption Discourse cited below, Edwards identifies the "angel of the Lord," the *mal'ak* YHWH, with Christ:

> So Christ appeared afterwards to Joshua in the form of the human nature, Josh. 5:13–15. . . . And so he appeared to Gideon, Judg. 6:11 etc. ["And there came an Angel of the Lord, and sat under an oak. . . . And the Angel of the Lord appeared unto him"]. So God appeared to Manoah, Judg. 13:17–20 ["For it came to pass, when the flame went up toward heaven from off the altar, that the angel of the Lord ascended in the flame of the altar"]. Here Christ appeared to Manoah in a representation both of his incarnation and death: of his incarnation in that he appeared in an human form, and of his death and sufferings represented by the sacrifice of this kid, which Christ now signified by ascending up in the flame of the sacrifice. . . . (197–98)

Compare Edwards's "Types of the Messiah": "when Manoah offered sacrifice by God's appointment, he that is called 'the angel of the Lord,' and who was the Lord (and whom I have proved to be the same person with the Messiah . . .), ascended in the flame of the sacrifice. . . ."[7] If, as Edwards says, "the main business of all this succession of prophets was to foreshadow Christ and the glorious redemption that he should accomplish" (202), what does Christ as "the angel of the Lord" foreshadow at the Red Sea, in the pillar of cloud guiding the Israelites, on Mount Sinai writing the Decalogue, and in the burning bush speaking to Moses? Types or shadows or prophecies are usually considered by exegetes to be proleptic figures pointing forward to their fulfillment, which in the case of the burning thorn bush that was not consumed is thought to be the virgin birth.

Throughout the Old Testament, according to Edwards, "Christ thus appeared time after time in the form of that nature he was afterwards to take upon him . . ." (198). On one hand, Christ, the second person of the Trinity, appeared "in the form of the human nature" to Moses, to Jacob, to Joshua, to Aaron, to Gideon, to Manoah, to Daniel, and to Ezekiel (197; 260); on the other, the Old Testament prophets were "types and shadows of Christ whereby his coming and redemption were prefigured" (136).[8] As Hans W. Frei has said, the "customary use of figuration was to show that Old Testament persons, events, and prophecies were fulfilled in the New Testament."[9] However, Edwards seems to be using figuration to prove that Christ, as the angel of the Lord and in "human form," was already present and active in the Old Testament. What is the background of his christology? What is its rhetorical purpose? To echo the question posed to Rabbi Joshua b. Karha by the heathen, why, in Edwards's Redemption Discourse and in "Types of the Messiah," did Christ speak to Moses from the thorn bush?

❖   ❖   ❖

"The Work of Redemption is a work that God carries on from the fall of man to the end of the world" (116). "It was begun immediately upon the fall and will be continued to the end of the world and then will be finished" (119). Edwards divides salvation history into "three periods," the "first reaching from the fall of man to Christ's incarnation" (127). Redemption, he asserts, was not "all wrought while Christ was upon earth"; it was not "begun and finished with Christ's humiliation" (117) but includes "all God's works that were properly preparatory to the purchase. . . ." The persons of the Trinity "do conspire" in the ongoing work of redemption, which includes "All that Christ does in this great affair as mediator in any of his offices, either Prophet, priest or King, *either when he was in the world in his human* [*form*], *or before or since*" (117–18; emphasis added). It is the "before" that mostly concerns us in this conspiracy. What, in Edwards's view, was Christ doing *before* "he was in the world in his human form"?

As we know, the Old Testament bears witness to numerous theophanies: in Edwards's words, "God revealed himself of old from time to time from the fall of man to the coming of Christ" (129). After the Fall (and here Edwards evokes the Anselmic theory of satisfaction), because he was "offended" by "offending mankind," God the Father "would have nothing to do with fallen man in a way of mercy but by a mediator" (130; 358). Therefore, we are told,

Christ graciously undertook to mediate between an "offended" God and man: "He immediately stepped in between a holy, infinite, offended majesty and offending mankind, and was accepted in his interposition . . ." (130).

> And therefore when we read in the sacred history what God did from time to time towards his church and people, and what he said to them, and how he revealed himself to them, we are to understand it especially of the second person of the Trinity. When we read after this of God's appearing time after time in some visible form or outward symbol of his presence, we are ordinarily if not universally to understand it of the second person of the Trinity. . . . And particularly *Christ often appeared in an human form*. (131; emphasis added)

Thus for Edwards, theophanies, revelations of God to Israel recorded in the Old Testament, are christophanies, as are divine acts of mercy. During the years of the Israelites' wandering and backsliding in the desert, Edwards states, "when Christ appeared to manage the affairs of his church in this period, he often appeared also in the form of that nature that he took upon him in his incarnation" (196). "So he seems to have appeared to Moses from time to time, and particularly at that time when God spoke to him face to face as a man, and he beheld the 'similitude of the Lord,' Num. 12:8. Then Moses beseeched him to show him his glory, which was the most remarkable vision that ever he had of Christ" (196–97). And Edwards proceeds by describing Moses's vision "when Christ passed by and put him in the cleft of the rock"; likewise, it seems, Christ appeared to Joshua "in the form of the human nature" and also to Manoah "in a representation both of his incarnation and his death" (197). Edwards's deliberate phrase, "in the form of," recalls Paul's letter to the Philippians: Christ, "being in the form [*morphe*] of God . . . made himself of no reputation, and took upon him the form [*morphe*] of a servant, and was made in the likeness of men" (2:6–8). It may be that for Edwards, the incarnation of Christ differs only in degree from the theophany/christophany in the burning bush.

However mediated, Edwards's christology has jumped back over fifteen hundred years or so to settle in between the second and fifth centuries, when in his view the "true church" was still in a pristine condition. By appropriating theophanies of the Old Testament to the discarnate (or preexistent) Christ, including the theophany in the burning bush, in which the names "Christ" and "the angel of God" are used as interchangeable, convertible terms, Edwards evokes the christologies of at least two early Church Fathers—Justin Martyr (ca. 100–ca. 165) and Tertullian (ca. 160–ca. 225). Both apologists are acknowledged by Edwards in the Redemption Discourse: "Justin Martyr, an eminent father in the Christian church who lived in the age next after the apostles"; "Tertullian, another eminent father in the Christian church who lived in the beginning of the following age" (391).[10] Tertullian writes in his polemical *Adversus Praxean*:

> It is the Son, therefore, who has been from the beginning administering judgment, throwing down the haughty tower, and dividing the tongues, punishing the whole world by the violence of waters, raining upon Sodom and Gomorrah fire and brimstone, as the Lord from the Lord. For He it was who at all times came down to hold converse with men, from Adam on to the patriarchs and the prophets, in vision, in dream, in mirror, in dark saying. . . . Thus was He ever learning even as God to converse with men upon earth, being no other that the Word which was to be made flesh.[11]

Reformation christology is nothing new (Karl Barth has said); it is a return to, a continuation of, traditions of the earliest Church.[12] The tendency to ascribe theophanies of the invisible God to the visible Son was general among Christian apologists such as Justin and Tertullian, who often used the term "Angel" to signify the preexistent, heavenly Christ. As a result, and aware of the perils of subordinationism in any form, Augustine argued in *De Trinitate* that "the theophanies recorded in the Old Testament should not be regarded, as the earlier patristic tradition had tended to regard them, as appearances exclusively of the Son."[13] "Whatever is affirmed of God is affirmed equally of each of the three persons."[14] Alluding to the burning bush theophany, Augustine explains: "In fact the whole passage of scripture about Moses at the burning bush makes it clear that it is the angel of the Lord speaking when it says 'The Lord said.' . . . But there are people who want to take the angel as meaning the Son of God speaking directly in his own person because the prophet calls him angel (Is. 9:6)."[15]

> If then [Augustine adds] you ask me how either the voices or the perceptible forms or likenesses were produced that occurred before the incarnation of the Word in order to prefigure that coming event, I answer that God worked them through angels. . . .[16]

> Acting in and through these angels, of course, were the Father and the Son and the Holy Spirit. Sometimes it was the Father who was represented by them, sometimes the Son, sometimes the Holy Spirit, sometimes just God without distinction of persons. Even if he appeared in visible or audible fashion, it was by means of his creation and not in his own proper substance.[17]

What Moses saw in the burning bush was a created angel, "an angel bearing the type of the Lord," Augustine declares in a homily on the Fourth Gospel delivered in the year 416. "Moses saw a cloud, saw an angel, saw a fire: all these are creatures. They bore the type of their Lord, not manifested the presence of the Lord Himself."[18] For Justin Martyr, on the other hand, it was the Son, called "Angel," who conversed with and appeared to the Patriarchs: the "Power" (*dynamis*) of the Father, Justin claims, may be called "the Glory of the Lord, now the Son, again Wisdom, again an Angel, then God, and then Lord and Logos. . . ."[19]

❖   ❖   ❖

"Christian typology is Christological," Jean Daniélou reminds us.[20] What deserves notice in Edwards (and in the writings of Increase Mather and Edward Taylor) is not the more or less arbitrary, more or less allegorized, two-part figure of type and antitype, wherein the type (the bush that burned but was not consumed) is said to be "fulfilled" or completed by its antitype (the virgin who "gave birth and remained pure," to cite the *Biblia Pauperum*, or the "great mystery of the incarnation and suffering of Christ," according to Edwards), but the version of christology that determines that figure.[21] For Edwards, as we have seen, the burning bush "was the growth of the earth, as the human nature of Christ in the Old Testament is represented to be. *Yet it had the divine nature of Christ in it, for this angel of the Lord that is said to appear in the bush has been proved to be the same with the Messiah . . .*" (emphasis added). We are in the realm of angel-christology.[22]

The parallels drawn by Edwards between the burning bush and the Messiah are informed by Jewish angelology: as intermediaries between God and his creation, angels may appear in human form, in the likeness of human beings. As well, Edwards's readings of the theophany in Exodus 3 evoke and depend on three Christian doctrines: the Trinity (which is really incompatible with angel-christology); the double nature of Christ, the "God-man" (358) ("the union of the divine with the human nature in one person," in Edwards's words [333]); and, most centrally, the doctrine of the preexistent Christ— God's Word, who was with the Father "in the beginning" (John 1:1) and (to recite Martin Werner's gloss on Paul) "could appear for the deliverance of the people of Israel, during the wandering in the desert in the form of a spiritual (*pneumatike*) rock which moved about and dispensed water."[23] From Jaroslav Pelikan's point of view, the doctrine of the preexistent logos was from earliest times "a means of correlating the redemption accomplished in Jesus Christ with the doctrine of Creation. Creation . . . revelation . . . and redemption could all be ascribed to the logos."[24]

Considered as a figure of speech, the preexistent logos serves to correlate before and after, early and late, prospect and retrospect, beginning and end, *arche* and *telos*. It may also reverse the accepted order of events. "For 'tis evident by the Old Testament," Edwards writes, "that the Messiah was not only to be the Savior of God's people that should be after his coming, but that he was the Savior of the saints in all ages from the beginning of the world";[25]

"Alpha and Omega are the names of the first and last letters of the Greek alphabet, as A and Z are of ours, and therefore it signifies the same as his being the first and the last, the beginning and the ending" (516; cf. Rev. 1:8). Origen argues that the Son of God is not "a new God. For the sacred Scriptures know that he is older than all created things; and it was to him that God said, concerning the creation of man, 'Let us make man after our image and likeness'" (Gen. 1:26).[26]

That for Edwards the Messiah (identified as Jesus Christ) is first and last, that he has mediated in salvation history "from the beginning of the world," evokes the Jewish Wisdom tradition. The text generally used by Christian exegetes to support the doctrine of the preexistent logos is Proverbs 8:22–23: "The Lord possessed me [Wisdom] in the beginning of his way, before his works of old. I was set up from everlasting, from the beginning, or ever the earth was." The identification of Wisdom with the preexistent Word (logos) of John 1 is reinforced in the Geneva Bible (1599): a marginal gloss to Proverbs 8:22–23 reads, "He declareth hereby the divinity and eternitie of this wisdome, which he magnifieth and prayseth thorow this booke: meaning thereby the eternall son of God Jesus Christ our Saviour, whom Saint John calleth the word that was in the beginning." Compare this passage from Edwards's *Miscellaneous Observations*:

> If Christ in the beginning created the heavens and the earth, he must be from eternity; for then he is before the beginning, by which must be meant the beginning of time; the beginning of that kind of duration which has a *beginning* and a *following*, before and after belonging to it. . . . So it is said, Prov. viii.22. &c. "The Lord possessed me in the beginning of his way, before his works of old."[27]

Proverbs 8 is echoed in Ecclesiasticus (Ben Sirach), part of the Jewish Apocrypha: "Wisdom hath been created before all things" (1:4). Some Christian exegetes conflate the figure of Wisdom (Heb. *hochma*; Gr. *sophia*) with the Glory of the Lord, with the Word or logos, and with the angel of God, the *mal'ak* YHWH. In rabbinic exegesis, the Targums especially, the angel of God and the Glory of the Lord, like the Lord himself, may be signified by the name of God's Presence, the glorious Shekinah. ("God spoke from the thorn bush," said Rabbi Joshua b. Karha to the heathen, "to teach you that there is no place where the Shekinah is not, not even a thorn bush.")

❖   ❖   ❖

What are the implications of Edwards's angel-christology, whereby Christ, the agent of creation and the mediator between an "offended" God and fallen man, is by a metonymy substituted for "the angel of God," the *mal'ak* YHWH, who appears to Moses in the burning bush, to Joshua at the battle of Jericho, to Manoah in a flame of fire? The question may be informed by reference to Calvin, for whom, as Heiko Oberman explains, the "eternal Word of God is the mediator and reconciler, not only since the Incarnation but already since the beginnings of creation."[28] Put otherwise by François Wendel, for Calvin, Christ's

> office as Mediator is closely connected with the Incarnation; yet in order to call the elect under the old Covenant, he was Mediator even before his manifesta-tion in the flesh, and he remains so after his death, "inasmuch as he appears today before the face and the majesty of God so that we may be heard in his name". Calvin also adds, in conclusion: "For this reason St Paul says that the love with which God loved us before the creation of the world had always been founded in Christ (Ephesians 1.4)."[29]

Moreover, in Calvin's revision of late-Jewish angelology, Christ becomes the head or chief of the angels. Alluding in the *Institutes* to the "chief angel," the *mal'ak YHWH* that appears to Abraham and to Manoah, Calvin explains that

> the orthodox doctors of the church have rightly and prudently interpreted that chief angel to be God's Word, who already at that time, as a sort of foretaste, began to fulfill the office of Mediator. For even though he was not yet clothed with flesh, he came down, so to speak, as an intermediary, in order to approach believers more intimately. Therefore this closer intercourse gave him the name of angel.[30]

(The "orthodox doctors" alluded to are Justin and Tertullian, we are told by John T. McNeill, the editor of Calvin's *Institutes*.) Calvin's discussion of the *mal'ak YHWH* continues with apposite proof-texts, including Jacob's struggle with the angel. (That particular angel was Christ because he was *vray Dieu*, not an *ange crée*.[31]) After all, Calvin reasons in the *Institutes*, if Christ were not the same God "who had always been worshiped among the Jews," why throughout the Old Testament is "Jehovah so frequently set forth in the per-son of an angel"? That the angel who appears in Judges 13:16, "refusing to eat bread, commands that a sacrifice be offered to Jehovah . . . proves that he is Jehovah himself. Therefore Manoah and his wife infer from this sign that they have seen not only an angel but God himself." In Zechariah 2, Christ is "the angel who sends the other angel."[32] Furthermore, argues Calvin, the in-vocative prayer of Genesis 48:16 ("the Angel which redeemed me from all evil") can only refer to Christ:

> If you take this verse as a reference to an ordinary angel, the words are absurd.
> . . . It is necessary to understand them of Christ, who is intentionally given

the title of *angel* because he has been the perpetual Mediator. Paul testifies that He was the leader and guide of the journey of his ancient people [through the wilderness].[33]

We are on shifting and sensitive doctrinal ground. From Calvin's perspective, Christ is "the subject matter of both testaments" (to cite Hans W. Frei);[34] furthermore, under the name of "angel," and as "mediator and reconciler," Christ was active in the Old Testament "in order to call the elect." Likewise, for Edwards, "Christ and his redemption are the great subject of the whole Bible" (290): "the sum and substance of both the Old Testament and the New is Christ and his redemption" (443). Not only the narrative sections of the Jewish Bible signify Christ; for Edwards (as for illustrators of medieval psalters) Christ is "the great subject of the songs of the Old Testament" (290). In short, "The Work of Redemption is a work that God carries on from the fall of man to the end of the world" (116); and from Edwards's point of view, and from the point of view of Justin Martyr and of Calvin, that redemptive work is carried on through the mediation of the second person of the Trinity, who, as the angel of the Lord, may appear in the burning bush, in the pillar of cloud, and at Penuel wrestling until dawn with Jacob: "And Jacob," Edwards declares, "had another remarkable confirmation of this covenant at Penuel . . . where Christ appeared to him in an human form, in the form of that nature [in which he was to appear]" (170).[35]

Compare this excerpt from Edward Taylor's *Christographia* sermons: "For Jesus Christ is the Same yesterday, and today, and forever. Heb. 13.8. He hath been Carrying on the work of a Mediator from the beginning. Hence Styled a lamb Slayn from the foundation of the World. Rev. 13.8. He was in the Burning bush, and with the Church in the Wilderness Act. 7.38, and the Captain of the Lords Host. . . ."[36] (Compare Edwards: "He was thus appointed the captain of the Lord's hosts and captain of their salvation, and always acted as such thenceforward, and so he appeared from time to time and will continue to act as such to the end of the world" [131].) Taylor is also convinced that the pillar of cloud guiding the Israelites through the wilderness "was moved by Christ himselfe, who pitched his tent in this cloud, Exo. 14.19. The Angell there is lookt upon to be Christ himselfe Styled Angel . . . by both Jewish Rabbies, & Christian Expositors."[37] (Likewise, Edwards writes: "Christ went before 'em in a pillar of cloud and fire" [176].) We shall move to some of those Rabbis and Expositors.

❖   ❖   ❖

The supposition that wherever in the Old Testament God appeared to the children of Israel—in the burning bush, at Sinai, at Penuel—it was the Son who so appeared lasted among the Church Fathers up to the time of Augustine. In popular culture, and in Calvinism, as it turns out, it lasted much longer: the *Biblia Pauperum*, for example, compiled almost one thousand years after Augustine, depicts (unmistakably) the cross-nimbed Son in the burning bush talking to Moses, who has reverently removed his shoes, while his father-in-law's sheep graze. ("The burning bush which is not consumed," the commentary beneath the plate reads, "prefigures the blessed Virgin bearing a child without defilement of her body."[38]) Calvin's extended gloss on the burning bush theophany in Exodus 3:2, "And the Angel of the Lord appeared unto him [Moses]," should be cited in full:

> But let us inquire who this Angel was? since soon afterwards he not only calls himself Jehovah, but claims the glory of the eternal and only God. Now, although this is an allowable manner of speaking, because the angels transfer to themselves the person and titles of God, when they are performing the commissions entrusted to them by him; and although it is plain from many passages, and especially from the first chapter of Zechariah, that there is one head and chief of the angels who commands the others, the ancient teachers of the Church have rightly understood that the Eternal Son of God is so called in respect to his office as Mediator, which he figuratively bore from the beginning, although he really took it upon him only at his Incarnation. And Paul sufficiently expounds this mystery to us, when he plainly asserts that Christ was the leader of his people in the Desert. (1 Cor. x.4.) Therefore, although at that time, properly speaking, he was not yet the messenger of his Father, still his predestined appointment to the office even then had this effect, that he manifested himself to the patriarchs, and was known in this character. Nor, indeed, had the saints ever any communication with God except through the promised Mediator. It is not then to be wondered at, if the Eternal Word of God, of one Godhead and essence with the Father, assumed the name of "the Angel" on the ground of his future mission.[39]

Thus, when Paul tells the Corinthians that the children of Israel "did all drink the same spiritual drink: for they drank of that spiritual Rock that followed them: and that Rock was Christ," Calvin understands him to have asserted "plainly" that Christ was present in the wilderness ("although at that time, properly speaking, he was not yet the messenger of his Father"). In the *Institutes*, Calvin asserts that the "only-begotten Son . . . became known of old to the Jews. In another place we have quoted Paul's view that Christ was the leader of the former deliverance" ("in the wilderness").[40]

If, as Calvin says, Christ, the second person of the Trinity, was indeed present at Horeb with Moses and at Penuel with Jacob; if throughout their forty-year journey in the wilderness, Christ was in the cloud guiding the Israelites ("his ancient people") toward Canaan, redeeming them, delivering them from bondage in Egypt; if he indeed "manifested himself to the patriarchs," what has happened to the proleptic, two-part figure of speech known loosely as typology? Consider these well-known examples: the rock that gave forth water when it was struck with Moses's rod is the type; its antitype is usually said to be the crucifixion, when blood and water flowed from Christ's side. The burning bush is the type; its antitype, according to Gregory of Nyssa, is "Mary's virginal maternity"; Clement of Alexandria thought the bush prefigured Christ's crown of thorns; Hilary saw in the bush "the Church surviving persecution."[41] Either way, if, as Calvin says, Christ addressed Moses from the burning thorn bush, is the discarnate Christ a figure or type of the incarnate Christ? If this is so, then presumably type and antitype are nothing more than degrees of revelation. A provocative remark of Paul Wernle's should be cited: "the novelty of Christianity can be no more than relative if we place ourselves at Calvin's point of view."[42]

My focus in the present chapter is not the vexed matter of Old Testament theophanies and their Christian apologists, but Edwards's angel-christology, which is informed by Justin, by Tertullian, and by Calvin's angelomorphic figures of speech. Some angels, Edwards writes, "had all along been the ministers of Christ in this affair of redemption" (301); those angels may be a part of the created "host of heaven" (Gen. 28:12). But in particular it is the angel of God, the being called *mal'ak YHWH*, that Edwards in the Redemption Discourse identifies as Christ appearing to the Patriarchs in his divine nature or in the "form" of the human nature. What distinguishes certain Old Testament passages, including the story of Moses and the burning bush and the story of Manoah and his wife, "is that it is impossible in them to differentiate between the Mal'ak and Yahweh Himself. The One who speaks or acts, i.e., Yahweh or the Mal'ak, is obviously one and the same person" (the not unbiased *Theological Dictionary of the New Testament* is cited).[43] In a study of Jewish and early Christian apocalyptic, Christopher Rowland describes the "angel of the Lord (*mal'ak YHWH*)" as an "angelic being who in some sense was regarded as communicating the appearance of God himself and who sometimes appeared in the form of a man (Gen. 18:2). This being was called by the name of God (Gen. 31:11–13), even though this attribution was derived from his function as God's representative."[44] Jon Levenson puts the matter this way: "It often happens in the Hebrew Bible that the line between God and his angel is so indistinct that the two can be interchanged artlessly."[45] Some scholars suppose that in the earliest version of certain theophanies (Jacob at Penuel and Moses at the burning bush, for example) the Patriarchs *were* confronted by God, face to face, as it were, but "that later scribes toned down the boldness of this concept by interposing an angel" (*Encyclopedia Judaica*).

At this juncture, I shall introduce another interposed, or interpolated, angel. It may be that a translator's error (or gloss) in the Septuagint, the early Greek version of the Hebrew Bible ("the Translation of the Seventy," Edwards calls it [273]), suggested to Justin and other exegetes of the early Church, including Origen, that the divine child, the messianic figure foretold in Isaiah, would be named "angel," or was to be an angel.[46] In a passage cited above, Augustine, alluding to Isaiah 9:6, refers us to an "angel" ("But there are people who want to take the angel as meaning the Son of God speaking directly in his own person because the prophet calls him angel"). Certainly that "angel" is present in the recension of the Latin Bible Augustine read, which had been translated from the Septuagint, not from the Hebrew. Alluding to the angel of Isaiah 9:6 (LXX), Martin Werner suggests that "the Greek translator of the Book of Isaiah was already identifying the Messiah with the 'angel of Jahwe'";[47] in any event, angel-christology was strongly underwritten by Jewish exegesis (the Septuagint, like Targum, is a form of biblical exegesis).

Evoking the key verse in Isaiah 9, Ambrose states, "Christ Himself is the Angel of the great council."[48] Likewise, Justin cites Isaiah 9:6 as proof-text for *his* angel-christology: "And when Isaiah calls Him [Christ] the Angel of mighty counsel, did he not foretell Him to be the Teacher of those truths which He did teach when He came [to earth]?" "He . . . is called at one time the Angel of great counsel, and a Man by Ezekiel, and like the son of man by Daniel, and a Child by Isaiah, and Christ and God to be worshipped by David, and Christ and a Stone by many, and Wisdom by Solomon. . . ."[49] Origen writes that the Son, as the Word, is "'the Angel of mighty counsel' and 'the rule came upon his shoulder.'"[50] Surprisingly, even Calvin alludes to an "Ange ou ambassadeur du haut conseill."[51] Nonetheless, in the Hebrew Bible, the messianic child of Isaiah 9:6 is not called "angel" at all; the word "angel" does not appear in that verse. The English Bible gets it right, of course, as does the Vulgate, which Jerome translated directly from the Hebrew, not from the Greek Septuagint: "For unto us a child is born, unto us a son is given: and the government shall be upon his shoulder: and his name shall be called Wonderful, Counsellor, The mighty God, The everlasting Father, The Prince of Peace" (Isa. 9:6; AV). To these names and titles of the wonderful child, the Septuagint translator adds, "the angel of mighty council": *Megales boules aggelos.* When, in *De Trinitate*, Augustine claims that "the prophet calls him [the Son of God] angel," he alludes to that "angel of mighty counsel."

Other details are relevant to an informed reading of Edwards. The Jewish philosopher Philo of Alexandria, a near-contemporary of Jesus, made the significant link between *aggelos* (angel) and *logos* (word or reason). Using the terms of Greek philosophy to allegorize the *mal'ak* YHWH of the Hebrew

Bible, Philo explains "the appearance of the angel of Yahweh to the Patri-archs" as the appearance of Logos or divine Reason.[52] To Philo, the Logos is the chief angel—"the oldest of the angels, such as he is called an archangel. The Logos is also the *mal'ak Yahweh*, who manifests himself in the theopha-nies" (Daniélou is cited).[53] For Philo (to follow James D. G. Dunn), "the Logos is nothing other than God himself in his approach to men." Apposite examples from Philo (set out usefully by Dunn) include: "of necessity was the Logos appointed as judge and mediator, who is called 'angel'." Philo also writes about "God's firstborn, the Word, who holds the eldership among the angels, their ruler as it were. . . ."[54]

Given the widespead messianic speculations of later Judaism, and given the "angel of mighty council" (or "counsel") in the Septuagint and the old Latin recensions of Isaiah 9:6, it may be only a step further to the identification of the preexistent Christ with the angel of the Lord, the *mal'ak YHWH*. What should not be forgotten, however, is the radical difference between the divine Logos as expounded in the Fourth Gospel, the Word that "was made flesh, and dwelt among us," and Philo's Logos, which is not a hypostasis, a being in any way separate from or other than God. Rather, as explicated by Dunn, in a "basic concept [that] remains firmly Jewish: *the Logos of God is God in his self-revelation.*"[55]

In the context of Edwards's *History of Redemption*, what I find most provocative about angel-christology is its well-documented role in the apolo-getic writings of the early Church. (I refer to "apologists" and "apologetic writings" in a broad sense.) "In Palestinian Judaism, particularly in the apoca-lyptic writings, *angels* were accorded a much more extensive role than hith-erto as intermediaries between heaven and earth, including that of interces-sors on man's behalf."[56] Thus, pre-Christian, and Jewish-Christian, angelology could provide "an opening" (as Dunn puts it) for the early Fathers to identify Christ as an angel.[57] Another opening, which can be mentioned here only in passing, has to do with the Septuagint, the Bible consulted by Justin and by Philo, and its tendency to alter the Hebrew phrase "sons of God" to read *aggeloi theou*, "angels of God," though sometimes the "sons of God" reading is preserved.[58] Then there is Philo's authoritative *logos-aggelos* identification, particularly his identification of the Logos or chief of angels with the *mal'ak YHWH*. Another "opening" for angel-christology is the tendency in the apologists' defense of Christianity to show that Christ was present "from the beginning": as the mediating angel of God, and in the "form" of his human nature, the discarnate Christ was active throughout the Old Testament. (Pelikan alludes to the apologists' "campaign to prove the superiority of Christian doctrine on the grounds of its antiquity."[59]) Tertullian, we have seen above, argues that it was the Son "who at all times came down to hold converse with men, from Adam on to the patriarchs and the prophets, in vision, in dream, in mirror, in dark saying."[60]

Justin too "makes a great play of the OT theophanies in his proof of the pre-existence of Christ, including those where the one who appears is identified as 'the angel of the Lord.'"[61] (Likewise, for Edwards, the "redemption of the children of Israel out of Egypt was by Jesus Christ as is evident, for it was wrought by him that appeared to Moses in the bush; for that was the person that sent Moses to redeem the people but that was Christ, as is evident because he is called the angel of the Lord, Ex. 3:2–3.") In his first *Apology* (written ca. 139), Justin explicates the theophany in the burning bush:

> For at that juncture, when Moses was ordered to go down into Egypt and lead out the people of the Israelites who were there, and when he was tending the flocks of his maternal uncle [*sic*] in the land of Arabia, our Christ conversed with him under the appearance of fire from a bush, and said, "Put off thy shoes, and draw near and hear." And he, when he had put off his shoes and drawn near, heard that he was to go down into Egypt and lead the people of the Israelites there; and he received mighty powers from Christ, who spoke to him in the appearance of fire. . . .[62]

The error of the Jews, Justin claims, is "to teach that the nameless God spoke to Moses" out of the midst of the bush, whereas the speaker was in fact God's Son, the Word of God, who is called "both Angel and Apostle." Thus when we read in Exodus, "the Angel of God spake unto Moses . . . and said I AM THAT I AM," that Angel was Christ "appearing sometimes in the form of fire and sometimes in the likeness of angels."[63]

The burning bush is explicated in Justin's *Dialogue with Trypho*, where proof-texts adduced in support of his angel-christology include the three angels who appeared to Abraham at the oak of Mamre (Gen. 18:1–2); Jacob and the angel of God at Bethel (Gen. 31:10–14); and Jacob wrestling with the man or angel at the ford of Jabok (Gen. 32:22–31).[64] Explaining to Trypho, a learned Jew of the second century, the true meaning of these events, Justin (who was entirely dependent on the Greek version or versions of the Jewish Bible) argues that "this same One, who is both Angel, and God, and Lord, and man, and who appeared in a human form to Abraham and Isaac, appeared in a flame of fire from the bush, and conversed with Moses."[65] It is not, to make an obvious remark, that for Justin the angel in the burning bush looks forward to or anticipates or predicts Christ; as the angel of the Lord, the discarnate Christ is conversing with Moses from the thorn bush (just as for Calvin, glossing Paul, Christ was "plainly" present in the wilderness with Israel). Thus Trypho replies to Justin: "For you utter many blasphemies, in that you seek to persuade us that this crucified one was with Moses and Aaron, and spoke to them in the pillar of cloud. . . ."[66]

Consider briefly a precursor of Justin's, Irenaeus (ca. 130–200), who, as Jean Daniélou confirms, "attributes all the theophanies of the Old Testament to the Son."[67] For Irenaeus, "the Word, who existed in the beginning with God, by whom all things were made, who was also always present with mankind, was in these last days, according to the time appointed by the Father, united to his own workmanship, inasmuch as He became a man liable to suffering."[68] Explicating the story of Moses and the burning bush, Irenaeus, like Justin and Jonathan Edwards, attributes the theophany to Christ:

"For Christ is the end of the law for righteousness to every one that believeth" [Rom. 10:4]. And how is Christ the end of the law if He be not also the final cause of it? For He who has brought in the end has Himself also wrought the beginning; and it is He who does Himself say to Moses, "I have surely seen the affliction of my people which is in Egypt, and I have come down to deliver them" [Exod. 3:7–8]; it being customary from the beginning with the Word of God to ascend and descend for the purpose of saving those who were in affliction.[69]

To return to seventeenth-century Puritanism: Samuel Mather (the eldest brother of Increase Mather) glossed the burning-bush theophany in terms that echo the Fathers and anticipate Edwards. According to the widely read *The Figures or Types of the Old Testament* (a series of sermons written between 1666 and 1668 and published posthumously in 1683): "The *second Person* Jesus Christ appeared to *Moses, Exod.* 3.2,4. For he is called *the Angel,* which agrees not so well to the first Person. *And* Moses *prays for his Good will,* Deut. 33.16. Therefore it was not any created Angel, but Jesus Christ, the Angel of the Covenant of Grace; as a *praeludium* to his Incarnation."[70]

❖   ❖   ❖

"The Angell there is lookt upon to be Christ himselfe Styled Angel . . . by both Jewish Rabbies & Christian Expositors. See Ainsworth on Exo. 14.19," writes Edward Taylor in *Types of the Old Testament.* Having cited Christian expositors early and late on the burning bush passage in Exodus 3, I shall turn to some of the Rabbis, or rather, the Rabbis as mediated by the separatist leader Henry Ainsworth (?1571–1622), "whose acquirements in rabbinical and oriental literature—as it was then understood—were equalled by few in Europe," according to the *Dictionary of National Biography.* Driven abroad to Amsterdam about the year 1593, where he served as the minister of the independent English Church, Ainsworth was the author of the much-cited *Annotations upon the Five Bookes of Moses* (written from 1616 to 1619, published in thirteen editions either singly or in various combinations between 1616 and 1639, and cited by every important Puritan and Congregationalist divine of the seventeenth and eighteenth centuries, including the Mathers and Edward

Taylor).[71] "Through Jewish contacts in Amsterdam he improved his Hebrew knowledge, the considerable extent of which is reflected in his writings" (*Encyclopedia Judaica*). Ainsworth's "memory abides through his rabbinical learning" (*Encyclopedia Britannica*, 13th edition).

What may have recommended the Rabbis to Ainsworth in the first place, despite the wrenching needed to accommodate their writings to his christology, is their adherence to the sacred text. As "arbitrary, forced, unhistorical, hairsplitting"[72] as some of it may be, rabbinic exegesis focuses on *sola scriptura*; it is also unmediated by the teachings of the despised Church of Rome. For Ainsworth, the Targums (Aramaic paraphrases of Hebrew Scripture) reflected the true spirit of the early Church: the Targum of Jonathan, "the Chaldee Interpreter," writes Ainsworth, protecting himself against charges of Judaizing, in "An Advertisement to the Reader," "is as ancient as the Apostles dayes if not more." "Ionathan that interpreted the Prophets, is reported to be the Scholler of Gamaliel, at whose feet our Apostle Paul learned the Law: and Onkelos who paraphrased on the Law, was not long after him."

"Wherever it was in any way possible," Sigmund Mowinckel tells us, "the rabbis read into the text references to the Messiah, the son of David."[73] Diligently turning to one rabbinic passage after another, Ainsworth at the same time performs a rhetorical trick by translating the Hebrew word for "Messiah," *masi^{a}h*, "the anointed one" (Aramaic, *m^{e}siha*), as "Christ." At this point, perhaps, the word "Messiah" should be clarified: as Mowinckel confirms,

> the Jews were awaiting a Messiah; and it was part of the message of Jesus, and later the central point in the teaching of His disciples, that He was this Messiah, "He that cometh" [Matt. 9:3].
> "Jesus Messiah", or in Greek "Jesus Christ", were His name and His title in the speech of the community, until the term "Christ" also began to be regarded as a personal name. . . .
> In later Judaism the term "Messiah" denotes an *eschatological* figure. He belongs to "the last time"; his advent lies in the future. To use the word "Messiah" is to imply eschatology, the last things.[74]

Put otherwise by John Ashton: "The *Messiah*, properly speaking, is a man anointed by God and sent by him at the end of time to assist him in establishing his kingly rule."[75] By naming the deferred Messiah of rabbinic writings "Christ," Ainsworth has appropriated those writings as discursive tools. Their value to him appears to be instrumental, but to what end? Nor does he tend to argue much with the Rabbis, who are smoothly conscripted into the service of Puritanism.[76] Like Justin's *Dialogue with Trypho*, Ainsworth's *Annotations upon the Five Bookes of Moses* reads like an apologetic, and one tool of

Christian apologists, as we have seen, is angel-christology. Another is metonymic substitution.

If, for Calvin, Christ is the substance and subject of the Old Testament, if "even before his manifestation in the flesh" he was actively mediating between an offended God and fallen man, calling the elect, for Ainsworth Christ is the subject and substance of rabbinic exegesis, including Talmud and the Aramaic Targums ("Chaldee paraphrases"), which are turned into christocentric proof-texts. A typical example is Ainsworth's gloss on Genesis 49:11. First the biblical text, taken by many Jewish and Christian exegetes to be a messianic prophecy: "Binding his foal unto the vine, and his ass's colt unto the choice vine; he washed his garments in wine, and his clothes in the blood of grapes." Digging up apposite bits of Targum and Midrash on this passage, Ainsworth claims:

> And so the Ierusalemy Thargun applyeth this to Christ, saying, *How faire is the King Christ, that shall spring up out of the house of Judah!* . . . Likewise in *Breshith Rabba,* speaking of this place, it is said; *he sheweth us that when the Christ shall come to save Israel, he shall make ready his asse, and ride upon him, and come into Israel with povertie.*

In the Targum, translated here from Aramaic by Robert Hayward, the apposite phrase reads: "How beautiful is King Messiah [$m^e siha$] who is destined to arise from those of the house of Judah." Ainsworth has substituted the personal name "Christ" for the delayed "King Messiah" of rabbinic theology, whose advent, as Mowinckel says, lies in the future.[77]

Let us proceed to Ainsworth's reading of the burning bush. As one might expect, the angel in the bush is Christ; indeed, in a rhetorical pattern familiar to us from Edwards, from Calvin, and from Justin Martyr, every appearance in the Old Testament of the *mal'ak* YHWH is identified with Christ, the second person of the Trinity, as is every mention in postbiblical Jewish writings of "Messiah" and of "King Messiah," of the ineffable name of God, of his Glory, and of his glorious "Presence," the Shekinah. Annotating the burning bush theophany in Exodus 3, Ainsworth props up his angel-christology with learned allusions to the Targumist ("the Chaldee paraphrast") and to "other Rabbines":

> Vers. 2. *Angell*] This was *Christ,* who in vers. 6. calleth himself the *God of Abraham;* named an *Angell;* as before in Gen. 48.16. therefore Moses blessing Israel, mentioneth the *good will of this dweller in the bush,* Deut. 33.16. where the Chaldee paraphrast added, *him whose habitation is in heaven;* meaning God. And other Rabbines acknowledged as much. . . .

Thus Ainsworth and the Rabbis are in accord: the "dweller in the bush" was Christ; the "Rabbines acknowledged as much." In fact, Hayward confirms, the "Chaldee paraphrast" of Deuteronomy 33:16 does *not* use the phrase "him whose habitation is in heaven." To force his christocentric reading of the verse, Ainsworth undoes the periphrasis in Targum Onkelos, in which, as is customary in rabbinic exegesis, the postbiblical noun *Shekinah* is used to speak about God's Presence and his dwelling place. In Hayward's translation, the passage properly reads: "May He Whose Shekinah is in heaven and Who appeared to Moses in the bush be favourable to him. . . ." Targum Pseudo Jonathan differs slightly: "May the God who appeared in the Glory of His Shekinah to Moses in the bush be favourable to him. . . ."[78] (Edwards writes: "This angel is said to dwell in this bush [Deut. 33:16], the more to represent the divine nature of the Messiah dwelling in the human nature."[79])

Likewise Ainsworth's reading of Genesis 32 and its midrash, Hosea 12:4, the story of Jacob ("and there wrestled a man with him until the breaking of the day"; "Yea, he had power over the angel, and prevailed"). The "man" that wrestled with Jacob, Ainsworth tells us, assimilating Michael, the chief archangel, to Christ, is

> called after, and by the prophet Hosee, *God*, and an *Angell*. . . . It was therefore *Christ* appearing in the forme of a man, (as before to Abraham). . . . And the ancient Iewish Rabbines acknowledged this Angell to be Christ; *Our Doctors of blessed memory* (saith R. D. Kimchi, on Hos. 12.4) *have said, this Angell was Michael.* . . . Michael, is Christ the *Archangel*. . . .

(Edwards also says that at Penuel, "Christ appeared to [Jacob] in a human form" [170].) Compare Ainsworth's reading of Exodus 14:19 ("And the angel of God [*mal'ak* YHWH], which went before the camp of Israel, removed and went behind them"); Ainsworth identifies the angel of God as Christ:

> Vers. 19. the *Angell*] that is, *Christ*, called *Iehovah*, Exod. 13.21. So the Hebrew Doctors have acknowledged this *Angell* to be *Michael the great Prince, who was made a wall of fire, betweene the Israelites and the Egyptians; Pirke R. Eliezer, chap.* 42. And others of them say *this Angell was (Shechinah) the presence* (or *Majestie*) *of God, and called a Angell and Prince of the World, because the government* of the world is *by his hand: R. Menachem upon this place.*

Likewise Ainsworth's christocentric reading of Exodus 13:21 ("And the Lord [YHWH] went before them by day in a pillar of cloud, to lead them the way; and by night in a pillar of fire"): for Ainsworth it was not YHWH but "*Christ* whom the Israelites tempted in the wildernesse" who went before them in the pillar of cloud. His gloss on Genesis 48:16, the "Angel which redeemed me from all evil," invokes the high authority of Rabbi Menachem:

Angell] *Christ*, the Angel of the covenant, Mal. 3.1. the Angel in whom Gods
name is, Exod. 23.20.21. called here Iakobs *Redeemer*, or *Deliverer*, which is the
title of God, Psal. 19.15. Esa. 32.14. and 47.4. The Rabbines acknowledge this
Angel to be God, saying; *hee mentioneth also Gods-majestie (Schechinah) when hee
saith, the Angell that redeemed me. R. Menachem on Gen 48.*[80]

When the three angels appeared to Abraham (Ainsworth glosses Genesis
18:2), they "seemed" to him to be "three men"; however, one of them was
Christ, for "Abraham acknowledged him as the *Lord*," whereas the other two
were "created *Angels.*" At the Akedah, the binding of Isaac (Gen. 22:11–12),
usually read as a figure or type of the crucifixion, the "*Angell* who speaketh as
God . . . was Christ himselfe." In brief, leaping midrashically from one
proof-text to another, from the Torah to Targum to the Rabbis and back again
(evoking "Our Doctors of blessed memory," even), Ainsworth refers to the
angel of God, the *mal'ak* YHWH, as "Christ," "Jehovah," "Jacob's Redeemer,"
"Michael the great Prince," and, finally, *Schechina*, a term, he informs us,
"used for the divine presence or Majesty of God, and *Christ dwelling with his
people*" (emphasis added).[81] For Ainsworth, then, it is not God's Presence, his
glorious *Shekinah*, that in the Hebrew Bible and postbiblical Judaism is
"dwelling with his people"; it is the second person of the Trinity, who has
taken over the Shekinah's place or *topos*, just as Christ has taken over the
topos of the *mal'ak* YHWH.[82] (Rabbi Joshua b. Karha replied to the heathen:
"God spoke from the thorn bush to teach you that there is no place where the
Shekinah is not, not even a thorn bush.")

Suddenly, and belatedly, what Ainsworth is doing makes some sense to me:
in the *Annotations*, Jewish messianic speculations and seventeenth-century
Puritan millennial speculations have been hopefully confused. So many
learned particulars have been brought into Ainsworth's text, and so diligently, that a very great matter must be at stake—not the conversion of the
Jews only, although that may be part of it, but the millennium, the final messianic reign within history. Extracanonical Jewish texts speak about two
major stages of redemption: the Messianic Age (or Age of Messiah) and the
world to come. In some rabbinic and cabbalistic writings, Israel's restoration
marks the opening of the Age of Messiah. That for Ainsworth Jesus Christ is
taken to be the subject of Jewish adventist writings suggests (to me) that they
are being read as prophecies (or eschatological types) of Christ's *second* advent, the delayed Parousia, which lies in the future. Just as the angel of the
Lord, the *mal'ak* YHWH who speaks to Moses from the bush, is identified
with Christ, so for Ainsworth the deferred Messiah of Judaism is identified
with Christ, whose second advent (it was believed in some Puritan circles)
will open the temporal Messianic Age.

❖   ❖   ❖

Ainsworth's *Annotations* circulated widely among divines in Europe and in America from the early 1620s. Increase Mather and his brother Samuel Mather leaned on them heavily, as did Edward Taylor. Edwards may or may not have known them at first hand (reading lists are incomplete, and no library catalogue has come down to us), but he did have Matthew Poole's huge *Synopsis Criticorum aliorumque Sacrae Scripturae Interpretum* (1669–76), a learned collection of treatises and annotations on the Bible, which cites Ainsworth as an authority on Targum, on Talmud, on late Jewish apocalyptic, and on other rabbinic texts.[83]

According to the widely known computations of some Rabbis, the year 1648 would mark the appearance of the Jewish Messiah. That Zoharitic year had been established by Gamatria (the numerical value of letters): the "Hebrew words *heble mashiah*, 'birthpangs of the Messiah,' have the numerical equivalent . . . which corresponds in the Hebrew calendar to the year 1648."[84] Other Rabbis and scholars discovered the year 1648 encoded in verses of Leviticus and Psalms.[85] To follow Abba Hillel Silver's *A History of Messianic Speculation in Israel:*

> As the year 1648 approached—the *Anno Mirabile*—the great year heralded by the *Zohar* and many subsequent teachers, the national fervour mounted. Fantastic hopes engulfed the whole of Israel, from Safed to London, from Morocco to Poland. The Rabbis of Palestine sent an encyclical prayer to be recited at dawn and in the evening in all the lands of the Diaspora, the recitation to be accompanied by lamentation and penance, asking for the restoration of the Kingdom of David and for the remission of the travailpangs of the Messianic times.[86]

Messianic fervor was also mounting in New England: in 1646 (we are told by Sacvan Bercovitch), Samuel Gorton, a radical New Englander,

> complained . . . about the settlers' "looking after, and foretelling so much . . . the calling of the Jews," and Increase Mather could say in 1710 (the year after he published his popular *Essay upon the Jews Conversion and the Millennium*), that "The Conversion of the Jews . . . has ever been received as a Truth in the Churches of *New-England.*"

"Long after 1648 had come and passed," Bercovitch writes, the ministers of New England still "discussed and prayed for the event. At times they undertook themselves to convert the Jews; they shared in the excitement through the 1660s—the crest of Shabb'tai Zvi's career—at the 'constant reports from sundry places and hands' about an influx of Jews to the Holy Land. . . ."[87]

But why did Samuel Gorton and Increase Mather pray for the "calling of the Jews"? Why did their "salvation" matter to those pious New Englanders one way or another? Because, for Mather (as for Jonathan Edwards), the conversion of the Jews was requisite to the opening of the millennium, the Messianic Age; and Mather, like Edwards, took the Jews' salvation to be their "calling" or conversion to Christianity. Paul's Epistle to the Romans is a proof-text cited generally by Puritan millenarians: "blindness [*porosis*] in part is happened to Israel until the fulness of the Gentiles be come in. And so all Israel shall be saved; as it is written, There shall come out of Sion the Deliverer, and shall turn away ungodliness from Jacob" (Rom. 11:25–26).[88] According to Poole's *Synopsis Criticorum*, Paul's phrase "all Israel" refers to the *whole* body of the Israelite people, to the fullness of Israel (with a few exceptions, who are literally "led for nothing," *pro nihilo*).[89] "Divines are wont to make the conversion of the Jews an immediate sign fore-running the day of judgment," Increase Mather writes in *The Mystery of Israel's Salvation* (1669). "The time surely draweth on apace."[90]

The time was still drawing on in 1739, when Edwards preached the series of thirty sermons published as *A History of the Work of Redemption*. At one time, we learn, the Jews "openly rejected Christ and ceased to be a professing people." "And then the Jews were rejected and apostatized from the visible church to prepare the way for the calling of the Jews which shall be in the latter days" (178–79).

> When they shall be called, then shall that ancient people that were alone God's people for so long a time be God's people again, never to be rejected more, one fold with the Gentiles. . . .
>
> Though we don't know the time in which this conversion of the nation of Israel will come to pass, yet this much we may determine by Scripture, that it will [be] before [the] glory of the Gentile part of the church shall be fully accomplished. . . . (470)

"Without doubt," Edwards says in "Notes on the Apocalypse," as soon as the Jews are called, and "lamenting their obstinacy," they will be restored to Israel, "because when their unbelief ceases, their dispersion, the dreadful and signal punishment of their belief, will cease too. As they have continued hitherto with one consent, to dishonor Christ by rejecting the gospel, so shall they meet together to honor him, by openly professing it with one mouth, and practice it with one heart and soul, together lamenting their obstinacy."[91]

❖   ❖   ❖

To read Edwards's Redemption Discourse in the context of second- and third-century Christian apologists such as Justin and Tertullian, and then to consider it in terms of the doctrine of the national conversion of the Jews, is to recognize the *History of Redemption* as a Calvinist apologetic. Edwards's designated opponents include Anabaptists, Quakers, Arminians, Socinians, Arians, Deists, Mohammedans, and, most centrally, the hated Church of Rome—"Antichrist" (405–16). Placing the "visible church" right at the beginning of the Old Testament, Edwards (like Calvin) takes up angel-christology, which was used rhetorically by the apologist Justin Martyr, who, like Edwards, was fighting on two fronts. On the one hand, relying on arguments from prophecy to prove the unity of God's plan, Justin was defending Christianity against heresy, Gnosticism in particular; on the other, he was converting the Jews.

When "Satan's visible kingdom on earth shall be destroyed," Edwards announces in the Redemption Discourse, "the church of Christ shall have easy work of it, as Joshua and the children [of Israel] had obtained that great victory . . . when the sun stood still, and God sent great hail stones" (466). (Earlier in the Redemption Discourse, we are told, "Christ fought as the captain of their host and cast down great hailstones" [193].) "Heresies and infidelity and superstition among those who have been brought up under the light of the gospel will then be abolished" (467). Rome, as predicted, will fall: along with Satan's despised "Mohammedan empire," the "kingdom of Antichrist shall be utterly overthrown" (468). Finally, and on the cusp of the millennium, "Jewish infidelity shall then be overthrown" (469).

> The Jews in all their dispersions shall cast away their old infidelity, and shall wonderfully have their hearts changed, and abhor themselves for their past unbelief and obstinacy; and shall flow together to the blessed Jesus, penitently, humbly, and joyfully owning him as their glorious king and only savior, and shall with all their hearts as with one heart and one voice declare his praises unto other nations.
>
> Nothing is more certainly foretold than this national conversion of the Jews is in the eleventh chapter of Romans. And there are also many passages of the Old Testament that can't be interpreted in any other sense. . . . (469–70)

(When at last all Israel is saved, to follow Increase Mather's gloss on the *mal'ak* YHWH of Zechariah 12:8, the Jews "shall be like unto the blessed Angels. They shall have most Seraphical gifts bestowed upon them, yea, *they shall be like to the Angel of the Lord, h.e.* they shall be like unto Jesus Christ, the Angel of the everlasting Covenant.")[92]

CHAPTER THREE

The Days of Messiah

Increase Mather and the Conversion of the Jews

The final reward and the ultimate good, endless and perfect, is the life of the World to Come; but the Days of Messiah belong to this world, and will be as the world customarily is, except that sovereignty will be restored to Israel.

Moses Maimonides[1]

Maimonides, who is accounted one of the wisest and soberest Writers amongst the Jews since their last fatal Dispersion in Tract. Saned. cap. 10. saith that Their wise Men are of the Belief that the Kingdom of the Messiah shall continue for a thousand Years. . . . And R. Eliezer says, The Days of the Messiah are a Thousand Years.

Increase Mather[2]

Good News for the Israel of God, and particularly for His New-English Israel. The Devil was never more let Loose than in our Days; and it proves the Thousand Years is not very Far Off.

Cotton Mather[3]

Great comets appeared in 1618, 1648, 1652, and 1654. The computations of the Zohar gave 1648 as the date of Messiah's appearance.[4] In 1651, the English millenary Mary Cary put the conversion of the Jews in 1656, the millennium in 1701.[5] Thomas Goodwin expected the millennium in 1700, the conversion of the Jews "by 1666 at the latest."[6] John (or Henry) Archer "dated the coming in of the Jews to 1650 or 1656, the start of the collapse of antichrist's 1260-year reign to 1666, and the commencement of the millennium

47

to around 1700."[7] For Thomas Brightman and Joseph Mede, the destruction of Rome and the millennium were imminent: Brightman predicted the Jews would be restored to their own land by 1650; "the last end of Antichrist" would expire in 1686.[8] John Napier, the Scots mathematician, advised that "the Day of God's judgment appears to fall betwixt the years of Christ 1688 and 1700."[9] Influenced by Rabbi Menasseh ben Israel, the Baptist preacher Henry Jessey said the Jews would be converted before 1658.[10] In 1655, Paul Felgenhauer of Bohemia, basing his chronology on "esoteric knowledge which had been prophetically revealed to him," predicted "the immediate advent of the Messiah and the restoration of the Jews."[11] John Cotton, Increase Mather's father-in-law and minister of the Congregational church in Boston, "set 1655 for the date of Christ's arrival in New England."[12]

In England, the year "most put forward" for the opening of the millennium was 1656; then it was 1666.[13] The mathematician William Oughtred "thought Jesus Christ might appear in person in 1656 to convert the Jews."[14] On October 24, 1655, in imitation of Christ's entry into Jerusalem, the Quaker leader James Nayler announced that he was Jesus and that Jesus was within him. Led through the mud by his disciples, who "kept up an ecstatic chant of *Holy, Holy, Holy,* and *Hosanna*" (or "Hosanna! Holy, holy! Lord God of Sabaoth!") he rode into Bristol on the back of a colt.[15] In 1665, Sabbatai Zevi, a kabbalist from Smyrna, announced formally that he was the Messiah. John Bull and Richard Farnham, "prophets who died in 1642, were believed by their supporters to have sailed away in a boat of bulrushes to convert the lost tribes."[16] Arise Evans, the Welsh author of *Light For the Iews: or, the Means to convert Them* (1656), convinced himself that "King *Charles Steeward* tis Gods chosen Vessel to deliver us all": "You may know King *Charles Steeward* to be the man that you look for, or your Messiah, as you call him, by the Star that appeared at his birth."[17] In *De Mille Annis* (1627), the German divine Johann Heinrich Alsted computed the messianic year to be 1694, a date he arrived at "based on the numbers in Daniel and . . . on the seals, trumpets, and vials of Revelation."[18] In 1623, the German shoemaker-theosophist Jacob Boehme admonished the Jews to "learn to know their Messiah, for the time of their visitation is at hand, wherein they shall be redeemed from the captivity of their misery and be made over again."[19] In the early 1650s, Thomas Tany (Theaurau John), a London goldsmith, "learnt Hebrew preparatory to setting out for Jerusalem 'to call the Jews' in a small boat which he had built for himself. He cried 'Ho for the holy wars in these nations beginning at France!'. . . He was drowned on his way to Palestine via Holland."[20]

❖   ❖   ❖

In 1666, Increase Mather, teacher of the Second Church in Boston, preached a series of lecture-sermons, *The Mystery of Israel's Salvation, Explained and Ap-*

plyed: or, a Discourse Concerning the General Conversion of the Israelitish Nation (London, 1669).[21] "The great and terrible day of the Lord, it is near, it is near," Mather predicts, reading as a sign of the end the Fire of London: "direful and astonishing desolations by fire, are a sign that the time is at hand wherein the Mystery of God shall be finished. . . . Now is it not so at this day, that the world seemeth to be all on fire?" (160). "But though this calamity be heavy, yet be comforted in that these awful tremendos dispensations are such, as that by the light of this fire we may see the *vial full* of the wrath of God is ready to be poured upon *the head of Rome*" (161). Fires, pestilence, earthquakes, wars, floods, "terrible Comets and many other amazing prodigies visible to the world": all proved "God is about some great work" (42). "The Lord then is roaring from on high to give us warning, that the great and notable day is coming" (161). "Indeed, a little before the conversion of the *Jews*, there will be the most terrible doings in the world that ever was heard of, in respect of wars and commotions, the waves of the Sea roaring, confused noise and garments rolled in bloud, bloud and fire, and vapour of smoke" (122). "It will be in a time of very great trouble when *Israel* shall be saved" (34). "Are not the powers of heaven shaking? . . . Do you not feel an earthquake at this day?" (162). "And what if the providential coming of Christ to destroy *Rome*, and to convert the *Jews*, should be signified by Comets and other prodigies?" (43). Prophesied by rabbinic calculations, by the "wickedness of the wicked" (39) and other birth pangs of the Messianic Age, the glorious millennium was at hand.

For Mather, Christ's *"providential coming* to destroy *Rome"* and also "his *personal coming* to begin that long, and last, and great day, when the Saints shall judge the world" were bound up with Israel's redemption as Mather and other Protestant millenarians imagined it (161). In 1650, six years before Cromwell readmitted the Jews to England (they had been expelled July 18, 1290), Rabbi Menasseh ben Israel (1604–1657) stated in *The Hope of Israel:* "Though we cannot exactly show the time of our redemption, yet we judge it to be near. For we see many prophecies fulfilled. . . ."[22] *The Hope of Israel* appeared in Spanish and in Latin; it then appeared in an English translation by Moses Wall. The second English edition (London, 1651), corrected in 1652, outlines its subject matter: "*The Hope of Israel:* written by Menasseh ben Israel, an Hebrew divine, and philosopher. Newly extant, and printed at Amsterdam, and dedicated by the author to the High Court the Parliament of England and the Councell of State. Whereunto are added some discourses upon the point of the conversion of the Jewes: by Moses Wall."[23] Introducing the recently published edition of Menasseh's text, Henry Méchoulan submits that "for the first time in history, relations between Jews and Christians are such that the former find themselves unburdened by the latter of all the sins of Israel. From now on universal salvation comes through the Jews, whom it is no longer proper to hate or despise, for they are, as it were, the keepers of the keys of the Kingdom."[24] Put otherwise, for Thomas Brightman, John Cotton, Joseph Mede, Thomas Goodwin, Hugh Broughton, Jeremiah Burroughs, John Davenport, William Twisse, John Owen, Henry Finch, and William Hooke, to name the most important Puritan millenarians cited in Increase Mather's *Mystery of Israel's Salvation*, the conversion or "calling" of the Jews was requisite to the creation of *"an heaven* established in the world" (143); "the last times are come," Mather announces, "and therefore the conversion of the *Jews* hasteneth" (38).

      ◈   ◈   ◈

Menasseh ben Israel "could not accept the second coming of Christ, or the prerequisite conversion of the Jews," Méchoulan writes.[25] In an essay of 1977, Mason I. Lowance, Jr., regards the conversion of the Jews as "an aspect of the millennial promise regarded as a crucial prerequisite by which the advent of the last things might be identified."[26] The phrase "crucial prerequisite" makes its way into a central chapter of Lowance's monograph of 1980, *The Language of Canaan*.[27] One comes across the word "prerequisite" again in an informed essay of 1990, *"Israel Redivivus:* the Eschatological Limits of Puritan Typology in New England," by Reiner Smolinski: "Puritan millennialists strongly asserted that the restoration and national conversion of the Jews was a *prerequisite* to the Second Coming; Christ's Second Advent was indefinitely postponed until such time as Israel's 'dry bones' were enlivened and restored to their ancient position of prominence."[28] Used in a messianic context, the word "prerequisite" evokes a distinguished study by Joseph Klausner, *The Messianic Idea in Israel* (1927; ET 1956), in particular a chapter called "The Prerequisites of Messiah's Coming."[29] Needless to say, for Klausner, those prerequisites do not include the conversion of the Jews to Christianity.

I am intrigued by the idea of prerequisite conversion. For Increase Mather, the conversion of the Jews was "necessary" for the opening of the millennium, the interregnum of peace on earth: "before the times of refreshing come," Mather says (echoing Acts 3:19), "when the Saints shall be free from the annoyance of every evil, it is necessary that *Israel* should repent and be converted and have their sins blotted out" (103). A note to Grant Underwood's "The *Hope of Israel* in Early Modern Ethnography and Eschatology" (1993) uses the phrase "crucial antecedent" to define the Jews' role in the Puritans' destiny. Citing Christopher Hill's "'Till the Conversion of the Jews'" (with its marvellous title), Underwood observes "how widespread in seventeenth-century England was the idea that the restoration and conversion of the Jews was the crucial antecedent to the millennium."[30] In the (exaggerated) view of Andrew Delbanco, the conversion of the Jews was "considered by virtually all Protestants to be an essential prelude to the advent of the millennium."[31] Méchoulan writes about "the precondition of the conversion of the Jews to Christianity."[32]

Prelude, precondition, prerequisite, antecedent, harbinger: the Jews' conversion, like the conversion of Saul of Tarsus, would be a work of grace. Jews would be "called," not forced, to convert. Mather thought their conversion would be effected "by Vision, as *Paul's* was, by a glorious manifestation of the person of the Son of God from heaven unto all the Tribes on earth, causing them to mourn" (90). Four decades later, in 1709, Mather's views have not changed much:

> As for the manner of their Conversion, I still encline (with Mr. *Mede*, Dr. *Twisse*, Dr. *Goodwin*, Mr. *Strong*, and others) to think that it will be effected as *Paul's* was, by a miraculous Appearance of Christ to some of them, and be carried on by the Preaching of the Gospel, with most glorious down pourings of the Holy Spirit therewith.[33]

"In no circumstances was coercion to be used," as Frank E. Manuel confirms, "for conversion had to be an act of free will and conscience."[34] Still, the Jewish conscience might be caught by messianic proof-texts drawn from Rabbis and Targumists.

Partly to that apologetic end, and to read the signs of the times, Puritan Hebraists were intent on studying the Rabbis' interpretations of Scripture. Since the first part of the sixteenth century (Katharine Firth tells us), "there had been two broad approaches to the proper use of Hebrew wisdom; one was to treat it and the Christian revelation separately, the other to attempt to reconcile them."[35] (Another was to burn it.)[36] Like the great seventeenth-century Hebraist Henry Ainsworth, Increase Mather wanted to reconcile them. Throughout *Mystery* are named, among Jewish exegetes (as cited by Mather), R. Akiba, R. Eliezar, R. Manesseh ben Israel, R. Kimchi, R. Solomon, R. Benjamin, R. Abrabaneel, Maimonides, R. Saadias, R. Ashe, Hillel, R. Samuel, R. Ketina, R. Ibn Ezra (or Abenezra), R. Moses-Ben-Nachman, Philo, and Josephus. Targum Onkelos (the Chaldee Paraphrase) and the Babylonian Talmud are cited, often by way of Ainsworth, whose *Annotations* on the Pentateuch were part of the Mathers's library.[37] Still, despite appeals to Jewish writings, there is what Grant Underwood has understatedly called "the minor matter of the Messiah's identity."[38] The Jews were (and are still) awaiting the *first* advent of their long-deferred Messiah.[39] Mather, on the other hand, was awaiting the *second* and penultimate advent of Jesus Christ, which in some Puritan circles depended on the conversion of the Jews.[40] We shall explore the background to Mather's eschatology.

❖   ❖   ❖

In 1709, responding to Richard Baxter's *The Kingdom of Christ* (1691), Mather described *The Mystery of Israel's Salvation* as "a large Discourse on *Rom.* 11.26. Printed at *London* in the year 1669. from which, as to the Sub-

stance of what is there asserted, I do not to this Day see any just Cause to re-
cede."[41] It is as an extended, apologetic gloss on Romans 11:25–26 that
Mather's *Mystery* should be approached. Paul's text reads:

> For I would not, brethren, that ye should be ignorant of this mystery, lest ye
> should be wise in your own conceits; that blindness [*porosis*] in part is happened
> to Israel, until the fulness of the Gentiles [*ethnon*] be come in. And so all Israel
> shall be saved: as it is written, There shall come out of Sion the Deliverer, and
> shall turn away ungodliness from Jacob. (Romans 11:25–26; AV)

Instead of "blindness," Mather points out in *Mystery*, Paul's phrase "may better be rendred, *hardness is happened to Israel*. The Greek word [*porosis*] noteth a
brawny hardness, a desperate obduration, such as maketh stupid and sense-
less: And they that have had to do with unbelieving Israelites, have seen the
truth of this" (91).

> And therefore when the Apostle saith, That *all Israel shall be saved*, this also is
> part of his meaning; That the whole nation of the *Jews* shall be *saved* from the
> blindness of their minds, *saved* from the unbelief of their souls, *saved* from that
> curse and wrath of God which lyeth upon them, and which hath remained
> upon many of them, for more than 2000 and divers hundreds of years. (11)

The Jews, says Mather, building on Paul's metaphor of spiritual blindness, "are
under perverseness and obstinacy of will, whence they shut their eyes against
the light, and grow blind against the Sun, that they neither do nor will believe. . . . But the day will come when they shall be freed from this
bondage, for they shall at last own and embrace the Lord Jesus Christ" (93).
Shortly they shall be converted from "the unbelief of their souls," which is to
say they shall be converted from (the "bondage" of) Judaism to a Puritan version of Christianity.

When the Jews are "saved," Mather predicts, stressing what Gershom
Scholem identifies as the "restorative" element in Jewish Messianism, they
"shall be repossessed of the land of their Fathers, and . . . shall have an ex-
ternal temporal glory and happiness above other people."[42] They "shall *partake*
of a Temporal *salvation*" (117). "Consider, That there will be a glorious inchoa-
tion and first fruits of that kingdom which the Saints shall possess at the great
day, even before Christ cometh from heaven to judge the earth. For the *Jews* (as
hath been shewed) shall be converted before the day of judgment" (143). As
for the timetable of these events, "the conversion of the *Jews* will not be till this
present state of the world is near unto its end." *Not* the world itself, it should be
noted, but "this present state" of the world will be "near unto its end"; the distinction is crucial to an informed reading of Mather and of other Puritan millenarians (Brightman, Cotton, and Mede, for example) who did *not* expect or
even want the world to end. They wanted the "light of the Messiah" to break

into history.[43] After "the *Jews* conversion," Mather predicts, will come "a glorious day for the elect upon earth, and . . . this day will be of very long continuance" ("Author's Preface"). It will be a time of "glorious tranquillity, which the most high (whose methods of divine providence, is to bring light out of darkness, good out of evil, order out of confusion, peace out of war) will establish on earth" (159). The millennium, the "glorious day," the temporary messianic kingdom, may last "for Generations": "Justly how long this glorious day shall continue, is not for us to say, for therein the Scripture is silent; Only it is evident, that it will be for Generations one after another" (57).

What is Mather's authority for a literal reading of Romans 11:26 and for his identification of Paul's "Israel" with the "blind" Jews of the seventeenth century? First of all, it is conferred by the marginal commentary of the Geneva Bible, trusted by Puritans long after the appearance in 1611 of the King James Bible. In the 1640s, we are told by Christopher Hill, the Geneva Bible was available "in pocketable editions, so that men could study it in the privacy of their homes, or could produce it in a church or ale-house to knock down an argument with a text."[44] Following Theodore Beza's annotations closely, the Genevan editors took the word "Israel" ("all Israel shall be saved") to signify non-Christians whose religion was Judaism.[45] In a 1610 edition of the Geneva Bible, for example, a note to Romans 11:26 (cited in part by Mather [51]) reads: "The blindness of the Iewes is neither so universal that the Lord has no elect in that nation, neither shall it be continuall: for there shall be a time, wherein they also (as the Prophets have forewarned) shall effectually embrace that, which they doe now so stubbornely for the most part reject and refuse." The Apostle (we read) "beateth this into their heads; that the nation of the Iewes is not utterly cast off without hope of recoverie."[46] Modified, the spirit of the Genevan gloss makes its way into the King James Bible as a headnote to Romans 11 (a 1613 edition of the Authorized Version is cited below. The same text appears in an 1880 edition of the AV; numbers in the headnote refer to verses):

> 1 God hath not cast off all Israel. 7 Some were elected, though the rest were hardened: 16 There is hope of their conversion. 18 The Gentiles may not insult upon them 26 For there is a promise in their salvation. 33 Gods judgments are unsearchable.

As well, high authority for a historical "calling" of the Jews is conferred by the Savoy Declaration of 1658, which in 1660 became the doctrinal basis of the Congregational churches. "As the Lord is in care and love toward his church . . . so, according to his promise, we expect that in the latter days, Antichrist being destroyed, *the Jews called,* and the adversaries of his dear Son broken, the churches of Christ . . . shall enjoy in this world a more quiet, peaceable and glorious condition than they have enjoyed" (emphasis added).[47] Who or what is "Antichrist," whose destruction is said to be coincident with the "calling" or conversion of the Jews? The Savoy Declaration (following Luther) identifies him as the Pope of Rome:

> There is no other head of the Church but the Lord Jesus Christ, nor can the Pope of Rome in any sense be head thereof; but he is that Antichrist, that man of sin and son of perdition that exalteth himself in the Church against Christ and all that is called God, whom the Lord shall destroy with the brightness of his coming.[48]

Three prophecies have been drawn together: the destruction of Antichrist, "son of perdition"; the "brightness" of Christ's coming; and the calling of the cast-off Jews. These events are to occur *before* the "glorious condition" of the churches can be enjoyed "in this world," to recite the Savoy Declaration. Thomas Brightman (1562–1607), someone "of very great note and worth," in Mather's words (107), was "one of the first divines of the Puritan school to reject the argument that the Jews' conversion must be placed at the very end of history." The calling of the Jews, Brightman thought, "would be part of a new and brighter era of history, and not the end."[49] This is to say that the "calling" or "conversion" of the Jews has been conflated with "restoration" and "redemption" as those words are understood in Jewish messianism. Taking their "apocalyptic paraphernalia" from Jewish writings, biblical and postbiblical, and from the Book of Revelation, Puritan millennialists such as Brightman, Mather, and Mede used them to fix chronologically the time of Jesus Christ's penultimate advent and the conversion of the Jews to Christianity.[50]

This brings us to Mather's concept of the "glorious day for the elect upon earth," which may continue "for Generations one after another." He is not looking to the end of the world, but to the end of conditions in this world— he is pressing for an "enduring transformation of the human condition within history."[51] The millennium, a temporal Canaan, will be *a kingdom of this world*," to cite Joseph Klausner's description of the Jewish Age of Messiah.[52] In Mather's program: when Rome burns and the "son of perdition" is destroyed "by the *Epiphany of the Lords presence*" (142), when the dispersed and exiled Jews have gathered together in "the land of their Fathers" and converted to Christianity, then the blessed age *on earth* will begin. The millennium is a time of leftover time, neither here nor there. It is a revision of Jewish messianism, wherein the Age of Messiah, as described by Marjorie Reeves,

> is conceived as within history, not beyond it. It is the very apotheosis of history, embodying a lineal rather than a cyclical conception of time. It is not a recurring phenomenon, a return to an Age of Innocence, but a climax towards

which the whole of history was moving. The optimistic strand in the Christian expectation of history derives from the Jewish hope of a Messianic Age.[53]

That hope is mostly political, as Klausner confirms (and as Marx knew): "the Messianic idea is primarily the hope for the fulfilment of the political expectations of the Jewish people; and these expectations remained more or less mundane."[54] There are in Jewish thought "two major stages of redemption, both of which will arise miraculously": the Messianic Age, or "days of the Messiah," and the life of the world to come.[55] Some Rabbis taught that the Messiah will reign over a restored kingdom of Israel to which all the Jews of the exile will return.[56] Nor, Scholem remarks, is their redemption a purely inward and private phenomenon: "Judaism, in all of its forms and manifestations, has always maintained a concept of redemption as an event which takes place publicly, on the stage of history and within the community."[57]

The pursuit of the millennium, to echo Norman Cohn's study of radical millenarianism,[58] was identified, correctly, as a Jewish pursuit. In Scholem's view, "political and chiliastic Messianism of important religious movements within Christianity often appears as a reflection of what is really Jewish Messianism." Scholem adds: "It is well known how vigorously such tendencies were decried as Judaizing heresies by their orthodox opponents in Catholicism and Protestantism alike."[59] So-called "Jewish opinions" and "Jewish dreams" are explicitly condemned as heretical in two sixteenth-century confessions: the Augsburg Confession of 1530, definitive for Lutherans, condemns those "who now scatter Jewish opinions that, before the resurrection of the dead, the godly shall occupy the kingdom of the world, the wicked being everywhere suppressed."[60] The Second Helvetic Confession (1566), accepted by Swiss Protestant Churches, reads: "We further condemn Jewish dreams that there will be a golden age on earth before the Day of Judgment, and that the pious, having subdued all their godless enemies, will possess all the kingdoms of the earth."[61]

It is because Judaism and radical millennialism were so closely linked in the popular mind that the very learned Joseph Mede (or Mead), toward the end of *Clavis Apocalyptis* (1627), feels called upon to defend himself from charges of Judaizing: "Saint Ierome doth so much charge the Millinaries with Iudaism," Mede admits. "But howsoever that opinion be true or false, whether those Fathers were in error or no; to be of the same minde with the Iewes is not always culpable."[62] Indeed, were we to dismiss all Jewish concepts, we would have to dismiss ideas of *"the world to come, Gehenna, and Paradise."* These are not found in the Old Testament, but are taken from the Rabbis: "Doe not we Christians consent with the Iewes in these things? Have not we the names likewise (*of the Kingdome of Heaven and the Day of Iudgement*) from the Iewish *Rabbins?* For where are those things read in the Old Testament? which yet are very frequent among the Iewish Doctors."[63] If New Englanders were like the Jews, it was not because they learned Hebrew, but because their sense of an ending was nothing if not an interpretation and revision of Jewish adventist writings about the temporal Age of Messiah.[64]

This much Mather admits: in his *Dissertation Concerning the Future Conversion of the Jewish Nation* (1695; published 1709), defending his millenarianism with strained appeals to biblical authority, he attempts to trace the "notion" of the thousand years to "the Prophets" via the *"Hebrew* Doctors." "The *Jews* cannot endure to read the *New Testament,"* says Mather condescendingly;

> nevertheless, some of them are affected with the *Book of Revelation,* for therein they find Mystical Numbers, such as 666, and 42 Months, Three Day and a half, &c. which they are delighted with, and they are taken with *John's* Description of the *New Jerusalem,* and the Allusions which are throughout to whole Book to Things which they are acquainted with is pleasing to them: And in particular *a Thousand Years glorious Reign with the Messiah* . . . is a Mystery which the *Hebrew* Doctors have not been altogether unacqainted with; having (no doubt) received that Notion, as well as that of the Day of Judgement, by Tradition from their Fathers, who had them from the Prophets.

To substantiate his point about the "Thousand Years glorious Reign," he invokes the "Jewish Opinions" of Maimonides, of the Babylonian Talmud, and of R. Eliezer, adding in Hebrew the words *atîd labô,* and translating them as "the glorious world to come."[65]

Prompted by Mather's appeal to "the Hebrew Doctors," we should look briefly at a complex subject—"the conception of the Jewish Messiah as it has become crystallized in Biblical Talmudic Judaism" (Klausner is cited).[66] Some scholars would write about "conceptions" of the Jewish Messiah, and about "messianisms."[67] My point is straightforward: what made such conceptions attractive to Increase Mather was certainly the political role assigned to the figure of Messiah, who, after "a preliminary judgment," would set up a messianic kingdom on earth.[68] The messianic king would redeem and restore an exiled nation—a nation in servitude. To follow Klausner, the Messiah "redeems the whole world from oppression, suffering, war, and above all from heathenism and everything which it involves. . . . For in the Messianic age all peoples will be converted to Judaism. . . ."[69] With accommodation, Klausner's phrasing can usefully be applied to the messianic-political hopes of Mather, for whom the demonized Roman Church embodied heathenism and everything it involved, especially idolatry. If in Judaism the messianic figure is "the king who will redeem and rule Israel at the climax of human history and the instrument by which the kingdom of God will be established,"[70] why should he not be the king (called "King Messiah" in the

Aramaic Targums) who, after destroying Rome and converting the Jews to Christianity, will open the millennium?

◈ ◈ ◈

Attempting to reconcile Jewish messianism with his chiliasm, thereby expediting the conversion of the Jews (if that is his intention in *Mystery*), Mather turns to the Rabbis for support, as we have seen. More problematically, he must coordinate the brief, brilliant, premillennial epiphany of Jesus Christ with the first appearance of King Messiah; thus prophecies normally applied by Christian exegetes to the incarnation and resurrection of Christ are projected into the future and applied to the Parousia. In a passage that echoes Joseph Mede, Mather's "Author's Preface" to *Mystery* sets out the "good and profitable use" to be made of Jewish writings:

> If any should further object that in some places in this *Discourse* there is too much weight laid upon *Rabbinical observations*, &c. To that I would say; far be it from us to give heed unto *Jewish Fables*; and since the *Jews* ceased to be the Church of God, and so have been forsaken of his Spirit, their writing (especially where they speak of Christ) are of far less worth than before that; yet I add, that there is a multitude of places in the New Testament (and in the old too) which no one can clearly understand, except he be acquainted with the *notions, customs, phrases*, &c. which were formerly in use amongst the *Jews*. Many terms are found in the New Testament, which are not in the old, but are in Jewish writings being in use amongst the Jewish Doctors whilst there was a Jewish Church, and from them . . . borrowed by the Apostles.

In connection with those Jewish writings, Mather (like Henry Ainsworth) uses the Greek word "Christ," a proper name of Jesus, just as if "Jewish Doctors" were anticipating *his* advent in particular. (From Mather's point of view, and from the point of view of seventeenth-century millenarians like Serrarius, the Jews *were* awaiting Jesus Christ; at his first advent, they had not recognized their Messiah in the form of a servant.)[71] On the other hand, opportunely, Mather will take up the term *Messias*. "Now the wretched *Jews* will not believe that Jesus Christ is he, that Jesus Christ is the true *Messias*, the Saviour of the world, therefore they live, they die in sin" (84).

If "Jewish writings" are "profitable," so are seventeenth-century Jews, who, according to Mather and like-minded exegetes, were preserved for "some great Work." Certain divines (we read in *Mystery*)

> lay much weight upon an argument drawn from the secret wonderful providence of God in preserving the *Jewish* Nation entire from mixing with other Nations where they are dispersed. The providence of God hath suffered other Nations to have their bloud mixed very much: As you know it is with our

own Nation, there is a mixture of *British*, *Roman*, *Saxon*, *Danish*, *Norman* bloud; but as for the body of the *Jewish* Nation it is far otherwise. (13)[72]

Compare Mather's *Dissertation Concerning the Future Conversion of the Jewish Nation*, which describes the *"Miracle by which God does preserve the Jewish Nation, distinguished from all others."* "It cannot be supposed," he confides, "that God would for Two Thousand Years preserve this People, scattered among other Nations, yet without mixing it self with them, if they were not preserved for some great Work."[73] The "great Work" for which Jews have been set apart and "preserved," we learn, is their "general conversion" to Christianity. From Mather's perch, the Jews have been kept intact to one end: to become Christians, and thus to fulfill the political ambitions of New England Puritans.

Indeed, Israel's "salvation," which "will be more wonderful than any of those former which heretofore have been" (77), is for Mather foreshadowed and prefigured in Hebrew Scripture: the Jews' deliverance from the captivity in Babylon is "a Type" of their deliverance (from the captivity of Judaism). The passage deserves to be cited in full:

> That deliverance of the *Jews* by *Cyrus* out of *Babylon*, was very wonderful, yet nothing so wonderful as this will be, as is evident, because that was but a Type of this, and therefore it is, that in many places in Scripture, the very same expressions are used to signifie both that deliverance out of *Babylon*, and this which is to come; so the Vision of the dry bones in *Ezekiel* doth firstly refer to the *Jews* captivated in *Babylon*, but principally to the forlorn estate of the *Jews* at this day, and the like may be said concerning many passages in other of the Prophets, that they do firstly concern the *Babylonian* condition of the *Jews*, but lastly their present condition; but because that deliverance was a Type of this, therefore this will be the more eminent and wonderful, for the Type must needs come short of the Anti-type. (78)

Comparing contemporary Jews to the "dry bones in Ezekiel" (a commonplace of conversion rhetoric), Mather regards the Jews' deliverance from the Babylonian captivity as "but a Type," a prefiguration, of their deliverance from Judaism at the hands of the Puritans. Furthermore, "this salvation will be more wonderful than that out of *Egypt*": just as the enslaved Children of Israel were redeemed from Egypt, so now they will be "saved from a state of death." For they are hopelessly scattered: "Now they are become like *a Lamb in a large pasture*, as the Lord threatned them it should be, *Hos. 4.16. i.e.* here a *Jew*, and there a *Jew*, scattered up and down the world" (80–81). Their ingathering will be a sign of the imminent fall of Rome and of the Turks, of the destruction of Antichrist, and of the glorious millennium.

Having come upon the loosely used terms "type" and "anti-type," we shall look briefly at Mather's approach to the argument from prophecy, an ap-

proach characterized by an indiscriminate use of sources, biblical and postbiblical, whose fulfillment is placed in the future. Predicting the wonderful
"Temporal salvation" of Israel (117) and "freedom from all persecution and
corporal oppressions" (118), Mather takes up verses from Psalms, from Isaiah,
and from Acts. Nor in their gloriously renovated state shall Jews any more op-
press their "poor brethren": this is proved with texts from James, from Ezekiel,
from Isaiah, and from 1 Samuel (119). Indeed, "after the Jews conversion,
such a government as that was, will be restored again amongst them. Isa.
1.26." At this point Mather cites an apposite verse from Isaiah, just as if the
Holy Ghost who spoke through the Prophets had all along been speaking
about the Jews' conversion to Christianity—as if the terms "redemption,"
"conversion," "resurrection," and "restoration" were fully interchangeable. If
in the context of Mather's *Mystery* one can refer to biblical "typology" at all,
it is nothing more than a way of manipulating, with hindsight, authoritative,
resonant texts to fit present rhetorical needs.

I am moving quickly through Mather's text, intending to pick up a few
threads later on. But one matter should be addressed here: from medieval
times until Luther, at least, there was, as Heiko Oberman has said, "the conviction that the talmudic books represent an obstacle to the conversion of the
blind Jews, leading finally to the burning of the Holy Books beginning in thirteenth-century France . . . and continuing in sixteenth-century Italy."[74]
That is not a conviction of Mather, who, like Puritan Hebraists before him
(Ainsworth and Mede come to mind), deftly converts rabbinic writings, including the Aramaic Targums, into proof-texts for the "calling" of the Jews to
Christianity. Often considered with approval as "philo-Semitism," his approach is high-toned anti-Judaism: it is a way of confiscating Jewish books.[75]
Alluding to the writings of "Jewish Rabbies" (Menasseh ben Israel and
R. Eliezer) on the "*resurrection* from the dead," for example, and proving that
the restoration of the Jews will be coincident with their conversion to Christianity, Mather proceeds to allegorize the Rabbis:

> It is evident, that this salvation of *Israel* will be wonderful, if we consider the
> state from which they shall be saved, from a state of death. I find that some of
> the Jewish Rabbies have an opinion that their *restauration* and the *resurrection*
> from the dead shall be contemporary. . . . What more wonderful than that
> the bodies of men which have been dead and rotting in their grave for ages,
> after-ages, should be raised and brought to life again? This is a mighty wonder:
> even so that the Jewish Nation, which have been perishing in a cruel grave, and
> there lain dead for many hundreds of years, to be made alive again, to say the
> least of it, is a wonder. (81–82)

It is not that at the resurrection numberless infinities will arise from a state of
death, as some Rabbis had taught; for Mather, the true sense of "the *resurrec-*

tion from the dead" is the conversion of seventeenth-century Jews to Christianity: "Now thus may we say concerning the *Jews* at this day, they remain in a state of sin, and therefore in a state of death: And how should it be other wise, as long as they reject him that *is the way, the truth, and the life?*" (84). The depiction of Jews coming to life like dry bones is underwritten by Romans 11:15 ("For if the casting away of them [the Jews] be the reconciling of the world, what shall the receiving of them be, but life from the dead?").[76] The influential Brightman imagines "the resurrection, is the full restoring of the Jewish nation, out of the dust of destruction, and their calling to the faith in Christ, whereby those that are dead in sinne are truly raised up againe. . . ."[77]

It is 1666, and rumour has it that Jews may at long last be coming to life. Even as Mather's sermons are being penned, there are "present stirrings which we hear are amongst the *Israelites*" (87): "when the day of *Israels* salvation cometh, we must first expect to hear that the Jews are gathered together out of one Countrey, and out of another Country, and making head toward their own Land, before we hear of their conversion . . ." (97). Again the Rabbis are badly used. In rabbinic Judaism, Klausner explains, there existed a "deep-rooted conviction that the dispersion of Israel would in the Messianic age return from the four corners of the earth to Palestine"; at that time, other nations would attempt to convert to Judaism.[78] Mather turns Jewish messianism on its head: when from the round earth's imagined corners thousands of Jews gather in Palestine to greet their Messiah, they will be converted to Christianity by a vision of Jesus Christ. John Davenport's "Epistle to the Reader" (which introduces Mather's *Mystery*) confirms the present stirrings:

> These Sermons being preached in a time when constant reports from sundry places and lands gave out to the world, that the *Israelites* were upon their Journey towards *Jerusalem*, from sundry Foreign parts in great multitudes, and that they were carryed on with great signs and wonders by a high and mighty hand of extraordinary providence, to the admiration and astonishment of all that heard it, and that they had written to others of their Nation, in *Europe and America*, to encourage and invite them to hasten to them. (A3–v)

Both Mather and Davenport allude to the self-proclaimed messiahship in 1665–66 of Sabbatai Zevi and to his followers, who in the mid-1660s had sold their goods and were making head faithfully toward Palestine. A few years later the "Messiah" had converted to Islam.

❖   ❖   ❖

Let us assume that Mather's *Mystery* is a missionary tract to convert the Jews, or even a tract to instruct Puritans on how best to approach the business of conversion. What arguments might induce Jews to embrace Christianity? After sixteen hundred years with "a vail of miserable blindness upon their hearts" (14), what might persuade those "children of *unperswadableness*" who are "under the power of Satan" (95) to acknowledge Jesus Christ as the true Messiah? ("It is now near 1600 years since the house of Israel was left unto them desolate; since which time the generality of the Jews have been in woful servitude, and hated and hissed at of all Nations, in almost all places of the world, as the Lord, many hundreds of years before it came to pass, threatned them, that for their disobedience it should be, *Deut.* 28.37" [10].) A remark of Heiko Oberman's about sixteenth-century attitudes to Judaism may be apposite: "After all, how does one grade degrees of anti-Judaism in a Christian world which is unable to decide whether it finds more self-confirmation in a Jewish mass conversion or in the stubborn blindness of those stricken by God?"[79]

I am interested in Reiner Smolinski's use of the word "bait" to describe Mather's approach to the conversion of the Jews: "Such promises of power and glory for the Jewish nation could also be employed as a bait to effect their conversion, Increase Mather asserted in his *Mystery*."[80] (Mather does not use the word "bait" anywhere in *Mystery*.) For Augustine, we may recall, the cross was the Devil's mousetrap, *muscipula diaboli*; the bait put out for the Devil was the humanity of Christ, which concealed the hook of his divinity.[81] In *The Mystery of Israel's Salvation*, the bait is rhetorical; but for whom is the bait intended, and what sort of hook might it conceal? First, when they are saved, Mather predicts (taking as his proof-text Zechariah 12:8, and citing on that verse the Aramaic Targum, the Septuagint, Walton's Polyglot Bible of 1650, and whatever else comes easily to hand), "the Tribes of *Israel* shall have converting grace bestowed upon them" (98). That "converting grace," we are assured, includes remarkable "gifts" of the spirit:

> they that are of low, mean, contemptible parts shall be so raised and enlaged [*sic*], that they shall be like unto *David*, who was a man of extraordinary gifts and qualifications; but what shall they then be who are as *David*? It followeth, *the house* of David *shall be as Elohim* (for so is the *Hebrew* word) i.e. like unto the blessed Angels. They shall have most Seraphical gifts bestowed upon them, yea, *they shall be like to the Angel of the Lord*, *h.e.* they shall be like unto Jesus Christ, the Angel of the everlasting Covenant. . . . (99)

Furthermore, as if being like unto David and Jesus Christ and the blessed Angels were not enough, they "shall be made the most gracious, holy people that ever were upon the earth" (100). Again, and it is easy to lose the thread (or redemptive line) of Mather's sermons, the "Tribes of Israel" must be converted to Christianity before those gifts are gratuitously bestowed; until then, they are "in the hands of Satan": "Thus may we say concerning the Church of *Israel*, God hath given her a Bill of divorce. . . . But there is a day coming, when God will receive them into favour again, and then they shall be under the powers of darkness no longer" (96).

Why is it that Jesus Christ does not come "immediately" to judge the world, Mather wonders? Why is his penultimate advent (to destroy Rome by fire and convert the Jews) deferred?

> because of *his long suffering towards us Israelities*, he is not willing that our nation should perish, but would have *all Israel to be saved*; now, if he should come immediately to judgment, then our Nation being at present without repentance, must needs perish amongst the ungodly that shall be consumed with fire. (104)

Mather's phrasing—"*us Israelites*" and "our Nation"—gives pause. Likewise, he insists, "there will a time come when upon earth *the Israel of God* shall be wholly freed from affliction" (120); "there will a day come when the *Israel* of God shall enjoy length of dayes as to natural or corporal life" (120). Regarding himself and his parishioners as "*us Israelites*," and in a pattern of rhetoric familiar to students of American literature, Mather has aligned the historical Israel and New England: the moral conversion of New Englanders ("spiritual *Israel*") and the conversion of seventeenth-century Jews ("carnal or natural *Israel*") are aspects of the same prophetic destiny (7).[82] According to Mather's reading of Paul, "there is a double *Israel* spoken of in the Scripture" (6). As the chosen people and faithful remnant, that "double Israel" was promised, and shall inherit shortly, the blessed earth, whereas Rome (or Babylon) and "those *black Priests* which wear the marks of *Baal*" shall "perish from off this earth" (115).

Prophecies of Israel's deliverance and restoration made by Ezekiel, by Isaiah, and by the Rabbis, or what Mather refers to as "those truths, which do so much concern the glory of *the kingdom of the Messias*" (126)—the era of harmony the wolf dwelling with the lamb, the fruitful earth with its vines and fig trees, the swords beaten into ploughshares—all these *topoi* are assembled and applied to the state of things *after* the conversion of the Jews and *after* the fall of Antichrist (the Pope), or, in other words, after Mather's political ambitions are fulfilled. "Justly how long this glorious day shall continue, is not for us to say, for therein the Scripture is silent; Only it is evident, that it will be for Generations one after another" (57). The Hebrew Prophets were not, then, writing about the reestablishment of the House of David and the glory of the historical Israel, or not only; nor, in Mather's view, were their prophecies fulfilled at the incarnation. Deciphered, unravelled, prophecies of Israel's restoration were intended for seventeenth-century New Englanders *and* for their unredeemed counterparts—the Jews.

More than halfway through *Mystery*, one happens on a telling section prompted by Joseph Mede's *Clavis Apocalyptis* (1627), acknowledged by Mather in a truncated marginal gloss. According to Mather,

> it giveth occasion of great offence to the *Jews*, when they perceive Christians deny that which their Prophets have so abundantly affirmed. It is not (as some have thought) the best way to deal with *Jews*, when they urge, that in the days of *Messias*, they must have such glory bestowed on them, as the like never was in the world, to tell them that all those things must be understood spiritually, and not literally, which in the Prophets look that way; but it were better yield to them, that they shall have such glory as the like never was, only that this must not be at *Messias* first appearing. (127–28)

When Mather considers "the best way to deal with *Jews*," and when he talks about giving "great offense to the *Jews*," which Jews does he have in mind? One should compare this long section from Mede (cited here in the 1643 translation by Richard More):

> I leave it to the judgement of learned men and great Divines to judge, whether this be not the best and easiest way to deal with the Iewes; not to wrest those plaine Prophecies touching things appertaining to the last and glorious coming of Christ, to his first coming; but to perswade them that they expect none other *Messiah*, who can fulfill all those things, namely changing those things that are to be changed (for a Christian must consent no further with the Iewes in any thing, than his profession doth give him leave) than that *Jesus* of *Nazareth* whom their Fathers have crucified. . . . For whilest that we wrest those plaine Prophecies touching things which shall be at the second coming of Christ to his first, the Iewes laugh at us, and they are hardned in their infidelitie.[83]

Mede's argument has its own logic: converting Jews cannot hinge on the distinction between literal and spiritual glory in the Age of Messiah (a Paulinism); it may, however, I suppose, hinge on the crucial difference between the first and second coming of the person Mather self-consciously calls *Messias*; it may hinge on what Grant Underwood, cited above, calls "the minor matter of the Messiah's identity." The matter was smoothed over by Menasseh ben Israel, whose messianism, as presented in *Vindicae Judaeorum* (London, 1656), "encouraged Protestant readers to think that God's Spirit was stirring the Jew to psychological readiness for the Second Coming." According to Menasseh (who was lobbying for the Jews' readmission to England), "that difference consists only in the circumstance of the time."[84] Mather too intends to reconcile Jewish and Protestant expectations: quoting the prophecy from Haggai 2 ("I will shake the heavens, and the earth, and the sea, and the dry land"), he adds: "The words are true concerning the second coming of the *Messias*, as well as concerning his first coming" (162). Mather's *Dissertation* adds:

The *Coming of the Messiah* is in many Scriptures in the *Old Testament* spoken of
as *one Day,* without any express Distinction of his First and Second Coming.
. . . The *Jews* therefore do not own Two comings of Christ. They say *Shiloh*
shall come, but where is it said he shall come twice? We reply, that such Things
are spoken concerning the Messiah as do necessarily imply a First and Second
Coming.[85]

Earlier we have thrown out the word "bait." On the subject of Christ's advent, Mather uses the word "snare": we cannot determine the time precisely,
for "God will have that day to come upon all the earth like a snare." ("For as a
snare [Gr. *pagis*] shall it come upon all them that dwell on the face of the
whole earth" [Luke 21:34–35].) "Nevertheless [Mather continues] we may
safely affirm in the general, that the time is nearer that most are aware of. Divines are wont to make the conversion of the *Jews* an immediate sign fore-
running the day of judgment" (141). The "day of judgment" referred to by
Mather is *not* the final judgment as it is usually understood in Christianity;
the careful reader of *Mystery* stumbles on the telling phrase "a first and an ultimate judgment" (139). Although the idea of a double judgment appears in
Revelation 20:1–10, Mather's phrasing evokes extracanonical Jewish texts
collected in the Apocrypha and Pseudepigrapha. The model of two judg-
ments—one to open the millennium, the other to close it—parallels, for example, the Ezra Apocalypse, visions supposedly seen by Ezra in Babylon
(chapters 3 through 14 of Second Esdras, written about 100 C.E. and com-
monly referred to as 4 Ezra). Explicated by Sigmund Mowinckel, there is "a
preliminary judgment," after which "a Jewish Messianic kingdom will be set
up on earth." The temporary kingdom may last a thousand years; it may last
four hundred years. "Then follows the general [or great] judgment, the destruction of the world. . . . Then comes the new creation, the new heaven
and the new earth, the resurrection, and the new state of bliss."[86] Along with
other details of Jewish apocalyptic, the two-stage program outlined by Mowinckel is essentially Mather's program. The conversion of the Jews he takes
to be "an immediate sign fore-running the [*first*] day of judgment" (141)—the
opening of the millennium, the Age of Messiah, the reign of the saints.

But is that sign to be awaited passively, as one waits for a traffic light to
change? If Mather is trusting in "glorious down pourings of the Holy Spirit,"
what is the point of worrying about "the best way to deal with *Jews*"? Surely
he must be engaged in a mission to proselytize. At the same time, I feel in-
creasingly uneasy about taking *The Mystery of Israel's Salvation* as a missionary
tract to convert Jews or even as an instruction book for proselytizers. Are any
Jews at all being reached by Mather's text in the late 1660s? In which ale
houses of New England are educated Jews sitting about, waiting to knock
down an argument with a rabbinic text? If "bait" is being put out, who will

swallow it? Jewish merchants did pass through Boston in the 1680s and 1690s, but only "small numbers" of Jews settled there, according to Jacob R. Marcus. By the 1730s, there were "enough of them in the city to create a community."[87]

In 1696, thirty years after *Mystery* was written, Increase's son Cotton Mather is still praying for the chance to convert a Jew "at some Time or other":

> This day [he records in his diary for July 18, 1696] from the Dust, where I lay prostrate, before the Lord, I lifted up my Cries; For the coming of the *Kingdome* of my Lord and for the Conversion of the *Jewish Nation*, and for my own having the Happiness, at some Time or other, to baptise a *Jew*, that should by my Ministry, bee brought home unto the Lord.[88]

Three years later his prayers were answered, more or less: according to a diary entry recording the receipt of a letter from Carolina, one Jew was converted with the assistance of Mather's "little Book," *Faith of the Fathers* (1699).[89] By the mid-1720s, however, Cotton Mather no longer believed that the conversion of the Jews was requisite to the millennium and the kingdom of the saints on earth. Rethinking the matter, he realized that the conversion alluded to in Romans 11 had taken place in the first century. "Alas," Mather writes in 1726, two years before his death, "I was a very Young Man; I understood not the true *Israel*; I *Recant*; I *Revoke*; and I now make my most Public *Retraction*."[90]

❖   ❖   ❖

Near the close of *Mystery*, Increase Mather presents himself as someone

> under special advantage to understand these mysterious truths *of God*; That is to say, such of us as are in an exiled condition in this wilderness. Indeed some came hither upon worldly accounts, but others there are that came into this wilderness purely upon spiritual accounts . . . so they might bear witness not only against the Name of the Beast, and against his character, but also against his Number . . . which is the number not of an Angel, but of a man, *h.e.* that so they might bear witness against all humane inventions in the worship of God. (163)

The world is controlled by demonic powers: "The Devil and the Pope are two great Authors of persecution" (68). John the Divine was "banished into the *Isle of Patmos*" in order "to see *Romes* destruction"; Daniel and Ezekiel were "exiles, when they saw Visions of God"; so Mather was exiled to New England in order to bear witness against "the Beast" and to see the "ruine of *Rome*" (163–64). The *Millennial Reign* was promised in Revelation 20 *"to them that have not worshipped the Beast nor received his mark.* Which comprehends not only the *Jews* yet to be converted, but many Protestants and Saints who never had the Honour (tho' they would have rejoyced in it) to die for Christ, or for bearing Witness to his Truth."[91] ("As for the *Jews converted* to the *Popish*

Religion, their Conversion was more to Antichrist than to Christ; they were perverted to the old Idolatry of their Fathers in Babylon.")[92]

It occurs to me that Increase Mather's most immediate concern is not the conversion of the Jews, but the "final destruction of Antichrist," the Pope of Rome (141). The Jews are requisite to the fulfillment of Mather's mundane political messianism. "Before this salvation of Israel be accomplished," he predicts, taking over Joseph Mede's chronology, itself a revision of rabbinic texts, "the Pope and Turk shall be overthrown and destroyed" (21); "the Jews shall be converted, when Antichrist is near unto his total ruine" (37–38). Meanwhile: "The Devil still reigns by his Vicar at Rome."[93]

If, in a literal reading of Romans 11:26, the salvation of "all Israel" is a prerequisite to the millennium, it is for Mather more or less coincident with the fall of Rome, which "will be destroyed before the coming of Christ" (143), who, in a premillennial advent (a first judgment) that will "precede the final Second Coming by hundreds of years," will destroy the Pope when the Jews are finally "saved."[94] That they have not been saved (converted) thus far, Mather argues—supporting himself with broad appeals to Targum—is because Jews despise "the Idolatry of image-worship"; until "Popery" with its "hideous Idolatry" is destroyed, the Jews cannot be expected to embrace Christianity, and "therefore it is a vain thing for us to expect any general conversion of the Jews, until such time as we hear that Rome is burnt with fire" (22–23).[95] "The Pope, (Anti-Christ) shall be destroyed before all Israel be saved" (22). "Rome shall be destroyed before the conversion of the Jews: as for the Pope and Turk, they shall be utterly destroyed after the Jews conversion, yet before or together with the consummate salvation of the Tribes of Israel" (34). "The utter destruction of all Antichristian power is in order of nature before, but in time it does synchronize with the consummate salvation of Israel" (34). (The idea of historical "synchronism" is Joseph Mede's.)

It is not that "bait" is being thrown out to Jews; Jews are being used as bait to catch New Englanders—"us Israelites"—many of whom remain in a "natural, unconverted state," to cite Some Important Truths About Conversion, Mather's "Sundry Sermons" published in 1674.[96] In Mather's economy of redemption, Jews are part of an eschatological chain, "that golden chain of salvation" (6) leading to the end of the Papacy, the end of the Turks, the end of Judaism, and the triumph of Puritanism. In a well-known essay, "The New England Puritans and the Jews," Arthur Hertzberg writes: "Every Jew who adopted the Puritan faith assured the Puritans that they were right: they were the true Israel."[97] It is more than that: every Jew who adopted the Puritan faith assured the Puritans that Rome and its doctrines were wrong.[98] Jesuits ("those black Priests which wear the marks of Baal" [115]) and their seventeenth-century missions to the New World, including French Canada, were especially wrong.[99] Below, in a passage of crude anti-Catholic polemic inter-woven with rabbinic hermeneutics, Mather prophesies the fall of Rome:

> As for the Year of the *Jews* Conversion, I cannot see that it is anywhere de-scribed in the Scriptures. The *Jews* themselves do not expect their Deliverance until *Rome* be first destroyed. . . . R. *Kimchi* is positive in his Assertions, that whatever the Prophets have said concerning the Destruction of *Edom* in the last Days *they have spoken it of Rome*. . . . There is undoubtedly *a Vial* to be poured out on *the Seat of the Beast*, before the *Jews* return. The *Beast* has his Seat (which he will needs have it called *Sedes Apostolica*) in *Italy*. I am per-swaded that the Time is at Hand when some strange Providence will cause the *Pope's* more peculiar Territories to be full of Darkness. After that Darkness the Light of Truth concerning the Mystery we are discoursing of, will appear with such Clearness as will leave no Room for Doubt or Disputation.[100]

The destruction of Rome and the conversion of the Jews have been con-flated (or synchronized); Jewish writings are taken out of their historical con-text and turned sharply against the Pope. At the start of this chapter, making note of comets and other harbingers of the millennium (messianic birth pangs), we read in Mather's *Mystery:* "Indeed a little before the conversion of the *Jews*, there will be the most terrible doings in the world that ever was heard of, in respect of wars and commotions, the waves of the Sea roaring, confused noise and garments rolled in bloud, bloud and fire, and vapour of smoke" (122). An atmosphere of catastrophe signals the fall of Babylon—the Church of Rome: "Certainly I do believe that the earthquake which the Lord of heaven and earth hath now begun, will not be over until *Babylon* fall and rise no more" (158). About the great Fire of London, Mather says, alluding to the vials of Revelation: "But though this calamity be heavy, yet be comforted, in that these awful tremendos dispensations are such, that by the light of this fire we may see the *vial full* of the wrath of God is ready to be poured upon the *head of Rome*" (160–61). "But Antichrist shall be utterly destroyed (as hath been shewed) when the salvation of *Israel* shall be consummate. Therefore when the beast shall be slain, and his body given unto the burning flame, there will be no more destruction in all the Lords holy mountain" (68).

❖   ❖   ❖

To claim that for New Englanders the conversion of the Jews was a crucial prerequisite to the millennium is in one sense true; at least, the causal con-nection between their conversion and the "times of refreshing" was true for Mather, as it was for his most important predecessors, Mede and Brightman. ("Now what do these *times of refreshing* note, but a day, wherein there shall be freedom from all persecution and corporal oppressions?" [118].) But again, if the Messianic Age is to be effected by "converting grace" (97) and "effusions of the spirit of God" (98), why place such weight on a historical event? "Three things come unawares," we are told by the Rabbis: "the Messiah, a found article, and a scorpion" (*Sanhedrin* 97a).[101] On the other hand, what if the Jews, or rumors about them, are being used by Mather as warning examples—as stock characters in a Puritan morality play, as allegories and doubles of ourselves, as propaganda? "Nay," he cries out in *Mystery*, "it is not possible for any creature, no not for the Devils themselves to be guilty of a greater wickedness, than that the whole Nation of the *Jews* was guilty of, when they rejected and crucified the Lord of life and glory. And yet for all this (which is a wonderful thing) the providence of God hath so ordered, that this people doth not cease to be a Nation, no, nor ever shall do" (74–75).

To the Puritan, Robert M. Healey has said, "the Old Testament was the history of a people living out the consequences of their apostasy"; thus it "became the lens through which the Puritan viewed all history, the fundamental principle of interpretation" by which to understand God's approach to his elect.[102] That as a nation the Jews should have survived to be converted is for Mather proof of God's saving grace.

> Certainly if the *Jews* shall be converted, then there is grace enough with God to convert and save the greatest sinners upon earth. For what guilt can there be greater, than the guilt which lyeth upon the miserable Nation of the Jews? As now a little to instance here, that so all may see and admire the infinite grace of God in Jesus Christ, encouraging the most vile and sinful among the children of the Apostate *Adam* to return unto him, that they may be saved by him. (171)

At this juncture in *Mystery*, there follows a catalogue of worn-out, obscene stories about Jews, who, depending on the exegete Mather turns to, are charged with idolatry, blasphemy, and ritual murder: if Jews no longer worship idols as they worshiped the golden calf, they anyway continue to worship "out of Christ . . . and that's Idolatry" (173). Moreover, "the heart of that people is desperately moved with envy and malice against the true Religion" (173). And so on, in a litany that includes poisoning wells and blood libel: the slander about Jews who once every year steal and crucify Christian children (175). Where, in mid-seventeenth-century Boston, is Mather going with his polemic? Why is he bothering to evoke such hardened sinners, unless they are proof-texts for some great end? Luther gave up on the Jews in 1543.

First, as we have seen, the Jews are living proof of God's grace: if such unbelievers can be converted, Mather reckons, "*the greatest sinners may be saved. . . . there is salvation to be had even for thee.*" Therefore "we should seek unto God continually that he would hasten the day of *Israels* salvation. Matters of prophecie and promise should be turned into prayer" (177). Using metaphors of turning, of wheels, and of overturning, Mather exhorts his audience to pray for the conversion of Jews they may have seen in illustrated Bibles. "Surely there is some great thing upon the wheel," he surmises. "When once the wheel is set a going, when once the Lord is upon the wing, he will come leaping over the hills like a Roe upon the mountains" (47). "It is prayer that sets the wheels of divine providence a going. It is prayer that turns the world upside down" (180).[103]

According to the situation one holds, the world turned upside down may not be such a good thing: "The Lord preserveth the strangers; he relieveth the fatherless and widow: but the way of the wicked he turneth upside down" (Ps. 146:9). The root of the Hebrew word *avvah*, rendered in the Authorized Version as "turn upside down," means to twist, to bend, to ruin, to distort, to pervert (I am told). The word occurs in Ezekiel's prophecy: "I will overturn, overturn, overturn it: and it shall be no more, until he comes whose right it is; and I will give it him" (21:27).[104] Converting Jews and their writings, biblical and postbiblical, is requisite to a more urgent overturning—political revolution, which for Mather is inseparable from "that kingdom which the God of heaven shall set up at the day of *Messias*" (178).[105] For Maimonides, Scholem has written, "the Messianic age is no highest good but only a preliminary stage in the final transition to the world-to-come."[106] It may be a catastrophe, but it's not the end of the world.

CHAPTER FOUR

Edward Taylor and the Feast of Tabernacles

The compassionate One! May he erect for us David's fallen booth [*sukkah*]. The compassionate One! May He make us worthy of the days of Messiah and the life of the World to Come.

Liturgy for the Feast of Tabernacles[1]

For the present subject matter of our discussion is the mystery of the true Feast of Tabernacles. For on this Feast the human Tabernacle is being set up as a tent for the one who put on humanity on our behalf.

Gregory of Nyssa, Sermon on the Nativity

Between March 1666 and January 1668, Samuel Mather (1626–1671), the eldest brother of Increase Mather, composed for his congregation of St. Nicholas's in Dublin a series of "elaborate sermons" on biblical typology. Published posthumously in 1683, *The Figures or Types of the Old Testament Opened and Explained* became for Edward Taylor and other Puritan divines "a handbook for the understanding of types," as Mason I. Lowance confirms.[2] From Samuel Mather's perspective, the "usefulness of the Old Testament to New Testament Saints" depends on "Gospel Truths" concealed within the Jewish Bible as nutmeats are concealed in nutshells. Thus readers are urged to "search into those ancient Administrations, because there is much Gospel there; tho' the Shell be hard, yet there is excellent Substance in the Kernel." To read the Old Testament profitably is to "distinguish between . . . the Shell, and the Kernel, the Shadow, and the Substance." The "Spirit and Substance, and Mystery of that Dispensation was Evangelical," Mather explains, "tho' it was involved in a legal Shell. . . ."[3]

Some of the hardest nuts to crack are "the *Types* and *Shadows* of the *Ceremonial Law*"; however, once broken ("if the Lord help us to break the Shell"), even they contain "precious Kernels of Gospel-Truths" and "glorious Myster-ies."[4] What Mather refers to as the "Ceremonial Law" (a rhetorical construct unheard of in Judaism) concerns sacrifices and ritual purification, the altar, priestly garments, and all festivals. To follow the Westminster Confession of Faith (1647): besides the "moral" law ("delivered by God upon mount Sinai in ten commandments"),

> God was pleased to give to the people of Israel, as a Church under age, ceremo-nial laws, containing several typical ordinances, partly of worship, prefiguring Christ, His graces, actions, sufferings, and benefits, and partly holding forth di-verse instructions of moral duties. All which ceremonial laws are now abrogated under the new testament.[5]

By "sticking in the Shell and Shadow" of the Ceremonial Law, the Jews re-jected "the Gospel, or the Thing itself," Mather says. As used by Mather and other Puritan divines, the term "Ceremonial Law" signifies for the most part anything in the Old Testament that resonates, however faintly, with the "ex-ternal Pomp and Splendor" of the Church of Rome. Driven into "Idolatry" by Satan, "Papists" have taken their "Popish Superstitions from the Jews, and from the Ceremonial Law."[6] (On the other hand, the Jews' "great stumbling Block at this day against the Christian Religion is, the Idolatry of the Popish Christians: For the poor blind Jews consider the Christian Religion no other-wise, but as corrupted with those Antichristian Abominations and Idolatries: And therefore their Conversion and Return is not to be expected till An-tichrist, that great stumbling Block, be removed out of the way.")[7]

The focus of this chapter on Edward Taylor is the Feast of Tabernacles (Feast of Booths, Feast of Ingathering—Sukkot, or "the Feast"), one of the three pilgrimage festivals of Judaism when all males are obliged to appear at the sanctuary in Jerusalem. Agricultural in origin, we are told, the great Feast was long regarded as a "general thanksgiving for the bounty of nature in the year that had passed"; during the fruit harvest, people dwelt in booths. In Leviticus, the booths are "given a symbolic meaning, and are brought into re-lation with the wandering in the wilderness"; the thanksgiving festival be-came a historical festival with an exact date and a prescribed ritual and liturgy.[8] The Tabernacles celebration includes the reciting of Psalms, espe-cially the Hallel (Psalms 113–18), flute-playing, numerous sacrifices, trumpet blasts (the blowing of the shofar or ram's horn), torch dances, prayers for rain, ritual water drawing, processions around the altar, and the lighting of the four great golden candelabra in the Temple courtyard.

Those aside, what underwrites the Christian typology of the Feast of Taber-nacles is its messianic significance. According to the final, visionary chapter of Zechariah, the Feast is in the Messianic Age to become a universal festival;

the surrounding nations "shall even go up from year to year to worship the King, the Lord of hosts, and to keep the feast of tabernacles" (14:16). Associated with redemption, the Feast anticipates the perpetual daylight of the Messianic Age when night will be as day: "And his feet shall stand in that day upon the mount of Olives"; "at evening time it shall be light"; "living waters shall go out from Jerusalem." Whoever fails to attend the Feast in Jerusalem, "even upon them shall be no rain" (Zech. 14:1; 7–8; 17).

The Rabbis found in the celebration of the Feast "the promise of the Messiah," we read in C. H. Dodd's influential work on the Fourth Gospel. (Christian exegetes, of course, found the messianic promise of the Feast fulfilled in the person of Jesus Christ.) Explicating the explicit allusions to the Feast of Tabernacles in John 7, Dodd writes:

> There is a somewhat vague notion [in postbiblical Jewish texts] that the Messiah might be expected to appear in the month Tisri, to which Tabernacles belongs. It is by no means impossible that the evangelist was acquainted with these eschatological associations.
>
> For him, at any rate, Tabernacles is the occasion when Jesus manifests Himself as Messiah in Jerusalem. His claims are canvassed in terms which show familiarity with various aspects of Jewish messianic expectation.[9]

As Samuel Mather reports in *Figures or Types*, the Feast of Tabernacles "began upon the fifteenth Day of the seventh Month, the fifteenth Day of *September*; and it lasted eight days. . . . The principal Rite and Ceremony of this Feast . . . was their *dwelling in Booths*, from whence it has its denomination, and is called the Feast of Booths, or Tabernacles. . . ."[10] There was "a three-fold *Mystery* in this Feast" (Mather echoes traditional Christian *and* Jewish exegesis): to put the Jewish people "in mind of their dwelling in Tents when they travelled through the Wilderness into the Land of *Canaan*"; to "instruct them that they were but Pilgrims and Strangers here below, Sojourners as it were in a Strange Land, passing through it to their own Country, towards their own Home"; and, most significantly for Mather and for Taylor, to hold forth "some principal thing concerning the Messiah."

> This Feast of Tabernacles [Mather writes] pointed them to the time when God himself would come to Tabernacle and pitch his Tent amongst Men. Therefore the Expression is in *John* 1.14. εσκήνωσεν *and the Word was made Flesh, and he came and did pitch his Tent amongst us*, dwell as in a Tent or Tabernacle amongst us. Wherein he refers to this great Institution and Feast of Tents or Tabernacles.

For Mather, the mystery concealed beneath or within the shell of the Feast of Tabernacles is the nativity—the time when God "would . . . pitch his tent amongst men." Christ was *not* born in the "depth of Winter," but in the fall: "the Birth of Christ was at the Feast of Tabernacles: Christ did then

Tabernacle in the Flesh"; "the time of his Birth was indeed in the seventh Month at the Feast of Tabernacles."[11] Indeed, "many learned Men confess there is a Mistake as to the Time, and that it must needs be at the Feast of Tabernacles, and not in *December*." After all, Mather submits, Augustus was "taxing all the World" at that time. "It is not likely that the Emperor would enjoyn all his subjects to travel in the depth of Winter to their own Cities." The "Shepherds were abroad watching and keeping their Flocks by Night, *Luke* 2.8. but it is not probable they were so in the depth of Winter." John the Baptist was "baptizing in *Jordan* at that time of the Year thirty years after, *Luke* 3.23. but it is not likely that he would choose out the coldest part of the Year for that Work. . . . The Winter even in those Climates was but a hard time to travel in, or to watch in."[12] That the Catholic Church celebrates Christ's birth in December is

> partly through the ignorance and unskilfulness which God was pleased to leave them to, as it were to rebuke them for their Superstition; and partly through their carnal compliance with the Pagans; which made the Bishop of *Rome* take the old *Saturnalia* and *Bacchanalia* of the *Pagans*, and to disguise them with a new Name, that those Festivities which had been kept before in the Devil's Name, might now be kept in Christ's own Name to his greater Dishonor.

Edward Taylor's sermon on the Feast of Tabernacles, delivered in the remote settlement of Westfield, Massachusetts, on December 26, 1697, follows some parts of Mather's text very closely. The "Celebrating of Christs birth in December," says Taylor, "is a delusion of the Enemy introduced by Superstition, & as another Heathenish Bachanall Feast: which was not taken up till the fourth Hundred year after Christ" (*Types*, 2, 531).[13] Christ was born in the fall, during the Jewish Feast of Tabernacles: "As to the Time of his Building his Tabernacle & dwelling in it in the World. & this was upon the fifteenth day of the Seventh month, i,e, September. for on this day they were to make and dwell in these booths" (2, 530). The "fifteenth of September [is] the beginning of the Feast of Tabernacles, & Christs Birthday" (2, 532). The Feast is a "Type" of the incarnation, a "Type" of Christ "as θεάνθρωπος [*theanthropos*], God man in one person"; it "contains the Mystery of Christs Personall Union in it, of the Godhead & Manhood together" (2, 528, 530). "The Whole time of the Feast of Tabernacles the people were to dwell in these Tabernacles to import that the Whole time of the Lord Christs being here, he must Tabernacle in our Flesh" (2, 531–32). Before focusing on Taylor's "Preparatory Meditation" 24, second series, whose controlling metaphor is the Feast of Tabernacles, I shall explore (or suggest) the history of an idea— that Jesus Christ was born in Bethlehem on the fifteenth day of Tishri, roughly from mid-September to mid-October, depending on the new moon.

❖   ❖   ❖

We begin in the fourth century. A typological connection between the nativity—Christ's "Building his Tabernacle & dwelling in it" (in Taylor's phrasing)—and the Feast of Tabernacles was ventured by the Cappodocian Father
Gregory of Nyssa (ca. 335–ca. 395) in a sermon written for the Feast of the
Nativity, 386 C.E. The sermon begins with a verse from Psalm 81 that alludes
to the trumpet blown on the Jewish New Year (Rosh Hashanah), the first new
moon of the month of Tishri. ("Blow up the trumpet in the new moon, in the
time appointed, on our solemn feast day" [81:3].) Moving from that trumpet
to the connection established by Paul between the trumpet and the logos (1
Cor.14:8), Gregory makes a useful distinction between a silver trumpet
(σάλπιγξ) and the trumpet "which the law calls horns" (κέρατανε), or, in
Hebrew, the *shofar*, the ram's horn blown ceremoniously at the New Year and
at the Feast of Tabernacles. (In the Jewish liturgy for the New Year, the *shofar*
is connected to the Akedah, or binding of Isaac, in particular to the ram
caught in the thicket by its horns and sacrificed in the place of Isaac [Gen.
22:13].)[14] Further on in Gregory's sermon, the trumpet of horn is said to be a
type of the "true unicorn"—a figure of Christ and of the virgin birth. The
central proof-text is the messianic Psalm 118, chanted (still) throughout the
Feast of Tabernacles and, until recently, part of the Roman liturgy for Christmas.[15] Here, in the opening section of Gregory of Nyssa's sermon on the nativity, the Feast of Tabernacles or Feast of Booths is a prefiguration of the
birth of Christ.

> David says *blow the trumpet in the new moon in the special day of your festival* [Ps.
> 81:3]. Now the ordinances of heavenly doctrine are in every way a matter of law
> for those who hear them. Therefore because the special day of our solemnity is
> present, let us now fulfil the law by becoming trumpeters of the sacred moon day.
> The trumpet [οάλπιγξ] spoken of by the law as the Apostle orders us to under-
> stand it is the Logos (1 Cor. 14:8). It must be distinct in respect of its sounds so
> that it can be clear to those who hear it. So then brethren let us also give out a
> sound which is bright and audible, in no way unworthy of the trumpet made from
> horn [κέρατανε]. For indeed the law prefigures the truth beforehand in the types
> of the shadow and it commands the sound to be made on the trumpets on the
> Feast of Tabernacles. *For the present subject matter of discussion of the Feast is the
> mystery of the true Feast of Tabernacles.* For on this Feast the human tabernacle is
> being set up [pitched] as a tent for the one who put on humanity [or clothed him-
> self as man] on our behalf. On [this Feast] our tabernacles which had fallen asun-
> der by death are restored by the one who built our dwelling from the beginning.
> So let us say what is said in Psalmody, joining in chorus with David of the great
> voice: "Blessed is he that cometh in the name of the Lord" [Ps. 118:26]. How does
> he come? Not by some kind of ship or vehicle [chariot, carriage]. But by virginal
> incorruptibility he journeys across [through] into human life. "He is our God, this
> is our Lord which has enlightened us" [118:27].[16] (emphasis added)

Thus, for Gregory of Nyssa, the birth of Christ inaugurated the "true Feast of Tabernacles." According to Jean Daniélou, Gregory's "interesting effort" to link typologically the Feast of Tabernacles with the Feast of the Nativity "was not followed up."[17]

But Gregory's effort *was* followed up. It was followed up by Samuel Mather and Edward Taylor, as we have seen above. It was followed up by Henry Ainsworth, Joseph Mede, Increase Mather, and Jonathan Edwards. However mediated—by the early Fathers, by the messianism of the Rabbis—we are dealing with an apologetic topos, directed partly against Rome and taken up by one Puritan exegete after another. Leviticus 23:34 reads: "The fifteenth day of this seventh month shall be the feast of tabernacles for seven days unto the Lord." Ainsworth's commentary on Leviticus, first published in 1616, explains that the Feast of Tabernacles was kept by the Jews "to figure out," or to prefigure, "the comming of Christ into the world at this time of the yeere":

> In the new Testament this feast is called in Greeke *Skenopegia*, that is, the *pitching of tents*, or *setting up of boothes*, Joh. 7.2. and so the LXX translated it in Deut. 16.16. This feast they kept, in remembrance of Gods favour to them in the wilderness, where they dwelt in booths . . . and to shew their thankfulnesse unto God for the fruits which in this moneth they reaped . . . and to figure out the comming of Christ into the world at this time of the yeere, to dwell in the Tabernacle of our flesh, who was *made flesh*, and *dwelt* (or *pitcht his tent*) among us Joh. 1.14. At this feast, Solomons Temple (a figure of Christs body, Joh 2.19.21) was dedicated with great solemnitie, and the Arke brought into it, 2 Chron. 5.2.3–7. This feast wee also are to keepe, Zech. 14.16–19, which things we doe by beliefe in Christ, that his grace is sufficient for us.[18]

Several points have been made in quick succession by Ainsworth: for Jews, the Feast of Tabernacles prefigured the "comming of Christ"; Jesus Christ was born in the fall, at the time of the great Feast; the typology is authorized by John 1:14, which states that the Word "pitcht his tent" among us; Solomon's Temple, a type of Christ's humanity, was dedicated at the Feast of Tabernacles. In part, Ainsworth's understanding of the Feast is based on the Tractate *Sukkah* and on the Aramaic Targums; both sources are acknowledged in his *Annotations*. As well, some of the Rabbis he consulted in Amsterdam believed their Messiah would arrive in Tishri, the month of the Feast of Tabernacles, whose festivities anticipated the joys of the messianic kingdom.[19] In an approach to Jewish eschatology we may recognize, Ainsworth has appropriated the messianic significance of the Feast as it is understood in Judaism to the first and second advents of Jesus Christ.

A brief excursus: Commenting on Gregory of Nyssa's sermon on the nativity, Daniélou believes that the connection made between the Feast of Tabernacles and the incarnation was not "followed up." Why, we may wonder, from the fourth century on, was the connection ignored by the Church? The answer may have to do with the dangers of millennialism. In a provocative study of the transfiguration, Harald Riesenfeld identifies "un caractère eschatalogique évident dans les fêtes de mois de Tisri et spécialement dans la fête des *Sukkot*."[20] On the one hand, Jewish messianism was indispensable for Christian apologists: Justin, Tertullian, and Irenaeus (all chiliasts) adapted a more or less standard catena of Old Testament texts to prove that Jesus was the expected Messiah. On the other hand, in rabbinic writings, the Feast of Tabernacles was connected to the temporal Age of Messiah; and Jerome, for example, was a "vitriolic opponent of chiliasm."[21] Jerome's commentary on Zechariah decries the "deceptive hopes" of Jews for whom the Feast of Tabernacles anticipated the joys of the millennial reign.[22] The kingdom promised in the book of Daniel would be celestial, not material; "the fable of one thousand years" must cease—*Cesset ergo mille annorum fabula*.[23] Likewise Augustine, who in *The City of God* "rejected as a 'ridiculous fable' the view that the thousand year kingdom of Christ in Revelation (20:1–6) would be a future earthly kingdom, interpreting it instead as a figure for the life of the Church in the present."[24]

That from the fourth century the pursuit of the millennium was widely considered a Judaizing heresy is well known. (See the preceding chapter on Increase Mather.) That Israel's messianic redemption was woven into the fabric of the Feast of Tabernacles is probably not so well known, although it was known to Jerome, who by 388 C.E. was in Israel "immersing himself in Hebrew studies."[25] Written before Jerome, Methodius of Olympus's *Banquet* reveals what Daniélou calls "traces of . . . rabbinic speculations." Methodius "sees the time spent by the Jews in tabernacles in the desert before they entered the Promised Land as a type of . . . 'the thousand years of rest' and 'the resurrection'."[26] As the Children of Israel travelled from the hardships of Egypt toward the Promised Land, so it is with us, Methodius writes in the *Banquet*, juxtaposing events of the Exodus journey and the ritual celebration of *Sukkoth*, the Feast of Tabernacles:

> I also, having started on the journey, I come out of the Egypt of this life, I come first to the Resurrection, to the true *Scenopegia* [Feast of Tabernacles]. There, having built my beautiful tent on the first day of the feast, that of the judgment, I celebrate the feast with Christ during the millennium of rest (*anapausis*), called the seven days, the true Sabbaths. Then, following Jesus Who has crossed the heavens, I start on my journey again, as they, after the rest of the Feast of Tabernacles, journeyed toward the land of promise, the heavens, not waiting

any longer in tabernacles, that is to say, my tabernacle not remaining any longer the same, but, after the millennium, having passed from a corruptible human form to an angelic grandeur and beauty. Then, going out from the place of tabernacles, having celebrated the feast of the Resurrection, we shall go towards better things, ascending to the house that is above the heavens.[27]

How did the messianic nature of the Feast as understood in rabbinic Judaism (and in another context by Jerome) influence the millennial expectations of seventeenth-century Puritans? Conversely, how did the millennial hopes of English and American Puritans dictate their eccentric typology, whereby the date of Christ's nativity is shifted from the winter wild to the fall? Pressing for the millennium to open, Increase Mather contends that Jews "deride at Christians" for celebrating the nativity in December, when really Christ's *conception* took place then (or will take place then; Mather's syntax is confusing). In the passage that follows, taken from Increase Mather's *The Mystery of Christ Opened and Applyed* (Boston, 1686), the name "Christ" may signify the delayed Messiah of Judaism *and* Jesus Christ:

> In my Text it was said *the Word was made flesh*, and the next words are, *and dwelt among us* [John 1:14]. The Greek word is [*eskenose*] which the ancients are wont to interpret [*skenos anelaben*] i.e. *Corpus assumptit*; He *tabernacled* among us. The Feast of *Tabernacles* did typify the Incarnation of Christ, whence the Jewes sappose [*sic*] that Christ will be born at the time when that Feast is by them observed; and they deride at Christians for keeping the Feast of Christ's Nativity in the *tenth* Moneth of the year, saying that they place the birth of Christ in the moneth, wherein they ought rather to place his Conception. However the Feast of Tabernacles which the Children of Israel kept in the seventh moneth, did signify that God would appear and dwell in our nature.[28]

Jonathan Edwards's *Some Thoughts Concerning the Revival* was published in 1743.[29] Focusing on the eschatological nature of *Sukkot*, which he knows looks forward to "the latter ages of the world," Edwards imagines the Feast of Tabernacles in terms of the great cosmic banquet—"that glorious spiritual feast, which God will then make for his Church." Glossing Zechariah's vision ("every one . . . shall even go up from year to year to worship the King, the Lord of hosts, and to keep the feast of tabernacles" [14:16]), Edwards thinks the prophet is alluding to our "unbelieving and disaffected" state. Those who do not keep the great Feast (spiritually), he warns, taking over the rain and drought and plague imagery from Zechariah 14, "shall all be smitten: that is, they shall have no share in the shower of divine blessing that shall then descend on the earth. . . ." In Judaism, the Feast of Tabernacles is the last feast of the year before "earth [is] destroyed by winter"; likewise, after the glorious messianic feast held for the redeemed remnant, "the lower world will be destroyed." Echoing rabbinic exegesis and applying it to the first and second advent of Christ (who was and shall be "born" at the time of the Feast of Tabernacles), Edwards recites the very ancient belief that the creation of the world *and* the salvation of Israel occur during the month of Tishri.[30] At the "great ingathering of the elect," Edwards promises, God will "set up his tabernacle among men" (cf. Rev. 21:3):[31]

> The world is supposed to have been created about the time of year wherein the Feast of Tabernacles was appointed; so in that glorious time God will create a new heaven and a new earth. The temple of Solomon was dedicated at the time of the Feast of Tabernacles, when God descended in a pillar of cloud and dwelt in the temple [1 Kings 8; 2 Chron. 7]; so at this happy time, the temple of God shall be gloriously built up in the world, and God shall in a wonderful manner come down from heaven to dwell with his church. *Christ is supposed to have been born at the Feast of Tabernacles*, so at the commencement of that glorious day, *Christ shall be born*; then above all other times shall the woman clothed with the sun . . . bring forth her son to rule all nations, Rev. 12. (emphasis added)

Edward Taylor respected the pious, learned millenarian Joseph Mede (or Mead; 1586–1638), whose widely read *Discourse* on the Feast of Tabernacles (published posthumously in 1643) is cited several times in Taylor's sermon on the Feast of Tabernacles. ("Now saith Mr. Mead, if John [Baptist] was born the 23 of April, Christ, who was born six months after, must be born the latter end of September" [2, 531].) According to Mede (who, like Ainsworth, appropriates to Christ's first advent the messianic nature of the Feast), "what this ceremony of *Tabernacles* aimed at [was] the mysterie of our Redemption by God in the *Tabernacle* of our flesh; or the *Incarnation* of Christ." Samuel Mather's knowledge of the Feast, as cited above, and the line of argument used to discredit the Feast of the Nativity and thus the Catholic Church (shepherds do not watch and keep their flocks by night in the depth of winter; Augustus would not have taxed all the world in the depth of winter; John the Baptist would not have gone into the Jordan in winter, and so on) are lifted straight from Mede's *Discourse* without acknowledgment.[32]

What strikes me particularly about Mede's *Discourse* is his gloss on John 1:14. The verse appears in the Authorized Version thus: "And the Word was made flesh, and dwelt among us"; the Genevan version (1599 edition) reads, "And that Worde was made flesh, and dwelt among us"; some versions render the last phrase "tabernacled among us." Mede's version of and annotations on the verse follow:

> But *of what thing concerning Christ to come it* [the Feast of Tabernacles] *was a Type*, it is not so express. . . . But by that which S. *John* saith, Chap. 1.14 Καὶ ο λόγος σὰρξ εγένετο καὶ εσκήνοσεν εν ημιν *The Word was made flesh and*

Tabernacled in us; for so signifies εσκήνοσεν[.] by this, I say, S. *John* should seem
to intimate That as the *Passover* was a Type of his *Passion, Pentecost* a *Figure* of
the *sending the Holy Ghost;* so should the *Feast of Tabernacles* be for a *Type* of his
Incarnation, when the Divine Nature *tabernacled* in our flesh, and the Word of
God became *Emmanuel, God with us.* For it is incredible that this principal
Feast should not be for a *Type* of *some principal thing concerning Christ.* . . .
And there is nothing but his *Incarnation* and *Nativitie* which can be applied
thereunto. . . .[33]

The Greek preposition εν can mean *in* or *among;* for Mede to say
that the *logos* tabernacled or dwelt "in" us rather than "among" us is to gloss
the incarnation spatially, in terms of an inner-outer model of enclosure. (One
recalls Samuel Mather's nutshell with its concealed kernel of truth—the
Gospel Mystery of the Feast of Tabernacles.) Ainsworth, too, as cited above,
describes "the comming of Christ into the world at this time of the yeere, to
dwell in the Tabernacle of our flesh." Increase Mather writes that "the Feast
of Tabernacles . . . did signify that God would appear and dwell in our nature." Taylor's allusions to John 1:14 are not phrased consistently; nevertheless, his sermon on the Feast of Tabernacles tends to follow Mede. "The Word
was made flesh, & dwelt in us. tabernacled in us. . . . Oh! that the Manhood should be the house, & the Godhead the Inhabitant. that the Finite
Nature Should bee the Tabernacle, & the Infinite Nature the Dweller
therein. What a wonder is here?" (*Types*, 2, 537). Is this not to emphasize the
distinction between the two natures of Christ? Throughout the Feast of Tabernacles, one dwells *in* a *sukkah*—a leafy booth or tabernacle made out of
boughs and branches and other natural, often woven, materials (as I explain
later). Yet Taylor is no Nestorian: "this Feast contains the Mystery of Christs
Personall Union in it, of the Godhead & Manhood together" (2, 530).[34]

Determined to move the date of Christ's nativity to Tishri, the month of
the Feast of Tabernacles, Puritan exegetes may in part be glossing John 1:14
in terms of God's gracious dwelling in Solomon's Temple. As Edwards says in
a passage cited earlier: "The temple of Solomon was dedicated at the time of
the Feast of Tabernacles, when God descended in a pillar of cloud and dwelt
in the temple" (1 Kings 8:10). It occurs to me that the model of inclusion we
are looking at may be endorsed by Calvin, whose idiosyncratic christology
emphasizes the *distinction* of Christ's two natures. "The two natures may not
be thought of as either fused or separated," Calvin writes in the *Institutes;* the
two natures are "distinct." Countering theologians who, "while meaning to
show the unity of the person . . . destroy either nature," Calvin argues,
"Christ would not have called his body a temple unless divinity, as distinct
from the body, dwelt therein."[35] Calvin also imagines that the Son "indwelt"
the flesh and "clothed" himself with the flesh.[36]

François Wendel explains: "What mattered above all to Calvin was to avoid anything that might be interpreted as a confusion of the divinity with the humanity"; from Calvin's point of view, "the distinction between the two natures is indispensable if we do not want to end by admitting a change in the divinity itself, brought about by the fact of the incarnation and necessarily equivalent to a diminution of it."[37] When Edward Taylor writes about the Feast of Tabernacles as "an Emblem of the Divine Nature distinct, & of the Humane Nature Compleat, Of the Nature of the Human, as a Booth" (2, 541), his christology emphasizes the difference, the distinction, between the divinity and the humanity in Christ. Booth-dwellers are not normally fused and confused with the booth wherein they dwell.

❖   ❖   ❖

Finally, after what may have been tedious groundwork, we arrive at Taylor's "Preparatory Meditation" 24, second series (dated December 25, 1697), whose epigraph, taken from John 1:14, is "Tabernacled amongst us," εσκήν-ωσε[v] εν ημιν (*eskenosen en emin*). The verb *eskenosen* (cognate with *skene*, the Greek word for "tent") means "to live or camp in a tent" and, transitively, "to pitch or inhabit a tent."[38] In the Greek Septuagint, the noun *skene* is used to translate two Hebrew words for "tent," *ohel* and *mishkan*; it is also used to render the Hebrew word for a leafy booth or pavilion or arbor, *sukkah*, whose plural is *sukkot*, whence the name given to the Feast: the Feast of Booths, or *Sukkot*. Taylor's Meditation 24 centers on a series of enclosures; all are interchangeable with the leafy *sukkah* of the Feast of Tabernacles.[39]

> My Soul would gazing all amazed stand
>> To see the burning Sun, with 'ts golden locks
> (An hundred sixty six times more than th'land)
>> Ly buttond up in a Tobacco box.
>> But this bright Wonder, Lord, that fore us playes
>> May make bright Angells gasterd, at it gaze.
>
> That thou, my Lord, that hast the Heavens bright
>> Pav'd with the Sun, and Moon, with Stars o're pinckt,
> Thy Tabernacle, yet shouldst take delight
>> To make my flesh thy Tent, and tent with in't.
>> Wonders themselves do seem to faint away
>> To finde the Heavens Filler housd in Clay.
>
> Thy Godhead Cabbin'd in a Myrtle bowre,
>> A Palm branch tent, an Olive Tabernacle,
> A Pine bough Booth, An Osier House or tower
>> A mortall bitt of Manhood, where the Staple
>> Doth fixt, uniting of thy natures, hold,
>> And hold out marvels more than can be told.

Thy Tabernacles floore Celestiall
 Doth Canopie the Whole World. Lord; and wilt
Thou tabernacle in a tent so small?
  Have Tent, and Tent cloath of a Humane Quilt?
  Thy Person make a bit of flesh of mee
  Thy Tabernacle, and its Canopee?

Wonders! my Lord, Thy Nature all With Mine
 Doth by the Feast of Booths Conjoynd appeare
Together in thy Person all Divine
  Stand House, and House holder. What Wonder's here?
  Thy Person infinite, without compare
  Cloaths made of a Carnation leafe doth ware
          (Stanzas 1–5)

Recalling the light imagery of John 1:9 ("the true Light, which lighteth every man that cometh into the world"), and evoking the radiance of the Feast of Tabernacles—the huge "golden candelabra . . . with four golden bowls atop them" that illuminated the Temple courtyard and (according to Rashi) shone out over the whole city of Jerusalem (Mishnah *Sukkah* 5.2–4), Taylor begins the Meditation with an image of the "burning Sun" (or Son). Whereas Taylor's "burning Sun" has "golden locks," golden hair like rays of the sun, those locks quickly modulate into contrivances for fastening a door or lid, which implicitly becomes the lid of a "Tobacco box," a small box for holding and carrying tobacco leaves. What amazes the poet and the "Angells" (who are "gasterd" at the sight) is to "see" the Sun "buttond up in a Tobacco box." (Just as the Sun is enclosed in its little box, so the phrase, "An hundred sixty six times more than th' land," is shut into, confined by, parentheses.) So far the four controlling images of Taylor's Meditation have been introduced: a "box" or covered dwelling-place for the Sun / Son who "pitched his tent . . . in our Nature"; leaves (including leaves of paper); brilliant illumination; and fastenings, or attachments.

In stanza 2, evoking Colossians 2:9 ("For in him dwelleth all the fulness [*pleroma*] of the Godhead bodily"), Taylor refers to Christ as "Heavens Filler housd in Clay," an image that evokes the doctrine of divine accommodation (condescension, *kenosis*, humiliation). One paradox in this stanza (stanzas, like tents, are enclosures, little rooms) concerns the size and grandeur of dwelling places. The "Heavens bright" with their "Sun," "Moon," and "Stars" are the Lord's "Tabernacle"; that he "should take delight / To make my flesh thy Tent, and tent with in't" is therefore cause for wonderment. In stanza 3, the Lord's "Tent" is described as a "Myrtle bowre, / A Palm branch tent, an Olive Tabernacle, / A Pine bough Booth"; or, in other words, a *sukkah*, whose name comes from its *sakak* or covering, its most essential feature.[40] Especially built each year in Tishri for the Feast of Tabernacles, a *sukkah* is a temporary structure, thatched so as to be a protection against the sun while allowing the stars to shine through at night.[41]

The *sukkah* of the Feast of Booths looks forward as well as backward: it commemorates the forty years in the wilderness when the Children of Israel dwelt in portable tents (not in *sukkot;* the biblical connection between the Exodus tents and the *sukkot* is made in Leviticus 24:43). It also, Daniélou remarks, prefigures "the *sukkot* in which the just are to dwell in the age to come."[42] For the prophet Hosea, the "Messianic time . . . appears as a return to the *ekklesia* of the desert when the people dwelt in booths":[43] "And I that am the Lord thy God from the Land of Egypt will yet make thee to dwell in tabernacles [Heb. *ohel*], as in the day of the solemn feast" (Hos. 12:9). Likewise Isaiah 32:18: "And my people shall dwell in a peaceable habitation, and in sure dwellings [Heb. *mishkan*], and in quiet resting places" (AV). The Geneva translators stay closer to the Hebrew: "And my people shall dwell in the tabernacle of peace, and in sure dwellings, and in safe resting places." Nor in the present context should the "eternal habitations" of Luke 16:9 be overlooked: "they may receive you into everlasting habitations" (*aionai scenai*). If indeed the verse is "an authentic saying of Jesus," we read in the entry under *skene* in the *Theological Dictionary of the New Testament,* "the logion shows that the idea of dwelling in eschatological *skenai* must have been familiar to Jesus himself."[44] (And if the saying is *not* authentic, messianic ideas current in Palestinian Judaism were, of course, familiar to Jesus.) But how should those eternal *skenai,* tents, tabernacles be visualized? Luther imagined them as eschatological *sukkot:* his Bible renders the *skenai* of Luke 16:9 as *die ewigen Hütten*—eternal huts. (The German name for the Feast of Tabernacles is *das Laubhüttenfest.*)

In later Judaism, even in the lifetime of Jesus, the Feast of Tabernacles was regarded as a foreshadowing of the Messianic Age, as we have seen: the Rabbis "connected the final harvest of the year with a harvest in the future—an ingathering of the nations to Jerusalem in the days of Messiah."[45] Shortly before the Messiah's advent, the trumpet of horn, blown at the New Year and at the Feast of Tabernacles, shall sound: "And it shall come to pass in that day, that the great trumpet [Heb. *shofar*] shall be blown . . ." (Isa. 27:13); "and the Lord God shall blow the trumpet [*shofar*]. . . . And the Lord their God shall save them in that day as the flock of his people" (Zech. 9:14,16). Geza Vermes has drawn our attention to a link made in rabbinic Judaism between the *shofar* and the "final salvation of Israel."[46] In sum, Taylor's imagery and typology in Meditation 24 depend on the messianic nature of the Feast as it was elucidated by the Prophets, by the Rabbis, and by some of the early Fathers: "Septembers fifteenth day did type the Birth / Of this thy tabernacle here on earth" (Stanza 6).

A few remarks about the term "Feast of Tabernacles" as it appears in the Septuagint and in the New Testament: In John 7:2, we are told that "the Jews' feast of tabernacles [σκηνοπηγία] was at hand." On the last day of the feast, Jesus urges the people to come to him for "rivers of living water." "In the last day, that great day of the feast, Jesus stood and cried, saying, If any man thirst, let him come unto me, and drink. He that believeth on me, as the scripture hath said, out of his belly shall flow rivers of living water" (John 7:37–38). For Taylor, as for many exegetes, including C. H. Dodd, Jesus's words recall the ritual water libations performed during *Sukkot*.[47] Daniélou explains the "living water" of John 7 as "an allusion to the ablutions of water on the last day of the Feast of Tabernacles." Furthermore, "In showing that it is He from whom living water is to come, Christ also shows that it is in Him that the reality prefigured by the feast of Tabernacles is fulfilled."[48] The noun *skenopegia* (which as Ainsworth says means "the erection of a tent") occurs nine times in the Septuagint. For example: "Three times a year shall all thy males appear before the Lord thy God in the place where he shall choose; in the feast of unleavened bread, and in the feast of weeks, and in the feast of tabernacles [LXX, σκηνοπηγίας]" (Deut. 16:16). Used in what Daniélou regards as "a very messianic context,"[49] *skenopegia* appears in Zechariah 14, part of the liturgy for *Sukkot*: "And it shall come to pass, that every one that is left of all the nations which came against Jerusalem shall even go up from year to year to worship the King, the Lord of hosts, and to keep the feast of tabernacles" (14:16). Aristotle, it seems, uses the word *skenopegia* for "the nest-building of swallows," but elsewhere it occurs "as a technical term of the Jewish language," almost always in connection with the Feast of Tabernacles (*Greek-English Lexicon of the New Testament*). (The image of swallows' nest-building is lovely: like a *sukkah*, a nest is a frail, lightly thatched, temporary abode, erected for ritual purposes.)

What is a tabernacle? Our English word "tabernacle" is rooted in the Latin *taberna*, "any slight structure used for a dwelling" (a hut, shed, booth, stall, or shop constructed of boards; it is cognate with "tavern"); in the Vulgate, *tabernaculum*, "a tent," signifies the Jewish tabernacle of worship (Lewis and Short). According to the *Oxford English Dictionary*, the word "tabernacle" signifies "a temporary dwelling; generally moveable, constructed of branches, boards, or canvas; a hut, tent, booth." (In Coverdale's version of Hebrews 11:9, Abraham is "a straunger in the londe of promes . . . & dwelt in tabernacles"; Wyclif, in a charming move, has the faithful Abraham dwelling in "litel housis"; the Geneva Bible says he "dwelt in tents"; the Authorized Version has him "dwelling in tabernacles"; the Revised Standard Version has him "living in tents." The Greek text reads *en skenais*.) Moreover, in the English Bible, "tabernacle" may signify "the curtained tent, containing the Ark of the

covenant and other sacred appointments, which served as the portable sanctuary of the Israelites during their wandering in the wilderness" (the tabernacle of worship, or tent of meeting, is never referred to as *sukkah* in the Hebrew
Bible). Used "figuratively," the word "tabernacle" may signify "the dwelling
place of Jehovah or of God"; the verb "to tabernacle" is used for the "sojourning of Christ on earth or 'in the flesh'" (OED). The word "booth," cognate
with "abode" and with "bower," is used more or less interchangeably with
"tabernacle" in its broad sense: a booth is a "temporary dwelling covered with
boughs of trees or other slight material"; like a tent or a stall, it may be covered with canvas or woven cloth (OED), as it still is in fairgrounds.

As for the Hebrew word *sukkah*: in the King James Bible, it is given indis-
criminately, arbitrarily, as "booth," "tabernacle," "pavilion," "tent," "covert,"
and "cottage." Englished verses of Hebrew parallelism make *sukkah* interchangeable with "lodge," with "secret place," with "dens," and with "lair."
Thus, "Jacob made booths [*sukkah*] for his cattle" (Gen. 33:17); "And there
shall be a tabernacle [*sukkah*] for a shadow in the daytime from the heat" (Isa.
4:6); "Israel and Judah abide in tents [*sukkah*]" (2 Sam. 11:11); "Benhadad
was drinking himself drunk in the pavilions [*sukkah*]" (1 Kings 20:16); "When
they couch in their dens, and abide in the covert [*sukkah*] to lie in wait" (Job
38:40); "He made darkness his secret place; his pavilion [*sukkah*] round about
him were dark waters" (Psalm 18:11); "And the daughter of Zion is left as a
cottage [*sukkah*] in a vineyard, as a lodge in a garden of cucumbers" (Isa. 1:8);
"Also can any understand the spreading of the clouds, or the noise of his
tabernacle [*sukkah*]?" (Job 36:29). "So Jonah . . . made him a booth
[*sukkah*], and sat under it in the shadow" (Jonah 4:5). Taking Jonah's booth as
a warning example, Edward Taylor reminds his congregation of a "most dread-
full curse" that will come upon those who "abidest out of this Tabernacle" of
Christ: "Now if the Gourd Leaves were Such a pleasant tabernacle Shaddow-
ing Jonas from the Scorching Sun beams, that when the Worm had destroyed
it, it did so afflict him that he chose rather to dy than Live. Jon. 4.8. How
sorely will the Wrath of God beate on thy Head that will not come into this
Tabernacle?" (*Types*, 2, 542). In the Hebrew Bible, as Taylor knew, Jonas's
"tabernacle" is a *sukkah*.

Let us recall the biblical context of *Sukkot*, the Feast of Tabernacles. In
Leviticus 23, Moses is instructed by the Lord to "Speak unto the children of
Israel, saying, The fifteenth day of this seventh month shall be the feast of
tabernacles for seven days unto the Lord" (Lev. 23:34).

> And ye shall take you on the first day the boughs of goodly trees, branches of
> palm trees, and the boughs of thick trees, and willows of the brook. . . .
> Ye shall dwell in booths seven days; all that are Israelites born shall dwell
> in booths: That your generation may know that I made the children of

Israel to dwell in booths, when I brought them out of the land of Egypt. (Lev. 23:40–42)

It seems the phrase "boughs of goodly trees" should read "the product" or "the fruit of goodly trees": "And you shall take on the first day the fruit of goodly trees, branches of palm trees, and boughs of leafy trees, and willows of the brook" (RSV). From earliest times, that fruit was understood to be an *etrog*, a kind of citron: Taylor remarks, "the Jerusalem Targum, & Chaldee, & so the Jewish Rabbies translate it the Pome Citron tree" (*Types*, 2, 529). Compare Ainsworth on that "fruit": "the Chaldee and the Targum Ierusalemy trans-lateth, *of the Pome-Citron tree.* So the Hebrew Doctors say, *the fruits of the goodly tree spoken of in the law, is the Pomecitron.*" (As almost always, his sources are acknowledged: "*Maimony* in *Shophar* and *Succah*, ch. 7. sect. 2.") The passage from Leviticus is both recalled and explicated in Nehemiah 8:14–16:

> And they found written in the law which the Lord had commanded by Moses, that the children of Israel should dwell in booths [Heb. *sukkah*; LXX *skene*] in the feast of the seventh month: And that they should publish and proclaim in all their cities, and in Jerusalem, saying, Go forth unto the mount, and fetch olive branches, and pine branches, and myrtle branches, and palm branches, and branches of thick trees, to make booths, as it is written. So the people went forth, and brought them, and made themselves booths, every one upon the roof of his house, and in their courts, and in the courts of the house of God. . . . And all the congregation of them that were come again out of the captivity made booths. . . .

How does the imaginative construct of a *sukkah* suggest to Edward Taylor "the true Feast of Tabernacles"—Christ incarnate? How does a *sukkah* become for Taylor an analogue to the conceptual language of John 1:14, wherein the Word tabernacled (*eskenosen*) among us (or in us), built or pitched his tent (or *sukkah*) among us (or in us)? Does John's term *eskenosen* make "the con-nection between the feast of the *scenai* and the feast of the Birth of Christ," as Daniélou suggests?[50] Or, and this is not impossible, does the connection in postexilian Judaism between the coming of Messiah and the Feast of Booths or Tabernacles determine John's use of the term? Let us recall the implicit se-ries of dwelling-places set out in the first three stanzas of Taylor's Meditation: the "burning Sun" in the "Tobacco box"; the "Heavens Filler" in "Clay"; the "Godhead Cabbin'd in a Myrtle bowre" (and in a "Palm branch tent, an Olive Tabernacle, / A Pine bough Booth, An Osier House or tower"). Each enclosure (including the parentheses in line 3) is metonymy for the thatched and leafy *sukkah* of the God-man, the *theanthropos,* who "pitched his tent in-deed in our nature." Taylor's sermon on the Feast of Tabernacles asserts:

"Christ Cabbining in our nature Spent his Whole time in this tent in the Work of Atonement" (*Types*, 2, 537); the "greate thing" in the Feast of Tabernacles is its depiction of the "Union" of the two natures of Christ:

> the Union of the Godhood to the Manhood . . . is held out to bee Such as is between a Booth, & the person in the Booth. So that the Godhead, which is Infinite, is described as the Inhabitant & the Manhood, which is finite, as the Tent in which this inhabitant Dwells. . . . Oh! . . . that the Finite Nature Should bee the Tabernacle, & the Infinite Nature the Dweller therein. What a wonder is here? (*Types*, 2, 536–37)

As well, each stanza of Meditation 24 constitutes a little "Tent" or "box" or "Booth" or "Tabernacle" or "Tenement," wherein the God-man, as subject of Taylor's Meditation, "dwelt" or "tabernacled" or cabined or "pitched his tent." Now in Stanza 3 come the lines,

> A mortall bitt of Manhood, where the Staple
> Doth fixt, uniting of thy natures, hold,
> And hold out marvels more than can be told.

The word "staple" is to my ears discordant. Of course a metal "staple" *may* be driven into the wood frame of a *sukkah* in order to hold the walls in place and to secure the boughs and foliage and hanging fruit to the roof beams. But to envision the Son's human nature, a "mortall bitt of Manhood," united by a "staple" to his divine nature (or, to invert the image, the divine nature united by a "staple" to the human frame), is to look for another sense of "staple"; the word can signify a threadlike "fibre of any particular variety or sampler of wool (in later use also of cotton flax, or other material for textile processes) considered with regard to its length and fineness" (OED, s.v. "staple," 3).[51] That sense of "staple" would unite and tie together human tissue with leaves, with woven and interlaced textiles, with texts, with the "golden locks" of Stanza 1, and with the "Canopee" or net of Stanza 4. Furthermore, the little word "bitt" ("A mortall bitt of Manhood") does not mean a bite, a little bit, a morsel, but may signify "one of the strong posts firmly fastened" in the deck of a ship "for fastening cables, belaying ropes, etc." (OED). Like a button, like locks, a "bitt" is used to fasten, to attach, to fix, to secure, to conjoin, but not to confuse: the "Godhead" is tied to Christ's "mortall bitt of Manhood." The two natures are *distinct*. Taylor's Meditation 40, second series, takes up a parallel image: "Thy Humane nature so divinely ti'de / Unto thy Person all Divine's a Spring."

That in Meditation 24 Christ's two natures, human and divine, are imagined as "fixt" (Stanza 3) or "Conjoynd" (Stanza 5) with a threadlike material evokes in the context of the Feast of Tabernacles the ritual *lulab*—branches of palm, willow (Heb. *aravot*), and myrtle (Heb. *hadasim*), bound together with palm fronds or bark.[52] The Hebrew word *lulab*, which means "date palm," is used metonymically by the Rabbis to refer to the bound festal bouquet. Carried in the right hand during the festival of *Sukkot*, waved in a prescribed manner during the recital of the great Psalm 118, the *lulab*, together with the unblemished citron or *etrog*, constitutes the "four species" of plant central to the feast (see Mishnah *Sukkah* 3.8). Ainsworth describes the *lulab* this way: "They binde the Palme-branch, and Myrtle, and willow branch, and make of them three, one bundle."[53] In rhetorical terms, the bound *lulab* is synecdoche for the *sukkah* covering: the *lulab* is a *sukkah* in miniature. (Taylor's image of the Sun "buttond up in a Tobacco box" may resonate with the unblemished yellow citron, the ritual *etrog*, housed in its container. Apparently, the Church Fathers saw in the *etrog* a symbol of the paradisal fruit of the tree of life.)[54]

For Taylor, "Thy Godhead Cabbin'd in a Myrtle bowre, / A Palm branch tent, an Olive Tabernacle, / A Pine bough Booth, An Osier House or tower" is a spatial correlative for the "uniting" in one person of Christ's two "natures" (Stanza 3). In one sense, Taylor is representing the person of the God-man as a *sukkah*, composed of two natures, the humanity and the divinity, united ("Conjoynd") just as the three species in a *lulab* are united and distinct.

> . . . and wilt
> Thou tabernacle in a tent so small?
> Have Tent, and Tent cloath of a Humane Quilt?
> Thy Person make a bit of flesh of mee
> Thy Tabernacle, and its Canopee?
>
> (Stanza 4)

(Taylor's question, "wilt / Thou tabernacle in a tent," echoes the transfiguration scene, with its "explicit allusion" [Daniélou] to the Feast of Booths:[55] "Then answered Peter, and said unto Jesus, Lord it is good for us to be here: if thou wilt, let us make here three tabernacles [*skenas*]; one for thee, and one for Moses, and one for Elias" [Matt. 17:4–5].) Unravelled, the five lines cited just above might read: heaven is your dwelling place and it canopies the whole world. Do you really want to tabernacle in this small and mean tent; do you really want to make my body ("a bit of flesh of mee") your *sukkah*? While the "Tent cloath" may be a hanging within the "Tent" (seventeenth- and eighteenth-century *sukkoth* were often richly decorated with tapestries), it also recalls the covering of the wilderness tent, at one time made of skins. The portable tabernacle of worship, for example, was covered with "rams' skins dyed red" (Exod. 39:34). Some Rabbis imagined that the eternal *sukkot* prepared for the righteous in the world to come would be covered with the skin of Leviathan.[56] (Others thought that the flesh of Leviathan and Behemoth will be eaten at the great messianic banquet.)[57]

Drawing together human tissue, woven cloth, and the catalogue of *sukkah* leaves (olive, myrtle, pine, willow, tobacco), Stanza 5 introduces another sort of leaf into Taylor's Meditation—a "Carnation leafe":

> Wonders! my Lord, Thy Nature all With Mine
>> Doth by the Feast of Booths Conjoynd appeare
> Together in thy Person all Divine
>> Stand House, and House holder. What Wonder's here?
>> Thy Person infinite without compare
> Cloaths made of a Carnation leafe doth ware.

The "Humane Quilt," the doubled tent-covering, has modulated into "a Carnation leafe" worn by the double-natured God-man, who is signified by the mimetic phrases "House, and House holder" and "Tent, and Tent cloath." Just as the tabernacle in the wilderness is covered by "rams' skins dyed red," just as the frail *sukkot* of the Feast of Booths are covered with foliage and other natural material, so for Taylor the incarnate Christ "doth ware" "Cloaths made of a Carnation leafe"—a double image of the fig leaves *and* the "coats of skin" worn by the fallen Adam and Eve (Gen. 3:21), and an undoing of the Fall.[58] Coincidently the (veined and lined) "Carnation leafe" alludes to "A Leafe" of Taylor's allusive and interlaced text, whose subject is the intimate connection between the incarnation and the Feast of Tabernacles: "Lord . . . make mee give / A Leafe unto thy Lordship of myself" (Stanza 11). Stanzas 6–8 of Meditation 24 read:

> What Glory to my nature doth thy Grace
>> Confer, that it is made a Booth for thine
> To tabernacle in? Wonders take place.
>> Thou low dost step aloft to lift up mine.
>> Septembers fifteenth day did type the Birth
> Of this thy tabernacle here on earth.
>
> And through this leafy Tent the glory cleare
>> Of thy Rich Godhead shineth very much:
> The Crowds of Sacrifices which swarm here
>> Shew forth thy Efficacy now is such
>> Flowing in from thy natures thus united
> As Clears off Sin, and Victims all benighted.
>
> But yet the Wonder grows: and groweth much,
>> For thou wilt Tabernacles change with mee.
> Not onely Nature, but my person tuch.
>> Thou wilst mee thy, and thee, my tent to bee.
>> Thou wilt, if I my heart will to thee rent,
> My Tabernacle make thy Tenement.

Should one happen to be dwelling in a *sukkah*, a "leafy Tent," during the Feast of Booths on a fine day in late September or early October, sunlight might filter in through the leaves and pine branches; according to the Rabbis, there must be more shade (covered space) than sun (open space), but enough open space for the stars to shine through. In itself, however, that *sukkah* is not the subject of the second stanza above (Stanza 7). Taylor's phrase "leafy Tent" refers to the God-man, Christ incarnate, wearing "Cloaths made of a Carnation leafe" as he pitches his tent, pitches his leafy *sukkah*, among us—as he *sukkahs* among us, as it were. So one presumes that "the glory cleare / Of thy Rich Godhead" that "shineth very much" has its source *within* Taylor's "leafy Tent," not without. Nor, I imagine, would that "glory" shine "through" in the sense that light shines through a window; the "glory" would shine throughout the human "Tent," the "Humane Quilt," which is more or less impermeable to light.

On the other hand, identifying Christ with the Spouse of Canticles 2:9 ("he looked forth at the windows, shewing himself through the lattice"), Taylor's sermon presents the human nature in terms of "Lattisses of the Manhood": just as the "Persons in these boughy, & leavy Tabernacles might easily be seen," Taylor writes, so "the glory of Christs Divine Person did Shine forth thro the Tabernacle of the Humane" (*Types*, 2, 531). (Compare John 1:14: "and we beheld his glory [*doxa*], the glory as of the only begotten of the Father.") Taylor's images of bright illumination recall the first stanza of the Meditation with the sun "buttoned up in a Tobacco box" (ingeniously, the word "Tobacco" is linked by assonance and consonance to the word "Tabernacle"). As well as signifying a small covered box for carrying tobacco around in the pocket, Taylor's "Tobacco box" may be imagined as a covered shed in which leaves of the tobacco plant are hung up on laths to dry.

❖   ❖   ❖

That said, what biblical evidence, what authority, is there for God's dwelling graciously among us in a *sukkah* rather than, say, in a tabernacle (Heb. *mishkan*) or in a tent (Heb. *ohel*)? However mediated—by Puritan divines, by the Fathers, by the Rabbis—what sacred texts does Taylor's precarious *sukkah*-christology, or *sukkah*-typology, depend on ultimately? Turning to the liturgy for the Feast of Tabernacles, we discover Psalm 76: "In Salem also is his tabernacle, and his dwelling place in Zion" (76:2, AV). The Morning Service for the first day of *Sukkot* renders the verse thus: "And so, His Succah was in Jerusalem." An intricate responsive reading follows: "Then He placed His Succah in Jerusalem among: the righteous modest ones; the splendid curtain; the ordered service; in a beloved Succah—and that is His Succah."[59] A midrash on Psalm 76:2 should be cited: "R. Berechia has said, In the beginning of the creation of the world, the Holy One, blessed be He, made Himself a booth [*sukkah*] in Jerusalem, in which, if one may so speak, he prayed."[60] But on what grounds does Rabbi Berechia imagine that the Holy One, blessed be He, is praying in a *sukkah*, when the word *sukkah* does not appear in Psalm 76? Why, in the liturgy for the Feast of Tabernacles, is "His Succah" placed in Jerusalem?

An answer is given by H. St. John Thackeray in his Schweich Lectures for 1920. The Hebrew word used in Psalm 76:2 is *sukkoh*, a word meaning "his covert or lair" ("In Salem also is his (*sukkoh*) and his dwelling-place [*meonah*] in Zion"). One scholar renders the verse this way: "In Salem also is his covert and his lair in Zion," images that evoke the lion of Judah. "On the other hand," Thackeray comments, the word "*Sukkoh* 'his covert' is hardly distinguishable from *Sukkah* 'a booth' or *Sukkatho* 'his booth'. Hence . . . modern commentators render 'his pavilion' (Kirkpatrick) or 'his bower' (Cheyne), and the ancients (Greek, Syriac, and Midrash) did likewise." In the context of Taylor's Meditation 24, Thackeray is especially helpful:

> The word "tabernacle" of our English Bible happily recalls the thought which could not fail to occur to every pilgrim at the Feast of Booths. JHWH is present with His worshippers, Himself observing the feast in the immemorial fashion; He too has His *Sukkah* in the Holy City. The Greek translator here writes o τό-ποσ αυτου, a euphemism for "His booth"; in the other festival Psalm (xlii.4, Gr. xli.5) he uses the two words εν τόπῳ σκηνης. The *Sukkah* or Booth of God is a remarkable phrase only found in these two Psalms and in one other which there is reason to connect with this feast (xxvii.5); it is not to be confused with his *Ohel* or Tent which is much more frequent.[61]

"The *Sukkah* or Booth of God": so according to the Psalms, and to the Rabbis' gloss on the Psalms, the Lord may dwell among us in a *sukkah* as well as in a tabernacle or in a tent of worship. Another biblical phrase is apposite here, "*sukkah* of David" (Amos 9:11), given misleadingly in the King James Bible as "the tabernacle of David." The Revised Standard Version has "the booth of David." That *sukkah* or booth has fallen: "In that day will I raise up the tabernacle [*sukkah*] of David that is fallen and close up the breaches thereof; and I will raise up his ruins, and I will build it as in the days of old."[62] A marginal note in the Geneva Bible interprets Amos 9:11 messianically: "I will send the Messiah promised and restore by him the spiritual Israel." Hence, for the Genevan commentators, to raise up the *sukkah* of David is by a metonymy to send the Messiah. From that link made between the fallen *sukkah* and the coming of Messiah (a reading supported by Acts 15:16) to the typological connection between the nativity and the Feast of Booths is only a further step; a *sukkah* is raised up, built, once a year, in the early fall, around the fifteenth of Tishri.

Let us return to Taylor's Preparatory Meditation 24, whose eighth and ninth stanzas are informed by his sermon on the Feast of Tabernacles: during *Sukkot*, he explains in parable, people go out of their houses to dwell in the *sukkah*, bringing necessary goods into the booth and working and sleeping there: "The Rabbies say at this feast they were to bring all their necessary goods out of their house into their Booths & do their work in them, Sleep in them, &c." Likewise, his congregation must go out of themselves to dwell spiritually in Christ "the Whole Week of this life" (2, 535).

> He that would have the blessing of God in the feast of Tabernacles must dwell in Tabernacles all the Dayes of the Feast. So must thou if thou wouldst have the Blessing of the Lord Christ Tabernacling in the Flesh, thou must go out of thine own House into Christ thy Tabernacle, & abide in him all thy dayes. thy Whole Week. thou must dwell in him, Walk in him, do all things in him. (*Types*, 2, 538)

Behind Taylor's Philonic allegory lurks the Mishnah: "All the seven days [of the festival] a man must make his *sukkah* his permanent [abode] and his house [his] temporary [abode]. If it rained, when is it permissible to leave? When the porridge becomes spoiled" (Mishnah *Sukkah* 2.9). In the final stanzas of Taylor's Meditation, the *sukkah* ("Tabernacle") is internalized, applied to the self, and reimagined as the poet's heart: whether Christ dwells or pitches his tent in that little chamber, or the poet dwells in Christ, is a matter of chiasmus (perhaps the most enclosed of poetic tropes) and of synecdoche, the trope of inclusion. Stanza 8 reads:

> But yet the Wonder grows: and groweth much,
>   For thou wilt Tabernacles change with mee.
> Not onely Nature, but my person tuch.
>   Thou wilst mee thy, and thee, my tent to bee.
>   Thou wilt, if I my heart will to thee rent,
>   My Tabernacle make thy Tenement.

Interchangeable with the *sukkah* and its metonymic equivalents—tent, bower, cabin, cottage, booth, tower, tobacco box (large and small)—the poet's heart is given out, rented out, in exchange for "rent in bliss." Meanwhile, "For Quarters in thy house," the Lord's house or *sukkah* (an "eternal habitation," perhaps), Taylor will pay "rent of Reverent fear," which I take to be the Meditation: the penultimate stanza includes, "Lord lease thyselfe to mee out: make mee give / A Leafe unto thy Lordship of myselfe."

The final stanza of Meditation 24 includes the phrase "The Tabernacles of the Righteous," cited knowingly by Taylor from Psalm 118, a central text in the *Sukkot* liturgy ("The voice of rejoicing and salvation is in the tabernacles of the righteous" [Ps. 118:15]).

The Feast of Tabernacles makes me sing
   Out thy Theanthropy, my Lord, I'le spare
No Musick here. Sweet Songs of praises in
   The Tabernacles of the Righteous are.
My Palmifer'd Hosannah Songs I'le raise
On my Shoshannims blossoming thy praise.

The poet alludes to his own "Palmifer'd Hosannah Songs": the elided word
"Palmifer'd" (palmiferous) again recalls the ritual *lulab* made up of palm, willow and myrtle branches; it also hints at the word "Psalm." Waving the *lulab*,
holding the *etrog*, those celebrating *Sukkot* chant Psalm 118 responsively:

> Save now, I beseech thee, O Lord: O Lord, I beseech thee, send now prosperity.
> Blessed be he that cometh in the name of the Lord: we have blessed you out of
> the house of the Lord. God is the Lord which has shewed us light. . . .
> (118:25–27)

The Hebrew word *hoshianna* means "Save, I Pray," or "Save, we beseech
thee." As Taylor read in Ainsworth and in Mede, the word *hosanna* may refer
to the festive wreath or bouquet itself.[63] Ainsworth says: *"Every day they went
about the Altar once, with the palme-branches in their hands,* and said O LORD
SAVE NOW, (or *Hosanna*) and O LORD PROSPER NOW, and *in the seventh day, they
went about the Altar seven times, &c. Maimony in Shophar . . ."* (on Lev.
23:40). Explicating Psalm 118:25, Ainsworth writes:

> *save now* or I *beseech thee save:* in Hebrue *Hoshianna,* or *Hosanna,* as it is
> sounded in Greek, Mat. 21.9.15. where the people and children welcome Christ
> into Jerusalem, singing *Hosanna the son of David,* that is, praying God most hye,
> *to save the King (Christ) who then came in the name of the Lord.*[64]

Furthermore, the word *hoshana* sounds very much like *shoshan* or *shoshan-*
nah, the Hebrew word for "lily." Singing out the Lord's "Theanthropy" in the
last stanza of the Meditation, Taylor gets double use from the word "Shoshannims": echoing the word *hoshana,* it connects the poet's "Sweet Songs of
praises," his "Hosanna Songs" (songs of salvation) to "blossoming" flowers
(perhaps by way of George Herbert's "Easter": "I got me flowers to straw thy
way; / I got me boughs off many a tree: / But thou wast up by break of day, /
And brought'st thy sweets along with thee"). No doubt influenced by a note
to Psalm 45 in the Geneva Bible and by Ainsworth, Taylor takes the word
"Shoshannims" to mean "a certaine tune or an instrument." Ainsworth
claims they are "Six-stringed instruments"; the word also "signifieth six-
leaved flowers, that is, Lilies."[65] Here is Taylor's informed description of cele-
brants at *Sukkot* singing out and carrying their *lulabim* "bound up in their
hands," liturgical actions that resonate in the scene of Palm Sunday, when

the people got boughs from many a tree and "strewd his [Christ's] way with Pine branches and sung Hosannahs to the Son of David":

> Touching the Manner of their Proceeding in this feast, It Was Such as that they Carried the branches of these bound up in their hands, & With joy Sang out their Hosannah & so some observe that the Branches came to be called Hosannas from the Song they Sang. In respect unto this when on another occasion Matt. 21.8.9. they strewd his way with Pine branches, & Sung Hosannahs to the Son of David, Hosanna in the Highest. & Hosannah, blessed is the King of Israel that cometh in the Name of the Lord. And tho this was at another time, yet they conferrd the Rites of the feast of Tabernacles on Christ as belonging to him. (*Types*, 2, 533)[66]

❖   ❖   ❖

Taylor's sermon on the Feast of Tabernacles alludes to, and misrepresents, Augustine's Homily on John 7: "Augustin saith Christ was in the booth. but the Shaddow hid the Light. He was at the Feast of Tabernacles, but it was Secretly" (*Types*, 2, 528). But Augustine does *not* say that Christ was in the booth, not at all: according to Augustine, "Christ was in the Scenopegia [the Feast of Tabernacles], but Christ latent." Which is to say that Christ is the mystery latent in the Feast of Tabernacles. In John 7:10 (Vulgate) we read that Christ went up to the Feast *non manifeste sed quasi in occulto*—"not openly, but as it were in secret" (AV)—εν κρυπτῳ, in the Greek text. Augustine elucidates the verse almost as if it were a model of textual concealment whereby one rhetorical trope is hidden in another: "He Himself was secretly latent in that holy-day. And yet, what I have been saying is itself latent from you. Then let it be manifested, let the veil be lifted up, and that appear which was in secret." Glossing the Exodus in terms of the Israelites' dwelling in booths on their way through the wilderness to the Promised Land, and equating the wilderness and the present age, the Promised Land and heaven, Augustine makes manifest the eschatological mystery of the great Feast:

> This feast-day, then; let us seek of which future thing it was the shadow. I have expounded what this Scenopegia was: it was the celebration of Tabernacles, because the people, after it was delivered out of Egypt, while on its way through the wilderness to the land of promise, dwelt in tabernacles. . . . Then let us mark ourselves, brethren; we have been brought out of Egypt where we were in bondage to the devil, as unto Pharaoh, where we were busied with works of clay in earthly desires, and therein had sore labour. . . . Brought out hence, we were made to pass through Baptism, as the Red Sea, (red, because hallowed by the blood of Christ,) with all our enemies dead that followed after us, that is, all our sins blotted out. At this present time then, before we come to the Land of Promise, that is, to the eternal kingdom, we

are in the wilderness [*in eremo*], in tabernacles. . . . That man is in tabernacles, who understands himself to be in the world, as a stranger in a foreign
land. That man knows himself sojourning in a strange land, who sees himself
to be sighing after the land of his home. . . .[67]

Augustine's homesickness is echoed by Samuel Mather: the Feast of Tabernacles, we read in *Figure or Types*, served to "instruct" the Jewish people "that
they were but Pilgrims and Strangers here below, Sojourners as it were in a
Strange Land, passing through it to their own Country, towards their own
Home."[68]

❖   ❖   ❖

Before the porridge spoils, I shall leave this chapter on Taylor and the Feast of
Tabernacles, but not without citing the distinguished twentieth-century
philosopher Franz Rosenzweig (1886–1929), who, in *The Star of Redemption*,
makes a connection other scholars have not made (as far as I can tell)—that
between the *sukkah* of the Feast of Tabernacles and "the manger in the
strange stable in which the redeemer comes into the world." What is "noteworthy" about the festival of Christmas, Rosenzweig writes, is that it "did not
conform to a holiday of the Jewish calendar like Easter and Pentecost." Yet in
the past centuries

> the festival has . . . undergone a development . . . which has brought it
> into a degree of proximity to the Jewish festivals of redemption. The house
> opens up to admit free nature. The hospitality of a warm room is extended to
> the snow-covered Christmas tree, and this opening up of the house to admit na-
> ture, and the manger in the strange stable in which the redeemer comes into
> the world, have their exact counterpart in the open sky admitted by the roof of
> the tabernacle-hut in memory of the tent of meeting which granted rest to the
> eternal people during its wanderings through the desert.[69]

Afterword

Reading events of the Old Testament as prefigurations of the New implies a "theology of history" (R. A. Markus is cited): by leading the Israelites "out of captivity from Egypt, in giving them his law through Moses, in calling them to repentance and new life through the prophets, God is always preparing his people for the final redemption to be accomplished in Jesus the Messiah. . . . The redemptive history is an educative process, a divine *paidagogia*, in which each stage has its due course in God's plan for men."[1] When Markus writes about "an educative process, a divine *paidagogia*," he is echoing Paul's letter to the Galatians: "Where the law was our schoolmaster [*paidagogos*] to bring us unto Christ, that we may be justified by faith. But after that faith is come, we are no longer under a schoolmaster [*paidagogon*]" (3:24–25). The people of Israel, according to the Westminster Confession of Faith (1647), were "a Church under age."[2]

For Markus, as for Oscar Cullmann, the redemptive history of the Old Testament is a *"preparation in time* for this Christ event," a tutorial, as it were, for the Christian revelation.[3] The model of advancing dispensations presupposes that things, persons, and events of the Old Testament (Moses, Isaac, Jacob, the marvellous rock, the burning bush, the Feast of Tabernacles) are messianic signs, types, shadows, and prophecies, whose significance is revealed by the New Testament. "We have found him of whom Moses in the law, and the prophets, did write"; "We have found the Messias, which is, being interpreted, the Christ" (John 1:45, 41). In the history of redemption written by Christian exegetes, Judaism is a "stage" with "its due course in God's plan for men": it is a station on the way to Christianity, which supersedes it.

Yet if the line of redemptive history moves forward in time incrementally from A to B—if, as Markus asserts, it is "an educative process, a divine *paidagogia*"—the recognition of that process moves backwards, horizontally, from B to A, back to the "signum" or "type." Typological exegesis is a "return to the Old Testament"; having seen the Old Testament fulfilled in the New, the Christian exegete attends to the Jewish Bible "precisely as foreshadowing this

95

fulfilment."[4] The two-part figure of speech generally known as figuralism or typology, defined by scholars in terms of the connection it makes between two
"real historical events," is a process of reading back into the Old Testament,
with hindsight, events of the New.[5] It is a retrospective and revisionary mode
of reading, whereby Scripture is attended to in terms of one event—the life
and death of Jesus Christ. It is a mode of spiritual perception.

I am struck by the "clothing" and "weaving" metaphors used by Markus to
illustrate the relation between Old and New Testaments:

> the New Testament reveals its detailed dependence on the Old—not simply as
> a literary influence, but as endowing the events recounted by the New Testa-
> ment writers with their significance. In clothing the New Testament story in
> Old Testament imagery and weaving narratives on patterns borrowed from the
> Old Testament, the writers are presenting the events they describe in terms of
> God's plan for the redemption of men.[6]

The Evangelists have clothed events in Old Testament imagery, Markus says;
they have woven narratives "on patterns borrowed from the Old Testament."
There may be an unusual twist here on Augustine's model of reading. "The
New Testament lies hidden in the Old, the Old Testament becomes plain in
the New"; "In the Old Testament, the Old is concealed, in the New the Old
is revealed." *In Vetere Novum lateat, et in Novo Vetus pateat.* Augustine's next
sentence begins: "The unspiritual fail to see this hidden meaning."[7] The Latin
verb *lateo* means "to lurk, be *or* lie hid *or* concealed"; "to be concealed *or* ob-
scure, to be unknown." Its opposite, *pateo,* means "to stand open, lie open, be
open"; it may also mean "to be clear, plain, well known, evident, manifest"
(Lewis and Short). By "clothing the New Testament story in Old Testament
imagery," by alluding to events of the Old Testament, the writers of the
Gospel sought to make clear and plain the underlying meaning (*hyponoia*) of
the Old Testament.

Cotton Mather revises the clothing metaphor. Presenting the Old Testament as a textile (tissue, veil, vellum, woven fabric) that can be explicated
(unfolded) and unpacked, he portrays the Gospel as a "Babe in Swadling
Cloaths": "the wise men that of Old were travelling and Enquiring after the
Lord Jesus Christ found Him a Babe in Swadling Cloaths and paid Respect
unto Him, King of the World. As many as are, and God forbid that any
should not be inquisitive after the Holy Child Jesus, may behold Him in the
Swadling Cloaths, which the *types* of the Old Testament Enwrapped Him
in."[8] After a hard journey, the Magi found Christ wrapped in "Swadling
Cloaths"; analogously, one infers, diligent readers may find him "Enwrapped"
in the types of the Old Testament. Samuel Mather, uncle to Cotton Mather,
urges us to "search into those ancient Administrations, because there is much

Gospel there." "The Spirit and Substance and Mystery of that Dispensation was Evangelical, tho' it was involved in a legal Shell."[9] Shells are to kernels as swaddling clothes are to infants, and as veils are to revelation.

We are looking at tropes of inclusion and involvement, whereby divinity is said to be enveloped, enfolded, obscured, enwrapped, implicated. Origen, in a homily on Leviticus, describes the "letter" of the Old Testament as a "vesture" covering the "spiritual sense" of the text:

> For the Word came into the world by Mary, clad in flesh; and seeing was not understanding; all saw the flesh; knowledge of the divinity was given to a chosen few. So when the Word was shown to men through the lawgiver and the prophets, it was not shown them without suitable vesture. There it is covered by the veil of flesh, here of the letter. The letter appears as flesh; but the spiritual sense within is known as divinity. This is what we find in studying Leviticus. . . . Blessed are the eyes which see through the letter's veil.[10]

For Cotton Mather, Christ is "Enwrapped" in the pliant "Cloaths" or *types* of the Old Testament. Origen's homily presents Christ's flesh as "suitable vesture"; then both flesh and vesture become metonymy for the "letter"—the literal or surface sense of the Old Testament covering the "divinity" or the "spiritual sense within." In ways I only intuit, the two natures of Christ, human and divine, have in Origen's text been accommodated to a twofold sense of Scripture: the "vesture" is meant to conceal *and* to reveal: the incarnation has become a model of reading. Like a "veil of flesh," the "letter" is an outer covering, and only "a chosen few" have the "knowledge" or "understanding" to see "through" the vesture or veil to the divinity.

❖   ❖   ❖

The twofold, christocentric model of reading, whereby the spiritual (hidden) sense of Scripture is involved in the literal sense as a kernel is involved in its shell, is approached in chapter 1 of the present study. That the Angel of Death did not "smite Israel," writes Melito of Sardis, who is echoed by John Chrysostom, is *because* the blood of the lamb sprinkled on the doorposts and lintels in Egypt was a type of the blood of Christ. In Chrysostom's interpretation of the binding of Isaac, the thing itself (*pragma*) was concealed; at the crucifixion, the matter was revealed and made plain. The *pragma* was common to both events "in a different degree of revelation."[11] For the Fathers, East and West, what is common to both events, the Akedah and the crucifixion, is "God in his revelatory action": "wherever God has revealed himself and will yet reveal himself, from the Creation on to the new creation at the end of time," writes Oscar Cullmann, "this 'Word,' which back then at this definite time became flesh, must be at work."[12] In Judaism, God's creating Word is not a hypostasis, a being in any way separate from or other than God; God's Word (called "Memra" or "Memra of the Lord" by the Targumists) is God in his self-revelation.

Indirectly, Cullmann throws light on an aspect of Jonathan Edwards's outline of redemptive history, the focus of chapter 2. By identifying the angel of the Lord (mal'ak YHWH) as Christ "in the form of the human nature," Edwards is reviving a pre-Nicene christology. Cullmann explains: "Whenever the subject of discussion is God's revelatory action—and to it belongs creation in a special degree—there in the Primitive Christian view, the subject of the discussion is Christ, the same person whose incarnation can be dated in an ordinary chronological manner."[13] By "Primitive" is meant the view of the Church Fathers up to the fifth century, when doctrine settled down. The revelatory action that concerns us in our discussion of Edwards is the story of Moses, addressed by the angel of the Lord, the mal'ak YHWH, from the burning bush; for Edwards, that angel is the preexistent Son, the second person of the Trinity, the vehicle or agency of revelation and creation.

To students of American literature, Edwards's christology may seem to be a rare fossil marked with concerns of second- and third-century apologists such as Justin Martyr, Irenaeus, and Tertullian. It is not so rare after all: reading back the presence of Christ into the Old Testament is a staple of Puritan writings. One finds it throughout the *Annotations* of Henry Ainsworth, whence it filtered broadly into colonial New England. One finds it in Taylor, whose sermon on the Feast of Tabernacles (a feast in which myrtle leaves figure) proposes that "the Angell or rather Christ himselfe was Seen among the Myrtle Trees Zech. 1.8. to import Christs presence with his Church."[14] For Taylor, as for Edwards, the pillar of cloud that led the Israelites through the wilderness was moved "by Christ himselfe, who pitched his tent in this cloud."[15] Increase Mather, in *Some Important Truths About Conversion, Delivered in Sundry Sermons* (1674), asserts that Jacob is wrestling with Christ (Gen. 32:24). Preaching on the necessity of solitary times for prayer and meditation, Mather tells his congregation: "*Jacob was left alone, and there wrestled a man with him until the breaking of the day.* He spent a good part of the night in secret prayer, none being there present but Christ and he."[16] Likewise, Increase's brother Samuel Mather identifies the angel in the burning bush as Christ: "The *second Person* Jesus Christ appeared to *Moses, Exod.* 3.2,4. For he is called *the Angel,* which agrees not so well to the first Person. And Moses *prays for his Good will,* Deut. 33.16. Therefore it was not any created Angel, but Jesus Christ, the Angel of the Covenant of Grace; as a *praeludium* to his Incarnation."[17]

As soon as the preexistent Christ is said to be present in some mode in the Old Testament, "the appearance of allegory sooner or later is almost inevitable," R. P. C. Hanson submits.[18] If that is so, the "inevitable" appearance of allegory may somehow be determined by the nature of an allegorical sign, which refers to something that *precedes* it.[19] According to the Fourth Gospel, the divine Word or Logos was "in the beginning, *en arche*" (John 1:1); in the Epistle to the Hebrews, God "made the worlds" (or ages, *aionas*) by or through the Son (1:2). Paul's letter to the Colossians describes the Son as "the image of the invisible God, the firstborn of every creature: For by him were all things created, that are in heaven, and that are in earth . . . And he is before all things, and by him all things consist" (1:15–17). So convinced were the early Fathers that the Son "was the agent in creation, that the first words of Genesis ["In the beginning God created the heaven and the earth"] were, by some of them, understood as 'by means of the Son God created heaven and earth'" (C. T. R. Hayward is cited).[20]

If the Son, the second person of the Trinity, is before all things, he is, of course, before the allegorical sign (the burning bush, the blood daubed on the lintels and doorposts, the myrtle, the pillar of cloud, the manna, the miraculous rock that gave forth water, Abraham and Moses). In the apologetic *Dialogue with Trypho*, Justin argues: "God begat before all creatures a Beginning . . . who is called . . . now the Glory of the Lord, now the Son, again Wisdom, again an Angel, then God, and then Lord and Logos."[21] Origen insists in *Contra Celsum* that the Son of God is not "a new God. For the sacred Scriptures know that he is older than all created things; and it was to him that God said, concerning the creation of man, 'Let us make man after our image and likeness'" (Gen. 1:26).[22] This sort of approach, Hanson remarks, "was to have a long and vigorous history in later Christian interpretation."[23]

❖   ❖   ❖

We seem to be addressing two subjects—typological exegesis and christology. On one level, however, they are the same thing. Whether the trope is called typological allegory, allegorical typology, figural allegory, prophetic allegory, or horizontal allegory, *typology is christological*; it is not another form of Hebrew parallelism.[24] The two-part figure of speech known as biblical typology is christocentric: it is structured around a center, the midpoint of Christian history, the incarnation. "By the events of this birth the true significance of all other events is defined," Auden writes in *For the Time Being*.[25] The "other events" include events of the Old Testament. In Christianity, there is a beginning, a middle, and an end; its midpoint (the pivot between B.C. and A.D.) is a historical event—two thousand years ago Christ appeared in history with the name of Jesus of Nazareth, and ever since it has been a matter of waiting for the end. In Judaism, on the other hand, the Messiah's *first* advent is deferred, and that deferral makes all the difference in Christian and Jewish models of reading.

In rabbinic exegesis and in the Hebrew Bible itself, events are clothed in the imagery of other events; the Exodus is interpreted and reinterpreted and rewoven by the Prophets, in the Psalms, and in postbiblical writings. The Targums, the Dead Sea Scrolls, and texts such as the Book of Jubilees draw out midrashically the event of the Akedah. Philo and the Rabbis allegorize Scripture in terms of hidden moral and ethical truths. But to insist, as some scholars do, on the presence of "typology" in the Hebrew Bible itself only serves to confuse two distinct models of history. Judaism does not define the significance of persons and events by reference to the incarnation. Judaism is informed by deferral and delay, by meaning deferred, by waiting. The exegete may never get to the point. In the line running through the Hebrew Bible, the Apocrypha, and postbiblical Judaism, there is no definitive *kairos* dividing chronology into time before and time after.[26]

That said, what is most striking about Puritan writings I have seen is the role played by Jewish exegetes and exegesis—the Targums, Josephus, Philo, the Talmud, medieval Jewish philosophy, the Lurianic Kabbala, and the seventeenth-century messianist Rabbi Menasseh ben Israel. In the first instance, Protestant scholars in England and in New England took their millennialism from Daniel and Revelation. They then turned to the uncoordinated program of Jewish messianism, which predicted "messianic birth pangs"—wars, fires, plagues, overturnings, and other catastrophes that were to announce Messiah's advent (outlined in chapter 3). Puritans pored over Jewish apocalyptic—Daniel, bits of Ezekiel and of Isaiah, *1 Enoch*, the second *Apocalypse of Baruch*, and the Ezra Apocalypse (*4 Ezra*). If Jews were awaiting the Age of Messiah—the time of fruitfulness when the redeemed will sit under their vines and fig trees—a group of Puritan chiliasts awaited Christ's transient, premillennial advent, which would signal the end of Antichrist (the Pope of Rome), the conversion of the Jews, and the opening of the millennium. These historical events had to be syncronized, and learned men such as Thomas Brightman and Joseph Mede did so by forcing one model of thought into another. A theology of history with a decisive midpoint (Christianity) was made to accommodate a history and a theology without a midpoint but with a highly developed eschatology.

Ideas about a temporal kingdom had been endorsed by the earliest apologists—Tertullian, Irenaeus, Justin. Increase Mather's *Mystery of Israel's Salvation* confirms this; he is scrupulous about giving sources. Yet for Mather and like-minded Puritans, the Fathers may be less important than the Rabbis, who were of two minds about redemption. Some of them (to cite David Daube) taught that not even Elijah knows the moment of redemption. "In fact it is sinful for a man to calculate the end. Nor may he do anything to hasten it, or for that matter to delay it. He must do his duty and wait." Other Rabbis, however, taught that "[s]in may delay redemption, holiness may hasten it—

though God may hasten it also freely, from mercy."[27] In the words of Joseph Klausner, "repentance and the keeping of the commandments were the pre-requisites of redemption, since they would bring about the great changes that must precede Messiah's coming."[28] For Puritan millennialists (who use the terms "conversion" and "repentence" interchangeably), a causal connection between the Jews' repentance and their final redemption was crucial. The "calling" or conversion of the Jews would signal that repentance; thus all Is-rael would be saved. Brightman thought that the Jews' "vocation" was "their calling to the faith in Christ."[29]

How convoluted the turnings are! Jewish texts, read in the original tongues by Brightman, Mede, Cotton, and the Mathers, are used rhetorically against the Church of Rome; then they are turned against Judaism. Even Henry Ainsworth employed his remarkable knowledge of postbiblical Judaism to make the Rabbis corroborating witnesses for Christianity. Already we have looked at swaddling clothes, vestures, and veils, but we have not come across nets. As everyone knows, one sort of net is "made of twine or strong cord, forming meshes of suitable size, used for the capture of fish, birds, or other liv-ing things" (*Oxford English Dictionary*). Introducing Cotton Mather's "Tri-paradisus," his editor remarks: "[B]y drawing for support on the works of mes-sianic Jews, as for instance, Rabbi Samuel Marochitanus's *Coming of the Messiah* (1648), Mather could cast out his net among the Jewish popula-tion."[30] Catching Jews with nets made out of rabbinic material is a distin-guishing mark of Puritan apologetics.[31]

Following Hans Joachim Schoeps's *Philosemitismus im Barock* (1952), scholars may dignify the Puritans' interest in Jewish texts with the term "philo-Semitism." David Katz's monograph of 1982 is called *Philo-Semitism and the Readmission of the Jews to England, 603–1655*.[32] In 1976, Frances Yates observed: "The Puritan movement was intensely philosemitic, He-braic, and Biblical in all its modes of expression."[33] One of those modes was Puritan apologetics. As defined in the OED, "philo-Semitism" is a "theory, action or practice directed in favour of the Jews." A "philo-Semite" is "one who is favourable to or who supports the Jews." Learning Hebrew and Ara-maic in order to decipher rabbinic texts and manufacture nets for Jews is to promote the end of Judaism. The term "philo-semitic millennialism" (which I have seen) is an oxymoron. One of Taylor's sermons justifies con-sulting the Rabbis (by way of Ainsworth and Poole) about details of Jewish ritual: "We cannot come to the knowledge of it, but by wading in the durty Channells of Rabbinical Foes to the Gospel." Somewhere those "durty Channells" may be connected to the "Dirty Pudle Water of Popish, & Eras-tian fopperies."[34]

❖   ❖   ❖

In some passages, the New Testament reflects controversy with Jews, and so it was useful to clothe events in imagery taken over from the Old Testament and to weave narratives "on patterns borrowed from the Old Testament" (to recite Markus). A century later, the Church Fathers were fighting on two fronts: Christianity had to be defended against heretics, and Jews had to be convinced of the Christian revelation. In both cases, Old Testament prophecies were used as messianic proof-texts to illustrate the unity of the divine plan. When we look at Puritan apologetics, their obsessive focus has become the Church of Rome. Again, those writings canvas the Old Testament as well as the Apocrypha and Pseudepigrapha. Brightman, Mede, John Cotton, Increase Mather, and Jonathan Edwards (as well as the Genevan editors) were convinced that prophecies given out so mysteriously in the book of Daniel (glossed in Revelation, in late Jewish apocalyptic, and in centuries of rabbinic material) signified without a shadow of a doubt the "idolatrous" Church of Rome. Pressing for the end was to press for the end of the papacy. Shortly the fifth vial in Revelation would be poured out on the seat of the beast; with the pouring out of the sixth vial and the arrival of the kings from the East, the Jews would be converted.

Finally, how is the Second Coming related to matters of biblical exegesis? Cullmann has identified the "tension" in redemptive history between the "already" and the "not yet"—the incarnation and the Parousia: "It is already the time of the end and yet it is not *the* end."[35] Building on Cullmann, Markus discusses the "two-fold spiritual sense" of Scripture. His phrasing bears scrutiny: for Aquinas, there is a twofold sense of Scripture—the literal sense of an event and its spiritual sense or *hyponoia*. In Aquinas's twofold model of reading, persons, things, and events of the Old Testament signify themselves *and*, at the same time, they signify something else: their spiritual sense. The spiritual sense, Aquinas says, "is based on and presupposes the literal sense."[36]

A "twofold spiritual sense," therefore, would be a *threefold sense* of Scripture, plotted along one continuous redemptive line. What the Old Testament had promised, Markus writes, "had come to pass—God had revealed his ways with men in Christ—and yet, it had still to come; the salvation he brought had still to be clinched and shown forth among men at his second coming in glory. Hence where the Old Testament points forward to its fulfilment, it has a double reference: it may point either to the Incarnation and its events, or the final consummation of earthly history, or to both."[37] Erich Auerbach describes the "one great drama whose beginning is God's creation of the world, whose climax is Christ's Incarnation and Passion, and whose expected conclusion will be Christ's second coming and the Last Judgment."[38] For Puritan chiliasts, that drama included a pause, a time of refreshing for all the saints who from their labors rest.

Until 1726, just two years before he died, Cotton Mather was convinced that the "progress toward the millennium could not be accomplished until Israel embraced the Messiah. In fact, with the miraculous intercession of Christ on the Jews' behalf at his return, then 'their Soul will Escape as a Bird out of the Snare of the Fowler.'"[39] Readers may recognize the "snare" Mather alludes to: "Our soul is escaped as a bird out of the snare of the fowlers: the snare is broken and we are escaped" (Psalm 124:7). In the Hebrew Bible, the word used (twice) in this verse for "snare" is *pach*; the Septuagint has *pagis*. Augustine's African psalter, we recall, had the soul caught in a mousetrap, *muscipula*; and from that mousetrap the soul is escaped. Jerome's Vulgate has: *anima nostra quasi avis erepta est de laqueo venantium; laqueus contritus est et nos liberati sumus*.

Notes

Foreword

1. Perry Miller, *The New England Mind: The Seventeenth Century* (1939; reprinted Cambridge, Mass.: Harvard University Press, 1954), 47.

2. "Self-Reliance," in Ralph Waldo Emerson, *Essays & Lectures* (New York: Library of America, 1983), 265.

3. Sacvan Bercovitch, "The Typology of America's Mission," *American Quarterly* 30 (1978): 135.

Chapter One

1. *An Exposition upon the Thirteenth Chapter of the Revelation*. By that Reverend and Eminent Servant of the Lord, Mr. John Cotton, Teacher to the Church at Boston in New England (London, 1655), 178. Compare 1 John 3:8: "He that committeth sin is of the devil; for the devil sinneth from the beginning. For this purpose the Son of God was manifested, that he may destroy [undo] the works of the devil."

2. Meyer Schapiro, "'Muscipula Diaboli,' The Symbolism of The Mérode Altarpiece," *Late Antique, Early Christian and Mediaeval Art*, Selected Papers (New York: George Braziller, 1979), 1–11; first published in *The Art Bulletin*, vol. 27, no. 3, September 1945, 182–87. Peter Lombard "in his widely read *Sentences* repeats almost word for word Augustine's fable of the mousetrap and the deceiver deceived" ("'Muscipula Diaboli,'" 2).

3. Schapiro, "'Muscipula Diaboli,'" 1; the Latin text is cited in note 3, p. 16; trusting the Latin text given by Jean Rivière, I have emended Schapiro's slightly: Sermo 263, "De ascensione Domini," Migne, PL 38, col. 1210. See also Sermo 130, col. 726, and Sermo 134, col. 745. Jean Rivière, *The Doctrine of the Atonement: A Historical Essay*, trans. Luigi Cappedelta, 2 vols. (London: Kegan Paul, Trench, Trübner, 1909), I, 166. (Translation of *Le dogme de la Rédemption*. Essai d'étude historique [Paris: Gabalda, 1905].) The most important, extended discussion of Augustine's mousetrap can be found in a monograph that is often inaccessible: Rivière's *Le Dogme de la Rédemption Chez Saint Augustine*, 3ième edition (Paris: Gabalda, 1933), 117–26 and Appendice VI, 320–38. According to Schapiro's note in an essay of 1959, "A Note on the Mérode Altarpiece," Rivière's book was "not available to me in 1945": *Late Antique*,

Early Christian and Mediaeval Art, Selected Papers (New York: George Braziller, 1979), 18n.

4. Schapiro, "'Muscipula Diaboli,'" 2. According to Rivière, the figure appears at least six times in Augustine's writings: "Tandis que la métaphore de la rançon est banale chez les Pères, celle de la souricière est propre à saint Augustin. Pour la plus grande joie des historiens satiriques du dogme, elle revient au moins six fois dans ses oeuvres oratoires, d'où il appert que la croix fut une «ratière» (*muscipula*) et le sang du Christ un «appat» (*esca*) auquel le démon se laissa prendre": *Dogme . . . Augustine,* 117.

5. Augustine, Sermon 130, cited in Schapiro, "'Muscipula Diaboli,'" 2; a complete English text of this sermon appears in Augustine, *Sermons on Selected Lessons of the New Testament,* 2 vols. (Oxford, 1845), 580–85. The excerpt cited is on 581–82. The Latin is given in Rivière, *The Doctrine of the Atonement,* 166.

6. Hastings Rashdall, *The Idea of Atonement in Christian Theology* (London: Macmillan, 1919), 323. Some exegetes find the locus classicus of the ransom theory in Irenaeus, *Against Heresies,* V.i.1 and V.xxi.3; see also III.xxxii.2. Others, however, do not trace the theory to Irenaeus; Foley, for example, thinks it was Origen who first formulated the theory and recognized the Devil's rightful claim, but in the context of the present study this does not really matter; George Cadwalader Foley, *Anselm's Theory of the Atonement,* The Bohlen Lectures, 1908 (London: Longmans, Green, 1909), 32–33. On the ransom idea and its relation to the early Church and to Luther, see Gustaf Aulén, *Christus Victor: An Historical Study of the Three Main Types of the Idea of Atonement,* trans. A. G. Hebert (London: SPCK, 1931), 162–72. Books about redemption written by Christian exegetes (each with an ax or two to grind) have been used in the present study as quarries for patristic material I could not have found without them.

7. Rashdall, *The Idea of Atonement,* 247. Anselm propounds his theory of satisfaction in the *Cur Deus Homo* ("Why the God man?"), which appeared in the year 1098.

8. David Daube, *The New Testament and Rabbinic Judaism* (London: Athlone Press, 1956), 268.

9. I paraphrase part of the extended entry s.v. *lutron* in the *Theological Dictionary of the New Testament,* ed. Gerhard Kittel and Gerhard Friedrich, 9 vols. (Grand Rapids, Mich.: Eerdmans, 1974).

10. Augustine, Sermon 130, vol. 2, *Sermons on Selected Lessons of the New Testament,* 581–82.

11. Daube, *The New Testament and Rabbinic Judaism,* 271.

12. Alexandre de Laborde, ed., *La Bible moralisée. . . .* 5 vols. Paris, 1911–1927, I pl. 48; cited in *Biblia Pauperum, A Facsimile and Edition,* ed. Avril Henry (Ithaca, N.Y.: Cornell University Press, 1987), 66, 135, n. 16.

13. One theologian, Gustaf Aulén, comments on the "very striking fact that Paul counts the Law among the powers that hold mankind in bondage. . . . In the patristic teaching, death and the devil are at once powers hostile to God and executants of God's judgment on sin. In the Pauline teaching, the Law of God is in one aspect a hostile power": *Christus Victor,* 83–84. From there it may be only a short step to or from Gnosticism, Marcion especially, although Aulén does not see it that way.

14. *Theological Dictionary of the New Testament*, s.v. *lutron*.

15. See Jon D. Levenson, *The Death and Resurrection of the Beloved Son: The Transformation of Child Sacrifice in Judaism and Christianity* (New Haven: Yale University Press, 1993): "The Johannine account of the crucifixion of Jesus with its explicit reference to Exod. 12:46 (John 19:36) provides powerful evidence that the 'Lamb of God' of John 1:29 is paschal. It might be retorted, nonetheless, that since the paschal lamb was never a sin offering, the clause 'who takes away the sin of the world' argues for a different animal, such as the sheep of Lev. 4:32–35, offered by a commoner in expiation of wrongdoing. The latter is, however, not necessarily a lamb, and we must not assume that the fine technicalities of sacrificial classification weighed heavily upon the minds of the evangelists as they drew upon biblical materials for their own purposes. Most importantly, the unclassifiable passover sacrifice of Exodus 12 does indeed have much in common with a sin offering, for it is through the blood of the lamb that lethal calamity is deflected, as the mysterious Destroyer is prevented from working his dark designs upon the Israelite first-born (vv 21–23). It is not at all hard to imagine that in the heated apocalyptic Judaism that served as the matrix of Christianity, the Destroyer would be transmuted into a personification of the Israelites' own mortal sins, and the blood of the paschal lamb would be seen as effecting not only an escape from death, but purification from moral pollution as well" (208–9).

16. J. N. D. Kelly, *Early Christian Doctrines*, 2d ed. (London: Adam and Charles Black, 1960), 398. *In Joh.* I, 29 (PG 73, 192).

17. *Midrash Rabbah*, Exodus, 3d ed., trans. S. M. Lehrman (London: Soncino Press, 1983), 213.

18. Geza Vermes, "Redemption and Genesis XXII: The Binding of Isaac and the Sacrifice of Jesus," in *Scripture and Tradition in Judaism, Haggadic Studies* (Leiden: E. J. Brill, 1961), 206.

19. Levenson, *The Death and Resurrection of the Beloved Son*, 44.

20. Gertrud Schiller, *Iconography of Christian Art*, vol. 2, *The Passion of Christ*, trans. Janet Seligman (Greenwich, Conn.: New York Graphic Society, 1972), 124–25; figs. 419, 420.

21. To anticipate chapters 2 and 4 of the present study: Jonathan Edwards's *A History of the Work of Redemption* interprets the Exodus in these terms: "He saved them, when others were destroyed, by the sprinkling of the blood of the paschal lamb, as God's church is saved from death by the sprinkling of the blood of Christ when the rest of the world is destroyed. God brought forth the people sorely against the will of the Egyptians when they could not bear to let 'em go, so Christ rescues his people out of the hands of [the] devil . . .": Jonathan Edwards, *A History of the Work of Redemption*, transcr. and ed. John F. Wilson, vol. 9 of *The Works of Jonathan Edwards* (New Haven: Yale University Press, 1989), 176.

On December 26, 1697, preaching to his congregation in the remote frontier settlement of Westfield, Masachusetts, Edward Taylor presents the incarnation in terms of God's "wonderfull befooling the Devill": just as the Devil drew our first parents into sin, so, in order to free us from bondage to sin and to death, God deceived the Devil. "God hath quite befooled the Divell in his drawing our first Parents into Sin," says

Taylor. "Doubtless the Divell did please himselfe on his Mischievous design of Stain-ing, & baining all man kinde by Sin eternally. But here you see his design is utterly broken . . .": Edward Taylor, *Upon the Types of the Old Testament*, 2 vols., ed. Charles W. Mignon (Lincoln: University of Nebraska Press, 1989), vol. 2, 538. This sermon, on the Feast of Tabernacles, is explicated in chapter 4 of the present study.

22. Augustine, *Homilies on The Gospel According to St. John*, vol. 1 (Oxford, 1848), 434.

23. Theodoret, *Qu. in Ex.* 27 (Schulze I.144). Cited in K. J. Woollcombe, "The Biblical Origins and Patristic Development of Typology," in G. W. H. Lampe and K. J. Woollcombe, *Essays on Typology* (London: SCM Press, 1957), 60.

24. To this established montage of types, the eighteenth-century poet A. M. Toplady added the "clift of the rock" where Moses hid when the glory of the Lord passed by (Exod. 33:22): "Rock of ages cleft for me, / Let me hide myself in thee; / Let the Water and the Blood, / From thy riven side which flowed, / Be of sin the dou-ble cure, / Cleanse me from its guilt and power." *English Hymnal*, Hymn 477.

25. Arthur Michael Ramsey, *The Glory of God and the Transfiguration of Christ* (Lon-don: Longmans, Green, 1949), 87.

26. Justin Martyr, *Dialogue with Trypho, a Jew*, chap. 111, *The Ante-Nicene Fathers*, vol. 1, ed. Alexander Roberts and James Donaldson (New York: Scribner's, 1913).

27. Oxford University, Bodleian Library; reproduced in Henry, ed. *Biblia Pauperum*, 14.

28. Schiller, *Iconography of Christian Art*, vol. 2, 125; figs. 420, 429, and 43.

29. I take the terms "event" and "afterlife" from a useful study of typology: A. C. Charity, *Events and their Afterlife: The Dialectics of Christian Typology in the Bible and Dante* (1966; reprint, Cambridge: Cambridge University Press, 1987).

30. Melito, *Homily on the Passion*; cited in Woollcombe, "Biblical Origins," 72.

31. Vermes, "Redemption and Genesis XXII," 206.

32. Chrystostom, *Apud Jo. Dam. parall.* (M.96.17A), cited in Woollcombe, "Bibli-cal Origins," 72.

33. Henri de Lubac, "'Typologie' et 'Allégorisme,'" *Recherches de Science Religieuse* 34 (1947), 180–226.

34. Vermes, "Redemption and Genesis XXII," passim. See also Levenson, *The Death and Resurrection of the Beloved Son*, passim.

35. Rosemary Woolf, "The Effect of Typology on the English Mediaeval Plays of Abraham and Isaac," *Speculum* 32 (1957): 807.

36. Woollcombe, "Biblical Origins," 73 (which I paraphrase here).

37. At the same time, a crucial distinction must be made between Philo and the Church Fathers: Philo was a Jew; he knew one sacred text—the Septuagint, the an-cient Jewish translation of the Hebrew Bible into Greek.

38. Augustine, *Quaest, in hept.* 2, q. 73; cited in Kelly, *Early Christian Doctrines*, 69. Cited also in Henry, ed., *Biblia Pauperum*, 40, n. 33.

39. Reproduced in Henry, ed., *Biblia Pauperum*, 13. I have also consulted *The Bible of the Poor* [*Biblia Pauperum*], *A Facsimile and Edition of the British Library Blockbook*

C.9 *d.2*, trans. and commentary by Albert C. Labriola and John W. Smelz (Pittsburgh: Duquesne University Press, 1990). See also *Biblia Pauperum: Facsimile Edition of the Forty-Leaf Blockbook in the Library of the Esztergom Cathedral*, ed. Elizabeth Soltesz (Budapest: Corvina, 1967).

40. Woolf, "The Effect of Typology on the English Mediaeval Plays of Abraham and Isaac," 807.

41. Henry, ed., *Biblia Pauperum*, 94, and 96.

42. Ibid., 98.

43. Augustine, *Homilies on the Gospel According to St. John*, vol. 1 (Oxford, 1848), 191 (on John 3:14).

44. Hastings, *Dictionary of the Bible*, s.v. "Leviathan."

45. Gregory of Nyssa, *Oratio catechetica magna*, 21–24 (PG 45, 60–66); cited in *The Later Christian Fathers*, ed. and trans. Henry Bettenson (Oxford: Oxford University Press, 1970), 142. Cited also in Schapiro, "'Muscipula Diaboli,'" 16, n. 7. See Rashdall, *The Idea of Atonement in Christian Theology*, 305, where he cites the Greek text. Following Gregory of Nyssa, Rufinus explains that "the object of the mystery of the Incarnation . . . was that the divine virtue of the Son of God—as though it were a hook concealed beneath the form and fashion of human flesh—might lure on the Prince of this world to a conflict, to whom offering His flesh as a bait, His divinity underneath might catch him and hold him fast with its hook, through the shedding of his immaculate blood." In Rufinus's somewhat overwrought prose, the blood marked on the doors in Egypt is linked to the saving blood of Christ and allegorized: "For He alone who knows no stain of sin hath destroyed the sins of all, of those at least who have marked the door posts of their faith with his blood. As, therefore, if a fish seizes a baited hook, it not only does not take the bait off the hook, but is drawn out of the water to be itself food for others, so he who had the power of death seized the body of Jesus in death, not being aware of the hook of divinity inclosed within it, but having swallowed it he was caught forthwith, and the bars of hell being burst asunder, he was drawn forth as it were from the abyss to become food for others." Cited in L. W. Grensted, *A Short History of the Doctrine of the Atonement* (London: Longmans, Green, 1920), 43.

46. Gregory of Nyssa, *Oratio catechetica magna*; cited in Rivière, *The Doctrine of the Atonement*, 125–26. (Rivière's translation is livelier than Bettenson's.)

47. Grensted, *A Short History of the Doctrine of the Atonement*, 43. See also Foley, *Anselm's Theory of the Atonement* 62–63 (PL 86, 680).

48. Athanasius, *Vita S. Antonii* 24 (PG 26, col. 880); cited in Rivière, *The Doctrine of the Atonement*, 165.

49. Augustine, Sermon 134, *Sermons on Selected Lessons of the New Testament*, Vol. 2, 608.

50. *Legenda Aurea*, in *The Golden Legend or Lives of the Saints as Englished by William Caxton* ed. F. Ellis. *The Temple Classics*, 7 vols. (London, 1900; reprint New York: AMS Press, 1973); cited by Henry, *Biblia Pauperum*, 142, n. 14.

51. Schapiro, "'Muscipula Diaboli,'" 7.

52. Cited in Aulén, *Christus Victor*, 119–20.

53. Cyril of Jerusalem. *Cath.* xii.15 (PG 33, col. 741); cited in Rivière, *The Doctrine of the Atonement*, 167–68.

54. Irenaeus, *Against Heresies*, III.xxiii; Roberts and Donaldson, eds., *The Ante-Nicene Fathers*, vol. 1.

55. Augustine, Sermon 261.1; cited in Bettenson, ed. and trans., *The Later Christian Fathers*, 222.

56. Grensted, *A Short History of the Doctrine of Atonement*, 43.

57. Foley, *Anselm's Theory of the Atonement*, 62 (PL 15, 1553, 1616).

58. Gregory of Nyssa, *Oratio catechitica magna*, 26; col. 68–69. Cited in Rivière, *The Doctrine of the Atonement*, 126.

59. H. E. W. Turner, *The Patristic Doctrine of Redemption* (London: Mowbray, 1952), 57. The pun had to be repeated.

60. Kelly, *Early Christian Doctrines*, 185.

61. Turner, *The Patristic Doctrine of Redemption*, 57, concerning the passage from Gregory of Nyssa.

62. John of Damascus, *Expositio Fidei Orthodoxae*, iii.27 (PG 94, col. 981), cited in Rivière, *The Doctrine of the Atonement*, 169; see also Rashdall, *The Idea of Atonement*, 319, and Foley, *Anselm's Theory of the Atonement*, 62.

63. *Epistle of Ignatius to the Ephesians*, chap. xix, in Roberts and Donaldson, eds., *The Ante-Nicene Fathers*, vol. 1.

64. Turner, *The Patristic Doctrine of Redemption*, 55.

65. Rashdall, *The Idea of Atonement*, 262.

66. Origen, *Com. in Math* xvi.8; cited in Rashdall, *The Idea of Atonement*, 259.

67. Gregory of Nyssa, *Oratio catechitica magna*, xxvi; in Foley, *Anselm's Theory of the Atonement*, 60–61.

68. Rashdall, *The Idea of Atonement*, 328, n. 5; citing *In Luc Exp.* ii.3 (PL 15, col. 1553). Ambrose also "states the transaction with the Devil in terms of civil rather than of criminal justice. Adam incurred a debt to the Devil which had descended like a burdened estate, with ever accumulating interest, to his posterity. Christ by His death wiped out the interest, but transferred the debt to Himself, and He is a 'bonus creditor'": Rashdall, 328, n. 5, citing *In. Ps.* xxxvi.46. See Rivière, *The Doctrine of the Atonement*, 163.

69. Schapiro, "'Muscipula Diaboli,'" 11.

70. Ibid., 7.

71. Cited in Foley, *Anselm's Theory of the Atonement*, 43–44; Foley is citing Frederic Huidekoper, *Christ's Mission to the Underworld* (Boston: Crosby, Nichols, and Company, 1854), 88.

72. Augustine, *In Ps.* CXL, PL 23, col. 1830; cited in Rivière, *Dogme . . . Augustine*, 327.

73. Rivière, *Dogme . . . Augustine*, 117.

74. Gerald Bonner, "Augustine as a Biblical Scholar," in *The Cambridge History of the Bible*, vol. 1: *From the Beginnings to Jerome*, ed. P. R. Ackroyd and C. F. Evans (Cambridge: Cambridge University Press, 1970), 550.

75. The only mousetrap that made its way into Jerome's Vulgate is part of a text he did not change—Wisdom, one of the Jewish Apocrypha. "Therefore even upon the

idols of the Gentiles shall there be a visitation: because in the creature of God they are become an abomination, and stumblingblocks [*temptationem*] to the souls of men, and a snare [*muscipulum*] to the feet of the unwise. For the devising of idols was the beginning of spiritual fornication, and the invention of them the corruption of life" (Wisdom 14:11–12, AV).

76. Rivière's Appendix 6 in "Muscipula Diaboli" is the source of my information about the nature of Augustine's African psalter; *Dogme . . . Augustine*, 320–38.

77. Rivière, *Dogme . . . Augustine*, 331.

Chapter Two

1. Exodus Rabbah ii.5; cf. Numbers Rabbah xii.4. Cited in Charles Taylor, *Sayings of the Jewish Fathers* [*Pirke Aboth*] (Cambridge: Cambridge University Press, 1897), 43.

2. Jonathan Edwards, *A History of the Work of Redemption*, transcr. and ed. John F. Wilson, vol. 9 of *The Works of Jonathan Edwards* (New Haven: Yale University Press, 1989), 175. Hereafter page numbers of the Redemption Discourse appear in the body of the text.

3. John F. Wilson's introduction to the Yale edition of *A History of the Work of Redemption* refers to Edwards's "high and conventional Christology" (54). Apart from angels themselves, there is from my point of view nothing "high" about Edwards's unsystematic christology, nor from the standpoint of Chalcedon or any other council is it "conventional." To cite Jean Daniélou on angel-christology: "One of the characteristics of theology which is genuinely archaic and Jewish Christian is the use of terms borrowed from the vocabulary of angelology to designate the Word and the Holy Spirit. 'Angel' is one of the names given to Christ up to the fourth century. After that the practice tends to disappear because of the ambiguity of the expression and the use made of it by the Arians. But in the second century the word was used in a restricted sense which constituted the ordinary form in which the Jewish Christian theology of the Trinity was cast." Jean Daniélou, *The Theology of Jewish Christianity*, trans. and ed. John A. Baker, vol. 1 of *The Development of Christian Doctrine Before the Council of Nicaea* (London: Darton, Longman & Todd, 1964), 117.

4. Jonathan Edwards, "Types of the Messiah," in *Typological Writings*, ed. Wallace E. Anderson and Mason I. Lowance, Jr., with David H. Watters, vol. 11 of *The Works of Jonathan Edwards* (New Haven: Yale University Press, 1993), 238–39.

5. Ibid., 238, n. 3.

6. Cf. Edwards, "Types of the Messiah," 244: "Joshua, in going before the children of Israel as the captain of the Lord's host and bringing them into the land of Canaan, did that which is spoken of in the books of Moses and Joshua themselves as the office of that angel of God's presence, who (as I have shown is evident by the Old Testament) was the same person with the Messiah."

7. Edwards, "Types of the Messiah," 314.

8. John F. Wilson, the editor of the Redemption Discourse, refers to Edwards's christology as a "literary strategy": "The literary strategy that completes this series ties together the whole 'history.' Edwards very occasionally declares that, beyond any outpouring of the Spirit, Christ was actually present among his people in manifestations

to Israel" (60). "Edwards' devices for inventing meanings or elaborating interconnections were relatively conventional. In effect, he availed himself of a series of literary strategies which involved claims about the revelatory power of isolated units in the narrative base. The strongest claim is the assertion that at several points Christ actually appeared to Israel before his incarnation. Slightly less strong claims concern a much broader class of materials: prophecies. A weaker level of claim, still very important, is made by typology. Here the individual or event is a figure that, while retaining its own integrity in the narrative base, yet discloses another reality. As we shall see, Edwards uses this method fully, but he feels free to apply typology less rigorously as well" (34). Wilson's phrase "isolated units in the narrative base" presumably signifies theophanies recorded in the Hebrew Bible. I cannot imagine what is achieved by his model of "strong," "less strong," and "weaker" levels of "claims." See also Wilson's "History, Redemption, and the Millennium," in *Jonathan Edwards and the American Experience*, ed. Nathan O. Hatch and Harry S. Stout (New York: Oxford University Press, 1988), 131–41.

9. Hans W. Frei, *The Eclipse of Biblical Narrative: A Study in Eighteenth and Nineteenth Century Hermeneutics* (New Haven: Yale University Press, 1974), 2.

10. Both Justin and Tertullian are cited by Edwards in Sermon 22 of the Redemption Discourse. In a footnote, the Yale editors tell us: "There were available to JE seventeenth- and eighteenth-century editions of classical and patristic authors, as well as numerous church histories in which references were made to classical authors. . . . Most likely JE culled these references, legends, and quotations from secondary works" (391, n. 7). For what reasons do the editors find it "likely" that Edwards knew the Fathers only at second hand?

11. Tertullian, *Adversus Praxean*, chap. 16; vol. 3 of *The Ante-Nicene Fathers* (New York: Scribner's, 1908).

12. To cite Heiko Oberman: "In a concise survey of the state of scholarship, Karl Barth shows, with quotations from Athanasius, Gregory of Nyssa, John of Damascus, Augustine and Thomas, 'das die Reformierten dies nicht etwa also eine theologische Neuerung, sondern in Fortsetzung der Tradition der ganzen älteren Christologie (mit Einschluss der griechischen) gesagt haben.'" Heiko A. Oberman, "The Theology of Calvin," *The Dawn of the Reformation: Essays in Late Medieval and Early Reformation Thought* (Edinburgh: T & T Clark, 1986), 247.

13. J. N. D. Kelly, *Early Christian Doctrines*, 2d ed. (London: Adam and Charles Black, 1960), 273.

14. Ibid., 272.

15. *The Trinity*, trans. and annotated by Edmund Hill, O.P. (Brooklyn, N.Y.: New City Press, 1991), 141–42. *The Works of Saint Augustine: A Translation for the 21st Century*, ed. John E. Rotelle, O.S.A. (Brooklyn, N.Y.: New City Press).

16. Ibid., 176.

17. Ibid., 144.

18. Augustine, *Homilies on The Gospel According to St. John*, vol. 1 (Oxford, 1848), 43.

19. Justin Martyr, *Dialogue with Trypho, a Jew*, chap. 61, in *The Ante-Nicene*

Fathers, vol. 1, ed. Alexander Roberts and James Donaldson (New York: Scribner's, 1913).

20. Jean Daniélou, *From Shadows to Reality: Studies in Biblical Typology of the Fathers*, trans. Dom Wolstan Hibberd (London: Burns & Oates, 1960), 24–25.

21. *Biblia Pauperum, A Facsimile and Edition*, ed. Avril Henry (Ithaca, N.Y.: Cornell University Press, 1987), 51.

22. Loren T. Stuckenbruck avoids the term "angel christology," using instead "angelomorphic" or "angelophanic Christology." See his learned, approachable *Angel Veneration and Christology: A Study in Early Judaism and in the Christianity of the Apocalypse of John* (Tübingen: J. C. B. Mohr [Paul Siebeck], 1995), 209n. Anyone concerned with late-Jewish angelology (including material from the Dead Sea Scrolls) will find Stuckenbruck's bibliography a crucial starting point for research.

23. Martin Werner, *The Formation of Christian Dogma: A Historical Study of Its Problem*, trans. S. G. F. Brandon (London: Adam & Charles Black, 1957), 128; the allusion is to 1 Cor. 10:4, wherein Paul may be revising an ancient Jewish legend, according to the distinguished scholars W. O. E. Oesterley and G. H. Box. The legend says "that for Miriam's sake (the sister of Moses) a marvellous well accompanied the Israelites; it was a rock that contained this well, and which followed the Israelites wherever they went": *The Sayings of the Jewish Fathers*, trans. W. O. E. Oesterley (London: SPCK, 1919), 64n.

Werner's controversial *Die Entstehung des christlichen Dogmas*, a work of more than seven hundred pages, first appeared in 1941. The English version is translated from a shortened form of the original, rewritten by the author, who argues that early Jewish Christians regarded Christ as an angel. Background to the angel-christology debate among contemporary theologians (up to the late 1950s) can be found in Werner's long footnote on page 130 of the English version of his text. See Daniélou, *The Theology of Jewish Christianity*, 117–46. See also Stuckenbruck, who in *Angel Veneration and Christology* alludes to "the sharp reaction among scholars during and after World War Two against Werner's one-sided thesis that as long as early Christian communities held the *parousia* to be imminent, Christ was primarily regarded as an angel," 208n. See the bibliography in John Reumann, "Martin Werner and 'Angel Christology,'" *The Lutheran Quarterly* 8 (1956), 357 (cited in Stuckenbruck, 124n, whose *Angel Veneration and Christology* brings the bibliography up to date).

24. Jaroslav Pelikan, *The Christian Tradition: A History of the Development of Doctrine*, vol. 1, *The Emergence of the Catholic Tradition* (100–600) (Chicago: University of Chicago Press, 1971), 188.

25. Edwards, "Types of the Messiah," 204.

26. Origen, *Contra Celsum* v. 37; cited in *The Early Christian Fathers*, ed. and trans. Henry Bettenson (Oxford: Oxford University Press, 1956), 241.

27. Jonathan Edwards, *Miscellaneous Observations*, vol. 2 of *The Works of Jonathan Edwards*, ed. Edward Hickman (London: William Ball, 1837), 500. On the Wisdom-Logos connection, see John Ashton, "The Transformation of Wisdom," in *Studying John: Approaches to the Fourth Gospel* (Oxford: Clarendon Press, 1994), 5–35.

28. Oberman, "The Theology of Calvin," 247.

29. François Wendel, *Calvin: Origins and Development of His Religious Thought*, trans. Philip Mairet (Durham, N.C.: Labyrinth, 1987), 230–31.

30. John Calvin, *Institutes of the Christian Religion*, vols. 20, 21 of the Library of Christian Classics, ed. John T. McNeill, trans. Ford Lewis Battles (London: SCM Press, 1961), I, xiii, 10.

31. E. David Willis, *Calvin's Catholic Christology: The Function of the So-Called Extra Calvinisticum in Calvin's Theology* (Leiden: E. J. Brill, 1966), 77n.

32. Calvin, *Institutes* I, xiii, 10.

33. John Calvin, *Commentaries*, trans. and ed. Joseph Haroutunian and Louise Pettibone Smith (Philadelphia: Westminster Press, 1958), 148.

34. Frei, *The Eclipse of Biblical Narrative*, 47.

35. "JE indicates intent to complete phrase": the reading in square brackets is conjectural. See the editors' note to the Yale edition of the Redemption Discourse, 170.

36. Edward Taylor, *Christographia*, ed. Norman S. Grabo (New Haven: Yale University Press, 1962), 404–5.

37. Edward Taylor, *Upon the Types of the Old Testament*, 2 vols., ed. Charles W. Mignon (Lincoln: University of Nebraska Press, 1989), vol. 2, 707.

38. Like the rod of Aaron that overnight "was budded, and brought forth buds, and bloomed blossoms, and yielded almonds" (Num. 18:8), the burning bush is a type of the incarnation: to follow Avril Henry, the "flame was the Spirit by whose divine power Mary remained unhurt at the conception of Jesus." On the relevant plate in the *Biblia Pauperum*, beneath the burning bush and the rod of Aaron, the texts read: "It glows and kindles but the bush is not consumed by fire"; "This is against nature: a rod bears a blossom." As Henry confirms in her commentary, "the God speaking from the bush is . . . the cross-nimbed second person of the Trinity." Henry, ed., *Biblia Pauperum*, 51.

39. Calvin, *Commentaries on the Four Last Books of Moses*, 61–62.

40. Calvin, *Institutes* II, ix, 1; cf. *Institutes* I, xiii, 10.

41. Cited in Daniélou, *From Shadows to Reality*, 224.

42. Cited in Wendel, *Calvin: Origins and Development of His Religious Thought*, 212–13.

43. Other passages cited in the *Theological Dictionary of the New Testament* (*aggelos*) are Gen. 16:7–13; 21:17–19; 31:11–13; Judg. 2:1–4. The subordinationism implicit in the Christian use of "Yahweh" terminology to speak about the God of Israel must have been discussed by someone.

44. Christopher Rowland, *The Open Heaven: A Study of Apocalyptic in Judaism and Early Christianity* (London: SPCK, 1982), 94–95. See also Rowland's "The Vision of the Risen Christ in Rev. i. 13ff.: The Debt of an Early Christology to an Aspect of Jewish Angelology," *Journal of Theological Studies*, n.s., vol. 31, pt. 1 (April 1980), 1–11.

45. Jon D. Levenson, *The Death and Resurrection of the Beloved Son: The Transformation of Child Sacrifice in Judaism and Christianity* (New Haven: Yale University Press, 1993), 45–46.

46. See the influential early essay by Adolphine Bakker, "Christ an Angel?: A Study of Early Christian Docetism," *Zeitschrift für die Neutestamentliche Wissenschaft*,

vol. 32, nos. 2/3 (1933): 257, passim. On Justin's ignorance of Hebrew, see the very useful entry "Hebrew Learning Among the Fathers" in the *Dictionary of Christian Biography*, ed. William Smith and Henry Wace (Boston: Little, Brown, 1880), vol. 2 of 4 vols., 851–72.

47. Werner, *The Formation of Christian Dogma*, 133.

48. Ambrose, *De Sacr.* II, 4; cited by Jean Daniélou, *The Bible and the Liturgy* (Notre Dame, Ind.: University of Notre Dame Press, 1956), 214.

49. Justin Martyr, *Dialogue with Trypho*, chaps. 76, 126.

50. Origen, *Comm. in Ioannen*, i. 37–38 (42); cited in Bettenson, *The Early Christian Fathers*, 212.

51. Calvin, *Institutes* II. xv. 1; the editors of the English version of the *Institutes* cite this in a note.

52. Kelly, *Early Christian Doctrines*, 22.

53. Daniélou, *The Theology of Jewish Christianity*, 118.

54. James D. G. Dunn, *Christology in the Making: An Inquiry into the Origins of the Doctrine of the Incarnation*, 2d ed. (London: SCM Press, 1989), 228, 220–21.

55. Dunn, *Christology*, 230. As Dunn explains, "Jewish Christians of the second and third centuries specifically affirmed that Christ was an angel or arch-angel" (132). Sometimes, according to Pelikan, Christ was identified with the archangel Michael, and as late as the fourth century was still called "prince of angels" by orthodox theologians—Greek, Latin, and Syriac (*The Christian Tradition*, vol. 2, 183).

56. Dunn, *Christology*, 129.

57. Dunn, *Christology*, 131.

58. Bakker, "Christ an Angel?," 261.

59. Pelikan, *The Christian Tradition*, vol. 1, 34.

60. In Dunn's informed and sober view, *"There is no evidence that any NT writer thought of Jesus as actually present in Israel's past,* either as the angel of the Lord, or as 'the Lord' himself": *Christology*, 158; emphasis in original.

61. Dunn, *Christology*, 132.

62. Justin Martyr, *The First Apology*, chap. 62, in Roberts and Donaldson, eds., *The Ante-Nicene Fathers*, vol. 1.

63. Justin Martyr, *The First Apology*, chap. 63.

64. Justin Martyr, *Dialogue with Trypho*, chap. 58.

65. Ibid., chap. 59.

66. Ibid., chap. 38.

67. Daniélou, *The Theology of Jewish Christianity*, 159.

68. Irenaeus, *Against Heresies*, III.xviii.1, in Roberts and Donaldson, eds., *The Ante-Nicene Fathers*, vol. 1.

69. Ibid., IV.xii.4.

70. Samuel Mather, *The Figures or Types of the Old Testament* (1705; reprint, New York: Johnson Reprint Corporation, 1969), 15.

71. Henry Ainsworth, *Annotations upon the Five Bookes of Moses, the Booke of the Psalmes, and the Song of Songs, or, Canticles* (London, 1627). This was the first edition with all parts in one binding. As I explain once more in a note to chapter 4 of the

present study, when citing Ainsworth I refer to the biblical text he is annotating; there is no point in referring the reader to page numbers. Copies of the *Annotations*, either singly or in various combinations, with or without his annotations on the Psalms, are available in libraries with extensive seventeenth-century holdings.

On Ainsworth, see Richard Reinitz, "The Separatist Background of Roger Williams' Argument for Religious Toleration," in *Typology and Early American Literature*, ed. Sacvan Bercovitch ([Amherst]: University of Massachusetts Press, 1972), 107–37, 121–27.

72. Sigmund Mowinckel, *He That Cometh*, trans. G. W. Anderson (Oxford: Basil Blackwell, 1959), 278.

73. Ibid., 283.

74. Ibid., 3.

75. John Ashton, *Understanding the Fourth Gospel* (Oxford: Clarendon Press, 1991), 235.

76. Sacvan Bercovitch, *The American Jeremiad* (Madison: University of Wisconsin Press, 1978), 73.

77. One may be accustomed to figural or typological readings of the two-part Bible, however far-fetched; thus "similar situation" parallels drawn by Christian exegetes and depicted in illustrated psalters, altarpieces, stained-glass windows, church ornaments, and paintings may be taken for granted: the burning bush and the virgin birth; the Red Sea and baptism; Noah's ark and the Church; the sacrifice of Isaac and the crucifixion; Aaron's budding rod and the incarnation; the manna and the eucharistic food; the rock that gave forth water and the crucifixion; the bunch of grapes carried by the spies and Christ; the serpent held up in the wilderness and the cross; and so on, from the early Fathers through the *Biblia Pauperum* and on to Edwards. But to discover (in Ainsworth) the Rabbis and rabbinic exegesis turned into corroborating witnesses for Christianity had for me the sudden effect of defamiliarizing typology, which revealed itself, not as the overarching trope of sacred history seen through the eye of God (as it is idealized by Erich Auerbach and others), but as *the* crucial two-part trope of Christian apologists, including Paul.

Of course, Marcel Simon has said this already: in order to show that "Christ and Christianity are manifest in every line of the sacred text," he writes, "the apologists had two methods open to them: the argument from prophecy, and the method of typological or allegorical exegesis. . . . The error of the Jews consists in the first instance in not realizing that the Messianic prophecies apply to the Messiah Jesus and can apply only to him. In the second instance, they have failed to perceive beneath the narrative sense of the narrative, legislative, or prophetic text the Christian revelation." *Versus Israel: A Study of the Relations between Christians and Jews in the Roman Empire*, trans. H. McKeating, The Littman Library of Jewish Civilization (Oxford: Oxford University Press, 1986), 147. What Ainsworth has done is to broaden the range of apologists' proof-texts; instead of limiting his activities to Scripture, he appropriates for Christianity the Talmud, Targum, and medieval Jewish writings.

78. For translations from the Aramaic Targums, I am entirely indebted to the generosity and patience of Robert Hayward (C. T. R. Hayward), an angel of very great counsel, who continues to guide me through the intricacies of postbiblical Jewish texts and their relation to Christian doctrine and liturgy.

79. Edwards, "Types of the Messiah," 238–39.

80. Calvin too, we recall, takes the angel of Genesis 48 to be Christ: "If you take this verse as a reference to an ordinary angel, the words are absurd."

81. Ainsworth, *Annotations*, on Exod. 33:14.

82. Edwards's identification of Christ with the *Shekinah* is a subject I have explored elsewhere; see Linda Munk, "His Dazzling Absence: The Shekinah in Jonathan Edwards," *Early American Literature*, vol. 27, no. 1 (1992): 1–30. Modified slightly, the essay appears as chapter 7 in *The Trivial Sublime: Theology and American Poetics* (London: Macmillan; New York: St. Martin's, 1992).

83. On Edwards's sources, see Stephen J. Stein's introduction in Jonathan Edwards, *Apocalpytic Writings*, ed. Stephen J. Stein, vol. 5 of *The Works of Jonathan Edwards* (New Haven: Yale University Press, 1977), 59. See also an important essay that is not always easily accessible: Thomas H. Johnson, "Jonathan Edwards' Background of Reading," *Publications of The Colonial Society of Massachusetts*, vol. 28 (December 1931) ("*Transactions*" 1930–1933), 193–222.

84. Marc Saperstein, *Jewish Preaching 1200–1800: An Anthology* (New Haven: Yale University Press, 1989), 289n.

85. Abba Hillel Silver, *A History of Messianic Speculation in Israel from the First through the Seventeenth Centuries* (New York: Macmillan, 1927), 252, 139. "When this year did not bring about the promised Redemption, the disciples [of Nathan of Gaza] found Gamatria for other years: 1675, 1680, 1686, 1692, 1706, 1710" (252).

86. Silver, *A History of Messianic Speculation*, 151.

87. Bercovitch, *The American Jeremiad*, 75; I presume Bercovitch is referring to Increase Mather's *A Dissertation Concerning the Future Conversion of the Jewish Nation, Answering the Objections of the Reverend and Learned Mr. Baxter, Dr. Lightfoot, and others. With an Enquiry into the first Resurrection* (London, 1709).

88. Romans 11:26 conflates two Old Testament prophecies: Psalm 14:9 ("Oh, that the salvation of Israel were come out of Zion! when the Lord bringeth back the captivity of his people, Jacob shall rejoice, and Israel shall be glad"); and Isaiah 59:20 ("And the Redeemer shall come to Zion, and them that turn from transgression in Jacob, saith the Lord").

89. Matthew Poole's commentary on Romans 11:25–26. Copies of Poole's *Synopsis Criticorum* (in Latin; I have not come across an English translation) are not hard to find in well-stocked rare book libraries. I have consulted a handsome edition held at Trinity College Library, University of Toronto.

90. Increase Mather, *The Mystery of Israel's Salvation, Explained and Applyed: or, A Discourse Concerning the General Conversion of the Israelitish Nation* (London, 1669), 141, 76.

91. Edwards, "Notes on the Apocalypse, in Stein, ed., *Apocalyptic Writings*, 135.

92. Mather, *The Mystery of Israel's Salvation*, 99.

Chapter Three

1. Maimonides, Mishneh-Torah (Ha-Yad ba-Hazaqah), Sepher ha-Madda, Hilkot-Teshuvah 9:2, cited in Joseph Klausner, *The Messianic Idea in Israel: From Its Beginning*

to the Completion of the Mishnah, trans. from the third Hebrew edition by W. F. Stinespring (London: Allen and Unwin, 1956), 415.

2. Increase Mather, *A Dissertation Concerning the Future Conversion of the Jewish Nation, Answering the Objections of the Reverend and Learned Mr. Baxter, Dr. Lightfoot, and others. With an Enquiry into the first Resurrection* (London, 1709), 29.

3. Cotton Mather, *Wonders of the Invisible World* (Boston, 1693); cited by Sacvan Bercovitch, "Images of Myself: Cotton Mather in His Writings (1683–1700)," in *Major Writers of Early American Literature*, ed. Everett Emerson (Madison: University of Wisconsin Press, 1972), 109.

4. Henry Méchoulan, introduction to Menasseh ben Israel, *The Hope of Israel*, English trans. Moses Wall, 1652, ed. Henry Méchoulan and Gérard Nahon, Littman Library of Jewish Civilization (Oxford: Oxford University Press, 1987), 47. To follow Marc Saperstein: "The Hebrew words *heble mashiah*, 'birthpangs of the Messiah,' have the numerical equivalent of 408, which correspond in the Hebrew calendar to the year 1648"; *Jewish Preaching, 1200–1800: An Anthology* (New Haven: Yale University Press, 1989), 289n.

5. Christopher Hill, *Antichrist in Seventeenth-Century England*, rev. ed. (London: Verso, 1990), 108n, 115.

6. Hill, *Antichrist*, 180. See also Peter Toon, ed., *Puritans, the Millennium and the Future of Israel: Puritan Eschatology 1600 to 1660* (Cambridge: James Clarke, 1970), 72.

7. Paul Christianson, *Reformers and Babylon: English Apocalyptic Visions from the Reformation to the Eve of the Civil War* (Toronto: University of Toronto Press, 1978), 211. In the years 1641 and 1642, Archer's pamphlet *The personall raigne of Christ upon earth* went through five printings, according to Christianson.

8. Katharine R. Firth, *The Apocalyptic Tradition in Reformation Britain 1530–1645* (Oxford: Oxford University Press, 1979), 174.

9. Christianson, *Reformers and Babylon*, 98.

10. Abba Hillel Silver, *A History of Messianic Speculation in Israel, from the First through the Seventeenth Centuries* (New York: Macmillan, 1927), 177. Jessey (Jesse) is mentioned in a letter of February 1655 written by Menasseh ben Israel to Paul Felgenhauer; cited in Silver, 168.

11. Silver, *A History of Messianic Speculation*, 164. Dedicated to Menasseh ben Israel, Felgenhauer's *Bonum Nuncium Israeli* appeared in 1655; he claimed to be Elijah the prophet.

12. In 1655, according to Cotton, the power of the Catholic Church would expire: Peter Toon, "The Latter-Day Glory," in Toon, ed., *Puritans, the Millennium and the Future of Israel*, 34. See also Mason I. Lowance, Jr., *The Language of Canaan: Metaphor and Symbol in New England from the Puritans to the Transcendentalists* (Cambridge, Mass.: Harvard University Press, 1980), 130. On Congregationalism, primarily in England, see Geoffrey F. Nuttall, *Visible Saints: The Congregational Way, 1640–1660* (Oxford: Basil Blackwell, 1957).

13. To cite Keith Thomas: "According to most commentators, this millennium had already begun. But in the seventeenth century various authors began to suggest that it was still to come. Of the many dates canvassed, 1666 was particularly popular, since

the number of the Beast who had first to be overthrown was 666 (Revelation, xiii, 18). An alternative date was 1656, since this was the number of years which were supposed to have elapsed between the Creation and the Flood." *Religion and the Decline of Magic: Studies in Popular Beliefs in Sixteenth- and Seventeenth-Century England* (1971; reprint, Harmondsworth: Penguin, 1991), 167–68.

14. Hill, *Antichrist*, 115.

15. R. A. Knox, *Enthusiasm: A Chapter in the History of Religion* (Oxford: Clarendon Press, 1950), 163. See also Ronald Matthews, *English Messiahs: Studies of Six English Religious Pretenders, 1656–1927* (London: Methuen, 1936). See also Richard H. Popkin, "Seventeenth-Century Millenarianism," in *Apocalypse Theory and the Ends of the World*, ed. Malcolm Bull, Wolfson College Lectures (Oxford: Basil Blackwell, 1995), 120.

16. Christopher Hill, "'Till the Conversion of the Jews,'" in *Millenarianism and Messianism in English Literature and Thought, 1650–1800*, ed. Richard H. Popkin, Clark Library Lectures, 1981–1982 (Leiden: E. J. Brill, 1988), 27.

17. Arise Evans, *Light For the Iews: or, the Means to convert them, in Answer to a Book of theirs, called The Hope of Israel, Written and Printed by Manasseth Ben-Israel, Chief Agent for the Jews here. 1650* (London, 1656), 16, 27. "I say, King *Charles Steeward*, Son of the late King *Charles* of *England*, is he whom you call your Messiah Captain and Deliverer, who will bring you to present happiness if you follow him" (20).

18. Firth, *The Apocalyptic Tradition*, 211. See also Toon, ed., *Puritans, the Millennium and the Future of Israel*, 53, and Silver, *A History of Messianic Speculation*, 169. Alsted's *De Mille Annis*, dedicated to Messianic calculations, was published in 1627.

19. Boehme, *Mysterium Magnum* (1623); cited in Silver, *A History of Messianic Speculation*, 163.

20. Hill, *Antichrist*, 115. On Thomas Tany, see also David S. Katz, *Philo-Semitism and the Readmission of the Jews to England, 1603–1655* (Oxford: Clarendon Press, 1982), 107. Ronald Matthews writes: "Thomas Tany, a London goldsmith, seems to have been on the verge of complete dementia. He has a fondness for high-sounding, meaningless, pseudo-Greek, Latin or Hebrew words, which intrude even into the titles of his books, as, for example, his *Aurora in Translagarum*. Tany had it revealed to him in 1649 that, though he had not suspected his descent before, he was a Jew of the tribe of Reuben. By divine command he assumed the name of Theaurau John, High Priest of the Jews, and Theau Ram Taniah, Leader of the People, claimed the thrones of England and France, and pitched a tent on Eltham Common, where the delivered Israelites were to gather before their departure for Palestine" (*English Messiahs*, xvi).

21. Increase Mather, *The Mystery of Israel's Salvation, Explained and Applyed: or, A Discourse Concerning the General Conversion of the Israelitish Nation* (London, 1669). All page numbers appearing in parentheses in the body of the present chapter refer to this text in this edition. Mather is cited frequently and directly; the text is hard to come by, and Mather's argument is not easy to follow. The problem with paraphrasing Mather's *Mystery* in shorthand is that scholars tend to recite their own or someone else's presuppositions.

22. Menasseh ben Israel, *The Hope of Israel*, 148; according to Henry Méchoulan,

Menasseh "very probably taught the young Baruch [Spinoza]," *The Hope of Israel*, 22. See also Silver, *A History of Messianic Speculation*, 187–92.

23. Méchoulan, in Menasseh ben Israel, *The Hope of Israel*, x. Wall was a friend of John Milton; see Richard H. Popkin, "A Note on Moses Wall," in *Hope of Israel*, 165–70.

24. *The Hope of Israel*, 47–48.

25. Ibid., 46; "But on a practical level, how could a restoration of the Jews of Palestine be envisaged, a restoration seen as a prerequisite for the second coming of Christ on earth?" (48). See Menasseh's cautious letter to the Bohemian chiliast Paul Felgenhauer; cited in Silver, *A History of Messianic Speculation*, 166–69.

26. Mason I. Lowance, Jr., "Typology and Millennial Eschatology in Early New England," in Earl Miner, ed., *Literary Uses of Typology from the Late Middle Ages to the Present* (Princeton: Princeton University Press, 1977), 247. A distinction should be made between "last things," an eschatological term, and the future hopes of New Englanders, who were not waiting for the end of the world.

27. Mason I. Lowance, Jr., *The Language of Canaan: Metaphor and Symbol in New England from the Puritans to the Transcendentalists* (Cambridge, Mass.: Harvard University Press, 1980), 135.

28. Reiner Smolinski, "*Israel Redivivus:* The Eschatological Limits of Puritan Typology in New England," *New England Quarterly*, vol. 63 (1990): 363; cf. 385. But again, for John Cotton and Thomas Brightman, the Second Coming (as the term is generally understood) was not really the issue. They were pressing for the millennium, which would be opened by Christ's penultimate advent.

29. Klausner, *The Messianic Idea in Israel*, 427. See also Silver, *A History of Messianic Speculation*.

30. Grant Underwood, "The *Hope of Israel* in Early Modern Ethnography and Eschatology," in *Hebrew and the Bible in America: The First Two Centuries*, ed. Shalom Goldman (Hanover: University Press of New England, 1993), 100.

31. Andrew Delbanco, *The Puritan Ordeal* (Cambridge, Mass.: Harvard University Press, 1989), 109. According to Luther, the future conversion of the Jews was *not* promised in scripture. Had he believed otherwise, history might have taken a different turn. Belief in a future conversion of the Jews was commonplace among English Puritans from about the first quarter of the seventeenth century.

32. Méchoulan, introduction, *The Hope of Israel*, 51.

33. Increase Mather, *A Dissertation Concerning the Future Conversion of the Jewish Nation*, 12.

34. Frank E. Manuel, *The Broken Staff: Judaism through Christian Eyes* (Cambridge, Mass.: Harvard University Press, 1992), 110.

35. Firth, *The Apocalyptic Tradition*, 152.

36. Heiko A. Oberman, "The Stubborn Jews: Timing the Escalation of Antisemitism in Late Medieval Europe," in *The Impact of the Reformation* (Grand Rapids: Eerdmans, 1994), 122–40, the quote is on page 132.

37. See Nicholas W. S. Cranfield, "From England to New England: The Protestant and Puritan Movement, 1600–1645," in Gerald T. Sheppard, ed., *The Geneva Bible*

(*The Annotated New Testament, 1602 Edition*) (New York: Pilgrim Press, 1989), 35. On the nature of the Messianic calculations of most rabbis cited by Mather, see Silver, *The Messianic Speculation in Israel*, passim.

38. Underwood, "The *Hope of Israel*," 97.

39. The Messiah, it is believed, will come "suddenly, unannounced, and precisely when he is least expected or when hope has been long abandoned": Gershom Scholem, "Toward an Understanding of the Messianic Idea," in *The Messianic Idea in Judaism* (New York: Schocken, 1971), 11. Even though it is dated, nontheologians might want to consult R. H. Charles's article "Eschatology of the Apocryphal and Apocalyptic Literature" in James Hastings's *Dictionary of the Bible* (Edinburgh, 1898), vol. 1, 741–49.

40. Among the authors of the secondary works I have read thus far, the only scholar who focuses on the crucial distinction between the middle advent and the final advent of Christ is Theodore Dwight Bozeman in his exemplary study *To Live Ancient Lives: The Primitivist Dimension in Puritanism* (Chapel Hill: University of North Carolina Press, 1988). Even the best-known historians tend to smooth away this radical strain in Puritan millennialism, perhaps because they have not consulted primary sources (Brightman and Cotton, for example), or because the model of a middle advent is unfamiliar, or because they have not bothered with Jewish apocalyptic texts, even though Mather depends on and cites them. Scholars interesting in exploring further the links between messianic ideas in Judaism and Puritanism might start with Peter Toon's chapter "The Latter-Day Glory" in Toon, ed., *Puritans, the Millennium and the Future of Israel*, 23–41. In 1978 Sacvan Bercovitch threw out a broad hint: describing the "apocalyptic fervour" of Rabbis in the seventeenth century, he mentioned the "excited exchange of millennial speculations among Jewish and Christian scholars. It issued in the expectation of a mass conversion of Jewry, in the Protestants' adoption of various tenets of Hebrew apocalypticism, and above all, in the belief that a momentous change was at hand, for the Jews first, and then mankind at large"; *The American Jeremiad* (Madison: University of Wisconsin Press, 1978), 74. What *were* the "tenets of Hebrew apocalypticism" adopted by Protestants, one wants to know? Which Jewish apocalypses were widely circulated?

Furthermore, it is not enough to talk about pre- and postmillennialism, as, say, Mason Lowance does in *The Language of Canaan*. The matter is not clear-cut: as Bercovitch notes, "pre- and postmillennialism are often present on the same movement, sometimes in the same thinker" (*The American Jeremiad*, 95). Nor, as Bozeman warns, should one confound expectations of the Second Coming (as the term is generally understood) and of the four last things with the Puritans' millennial fervor. There is a general confusion of terms in discussions of Puritan millennialism. Even Philip Gura does not work through the paradigm of the so-called middle advent, noting that the conversion "of the Ten Lost Tribes of Israel . . . would immediately precede Christ's second coming": *A Glimpse of Sion's Glory: Puritan Radicalism in New England, 1620–1660* (Middletown, Conn.: Wesleyan University Press, 1984), 133. In one sense Gura is right, but only if he makes clear that Christ's second coming is the penultimate one.

In the (unpaginated) "Author's Preface" to *The Mystery of Israel's Salvation*, Increase Mather insists that he does "not think that there are any more than two personal comings or Residencies of Christ upon the earth, spoken of in the Scripture. Nor do I believe that Christ will reign personally upon the earth a thousand years before the day of judgment. Only I conceive that *the great and last day* so much celebrated by the Prophets and Apostles, will begin at the final destruction of Antichrist, even then when *the thousand Apocalyptical years* shall begin." In other words, the "last day," inaugurated by Christ, begins a thousand years, more or less, before it ends. In the treatise itself, we read about a "personal appearance" of Christ to destroy Antichrist *and* about Christ's "personal residence upon earth" at the last judgment (105). Mather makes a guarded distinction between Christ's brief "appearance" and his "residency." He also talks about "a first and an ultimate judgment. For as in a day there is an evening and a morning, so in this great day, even the day of judgment, there is an evening and a morning: The one containeth that blessed thousand years *John* speaketh of, the other containeth that space which shall be between the resurrection of the unjust, and the time when Christ shall give up his Mediatory kingdom, when God shall be all in all" (139; cf. 105). Mather was influenced by the millennialism of his father-in-law, John Cotton, as well as by Mede, Alsted, and Brightman; ultimately their models stem from Jewish apocalyptic, often by way of Revelation, whose eschatology is continuous with intertestamental apocalypses. Bozeman's chapter "Puritan Millennialism," with its meticulous documentation, is a key resource for scholars interested in apocalyptic models in American literature. I'd start with Toon's *Puritans, the Millennium and the Future of Israel*, though.

41. Increase Mather, *A Dissertation Concerning the Future Conversion of the Jewish Nation*, 11.

42. See Scholem's discussion of "restorative" and "utopian" messianism, "Toward an Understanding of the Messianic Idea," 21–24 and passim. The same terms are used by Lawrence H. Schiffman in *Reclaiming the Dead Sea Scrolls: Their True Meaning for Judaism and Christianity* (New York: Doubleday, 1995), 315.

43. Scholem, "Toward an Understanding of the Messianic Idea," 10.

44. Christopher Hill, *The World Turned Upside Down: Radical Ideas During the English Revolution* (Harmondsworth: Penguin, 1991), 93. I'm not sure those "pocketable" editions included notes; the few I examined in the Bodleian Library did not.

45. Mather makes direct reference to Beza's annotation: "*Beza* in Rom. 11.26" (*The Mystery of Israel's Salvation*, 17; cf. 9, 57). To follow Iain H. Murray: "Neither Luther nor Calvin saw a future general conversion of the Jews promised in Scripture; some of their contemporaries, however, notably Martin Bucer and Peter Martyr, who taught at Cambridge and Oxford respectively in the reign of Edward VI, did understand the Bible to teach a future calling of the Jews. In this view they were followed by Theodore Beza, Calvin's successor at Geneva." *The Puritan Hope: A Study in Revival and the Interpretation of Prophecy* (1971; reprint, Edinburgh: Banner of Truth Trust, 1975), 41. I am grateful to Sheridan Gilley, who directed me to Murray's provocative study.

46. Geneva Bible (London: Christopher Barker, 1610). The same commentary ap-

pears in annotated editions of 1599 and 1602 that I have seen. The 1560 edition simply reads: "He sheweth that the time shal come that the whole nation of ye Iewes thogh not every one particularly shalbe joyned to the Church of Christ." Scholars sometimes forget that in the mid-seventeenth century, eight editions or more of the King James Bible were published with the Genevan notes; see Christopher Hill, *The English Bible and the Seventeenth-Century Revolution* (Harmondsworth: Penguin, 1994), 66.

47. Gerald Bray, ed., *Documents of the English Reformation* (Cambridge: James Clarke, 1994), 538–39. Peter Toon suggests that "the chief architect of this paragraph" in the Savoy Declaration was John Owen, the leading theologian of the Congregationalists: *Puritans, the Millennium and the Future of Israel*, 37.

48. Bray, ed., *Documents of the English Reformation*, 538. In *Table Talk*, Luther writes: "Anti-Christ is the pope and the Turk together . . . the spirit or soul of Anti-Christ is the pope, his flesh or body the Turk"; cited in Silver, *A History of Messianic Speculation*, 122n. Compare a pronouncement made in 1588 by James VI of Scotland, later King James I of England: "The pope is antichrist, and popery is the loosing of Satan, from whom proceedeth the false doctrine and the cruelty to subvert the kingdom of Christ"; cited in Christianson, *Reformers and Babylon*, 95.

49. Murray, *The Puritan Hope*, 45, 46. On Brightman, see Katharine R. Firth, *The Apocalyptic Tradition*; William Lamont, *Godly Rule: Politics and Religion, 1603–60* (London: Macmillan, 1969); Richard Bauckham, *Tudor Apocalypse: Sixteenth Century Apocalypticism, Millenarianism, and the English Reformation, from John Bale to John Foxe and Thomas Brightman* (Oxford: Oxford University Press, 1987); and Peter Toon, ed., *Puritans, the Millennium and the Future of Israel*. A useful if exaggerated appraisal of Brightman's influence is made by Avihu Zakai, "Exile and Kingdom: Reformation, Separation, and the Millennial Quest in the Formation of Massachusetts and Its Relationship with England, 1628–1660," Ph.D. diss., Johns Hopkins University, 1983. This dissertation with an updated bibliography was published in 1994 under the title *Theocracy in Massachusetts: Reformation and Separation in Early Puritan New England* (Lewiston, N.Y.: Edwin Mellen Press, 1994). In 1992, a misleadingly titled book by Zakai appeared, *Exile and Kingdom: History and Apocalypse in the Puritan Migration to America* (Cambridge: Cambridge University Press, 1992); despite its title, however, this is *not* the dissertation of 1983, although there is a good deal of overlapping. As published (or rather printed) by the Mellen Press in 1994, the original dissertation has not been edited or proofread, and only the most generous reader will not lose patience with inconsistencies, repeated mistakes, and the overall slipshod production.

50. The term "apocalyptic paraphernalia" is used by Silver, *A History of Messianic Speculation*, 32; he is speaking about millennial ideas in the early Christian Church.

51. The phrasing is Theodore Bozeman's by way of Norman Cohn (Bozeman, *To Live Ancient Lives*, 199). On the millennium and America, see (among many other books and articles) J. F. Maclear, "New England and the Fifth Monarchy: The Quest for the Millennium in Early American Puritanism," *William and Mary Quarterly*, vol. 32 (1975): 223–60; and Stephen Foster, *The Long Argument: English Puritanism and the Shaping of New England Culture, 1570–1700* (Chapel Hill: University of North Carolina Press, 1990).

52. Klausner, *The Messianic Idea in Israel*, 517.

53. Marjorie Reeves, *The Influence of Prophecy in the Later Middle Ages: A Study in Joachimism* (Oxford: Clarendon Press, 1969), 296.

54. Klausner, *The Messianic Idea in Israel*, 418. See also Sigmund Mowinckel, *He That Cometh*, trans. G. W. Anderson (Oxford: Basil Blackwell, 1959), 7: "The Messiah is he who shall restore Israel as a people, free her from her enemies, rule over her as a king, and bring other nations under her political and religious sway." To follow Harold Fisch: "The theme of salvation was for the Hebrew the theme of History, not of Metahistory"; *Jerusalem and Albion: The Hebraic Factor in Seventeenth-Century Literature* (London: Routledge & Kegan Paul, 1964), 95.

55. *Encyclopedia Judaica*, ed. C. Rott, 16 vols. (Jerusalem: Macmillan, 1971) s.v. "Redemption"; see also Hastings's *Dictionary of Religion and Ethics* under "Salvation (Jewish)."

56. *Encyclopedia Judaica*, s.v. "Messiah," vol. 11: 1407.

57. Scholem, "Toward an Understanding of the Messianic Idea," 1. Maimonides "regards the Messianic age as restorative and as a public event realized in the community," 31.

58. Norman Cohn, *The Pursuit of the Millennium: Revolutionary Millenarians and Mystical Anarchists of the Middle Ages*, rev. and exp. ed. (New York: Oxford University Press, 1970).

59. One such movement, Scholem adds, is the "radical wing of the Puritans"; "Toward an Understanding of the Messianic Idea," 16.

60. Bray, ed., *Documents of the English Reformation*, 613; see also Martin A. Noll, *Confessions and Catechisms of the Reformation* (Grand Rapids: Baker Book House, 1991).

61. Arthur C. Cochrane, ed., *Reformed Confessions of the Sixteenth Century* (Philadelphia: Westminster Press, 1966), 245–46. Cited also in Toon, ed., *Puritans, the Millennium and the Future of Israel*, 19. See also Firth, *The Apocalyptic Tradition*, 174–75.

62. Like Augustine, Jerome (ca. 342–420) was an opponent of chiliasm: his commentary on the messianic vision of Zechariah 14 derides the "deceptive hopes" of Jews, for whom the Feast of Tabernacles signified the earthly millennial reign. Jean Daniélou, *The Bible and the Liturgy* (Notre Dame, Ind.: University of Notre Dame Press, 1956), 338.

63. The English translation of 1643 is cited. Joseph Mede, *The Key of the Revelation, searched and demonstrated out of the Naturall and proper Characters of the Visions. With a Coment thereupon, according to the Rule of the same Key published in Latine by the Profoundly Learned Master Joseph Mede . . .* Translated into English by Richard More . . . With a Praeface written by Dr Twiss now Prolocutor in the present Assembly of Divines (London, 1643), 134. Among Mede's students at Cambridge were Milton and Henry More. On Mede's influence see Christianson, *Reformers and Babylon*, 93–132.

64. Assessing Brightman's importance in seventeenth-century millennial thinking, Avihu Zakai, like other historians of the period, ignores the well-documented Jewish influences on English and American Puritans. Their writings are not considered, even. It is not enough to say that "Brightman transformed the millennium into an attain-

able, historical goal to be realized in an immediate future by the saints and Christ under some terrestrial reign," as Zakai does. In Jewish messianism, the millennium was nothing if not a "historical" goal to be enjoyed under a "terrestrial reign." Nor *ex nihilo* did Brightman "infuse the millennium into time and history" (*Theocracy in Masssachusetts*, 87). If "Brightman envisaged the Kingdom of God to be within the framework of history" (90), he is following Jewish adventist writings. Zakai claims: "Without the eschatological and millennial context provided so well by Brightman, the Puritan migration to, and the Puritan commonwealth in, Massachusetts can hardly be completely understood" (*Theocracy in Massachusetts*, 101). But Brightman's "framework" was ready-made. Without the millennial context provided by *Jewish* writings, canonical and extracanonical, Puritan eschatology cannot be understood. Zakai's views are echoed in (or adumbrated by) his *Exile and Kingdom:* "With Brightman, therefore, the millennium was immersed in time and history" (50); "This was the sense of the imminent fulfillment of prophetic revelations within the boundaries of time and history, a sense of the millennium at hand, that Brightman infused into English apocalyptic tradition in the early seventeenth century" (53). Educated Puritans, who knew that the Catholic Church was dead set against chiliasm, were reading Jewish writings carefully for clues about the date of the millennium. For a mild corrective to Zakai, see Bozeman's chapter "Puritan Millennialism" in *To Live Ancient Lives*.

65. Increase Mather, *Dissertation Concerning the Future Conversion of the Jewish Nation*, 29–30.

66. Klausner, *The Messianic Idea in Israel*, 519.

67. See the collection of essays by several hands in the provocatively titled *Judaisms and Their Messiahs at the Turn of the Christian Era*, ed. Jacob Neusner, William S. Green, and Ernest Fredericks (Cambridge: Cambridge University Press, 1987).

68. Mowinckel, *He That Cometh*, 277.

69. Klausner, *The Messianic Idea in Israel*, 521.

70. We so read in the *Encyclopedia Judaica*, vol. 11, 1407.

71. See Méchoulan's introduction, *The Hope of Israel*, 50.

72. Compare Jonathan Edwards: "Besides the prophecies of the calling of the Jews, we have a remarkable seal of the fulfillment of this great event in providence by a thing that is a kind of continual miracle, viz. the preserving them a distinct [nation] when in such a dispersed condition for above sixteen hundred years. The world affords nothing like it—a remarkable hand of providence"; *A History of the Work of Redemption*, transc. and ed. John F. Wilson, vol. 9 of *The Works of Jonathan Edwards* (New Haven: Yale University Press, 1989), 447.

73. Increase Mather, *A Dissertation Concerning the Future Conversion of the Jewish Nation*, 11.

74. Oberman, "The Stubborn Jews," 132.

75. I am certainly not the first to identify the term "philo-semitism" as an example of doublespeak: Norma Perry, writing about pro-Jewish currents in seventeenth-century England, points to "a wave of sympathy, paradoxically called philo-semitism (paradoxically, since it involved the desire to convert the Jews to Christianity and thus put an end to Judaism) although many remained hostile": "Anglo-Jewry, the Law, Religious Conviction, and Self-interest (1655–1753)," *Journal of European Studies*,

vol. 14 (1984): 18. See also Jonathan Israel, *European Jewry in the Age of Mercantilism, 1550–1750* (Oxford: Clarendon Press, 1985).

76. The Genevan gloss to Romans 11:15 reads: "It shall come to passe that when the Iewes come to the Gospel, the world shall as it were quicken againe, and rise up from dead to life."

77. Thomas Brightman, "To the friendly reader," in "A Most Comfortable Exposition of the last and most difficult part of the Prophecy of Daniel," included in Brightman's *The revelation of Saint Iohn Illustrated with Analysis and Scholions. Wherein the sense is opened by Scripture: and the Events of things foretold, shewed by Histories Together with A most Comfortable Exposition of the last and most difficult part of the Prophecy of Daniel Wherein the restoring of the Jewes, and their calling to the faith of Christ, after the overthrow of their three last enemies, is set forth in lively colours* (Amsterdam, 1644), 298. Brightman died in 1607. *A Revelation of the Revelation* (without the exposition of Daniel) was first published abroad in 1615. In *The Wonder-Working Providence of Sions Saviour in New England* (1654), Edward Johnson depicts the conversion of the Jews in terms of dry bones coming to life: "And now you antient people of Israel look out of your Prison grates, let these Armies of the Lord Christ [in America] provoke you to acknowledge he is certainly come, to put life into your dry bones." Cited in Bercovitch, *The American Jeremiad*, 79.

78. Klausner, *The Messianic Idea in Israel*, 470.

79. Heiko A. Oberman, "Three Sixteenth-Century Attitudes toward Judaism: Reuchlin, Erasmus, and Luther," in *The Impact of the Reformation*, 87.

80. Smolinski, *"Israel Redivivus,"* 381.

81. See chapter 1 of the present study.

82. On "literal" and "spiritual" Israel, see Bercovitch, *The American Jeremiad*, 32–47.

83. Mede, *The Key of the Revelation*, 134–35.

84. Underwood, "The *Hope of Israel* in Early Modern Ethnography," 97. In Menasseh's *Vindicae Judaeorum* (London, 1656), he cites Isaac La Peyrère, the French millenarian: "For, as a most learned Christian of our time has written, in a French book, which he calleth *Rappel of the Iewes* (in which he makes the King of France to be their leader when they shall return to their country), the Iewes, saith he, shall be saved, for yet we expect a *second* coming of the same Messiah, and the Iewes believe that that coming is the *first* and not the second, and by that faith shall be saved; for that difference consists only in the circumstance of the time." Cited in Popkin, "Seventeenth-Century Millenarianism," 131, n. 37. In the phrase "the circumstance of the time," the second "the" is omitted in Popkin's citation, whereas in Underwood's précis of the same passage, a "the" is included, which makes more sense (Underwood, "The *Hope of Israel* in Early Modern Ethnography," 97).

85. Increase Mather, *A Dissertation Concerning the Future Conversion of the Jewish Nation*, 14.

86. Mowinckel, *He That Cometh*, 277. See also H. H. Rowley, *The Relevance of Apocalyptic: A Study of Jewish and Christian Apocalypses from Daniel to the Revelation*, rev. ed. (New York: Associated Press, 1964), 115–18.

87. Jacob R. Marcus, *The Colonial American Jew 1492–1776* (Detroit: Wayne State University Press, 1970), vol. 1, 303.

88. Cotton Mather, *Diary of Cotton Mather, 1681–1724*, 2 vols., *Collections of the Massachusetts Historical Society*, 7th ser. 7–8 (Boston, 1911–12), 1:200. Cited in Smolinski, "*Israel Redivivus*," 382.

89. One critic uses the word "obsession" to describe Cotton Mather's urge to convert Jews: "his ambition to be the means of converting a Jews to Christianity was very nearly an obsession for him"; Louis H. Feldman, "The Influence of Josephus on Cotton Mather's *Biblia Americana*: A Study in Ambiguity," in *Hebrew and the Bible in America,* ed. Goldman, 140.

90. Cotton Mather, *The Threefold Paradise of Cotton Mather* (an edition of "Triparadisus"), ed. Reiner Smolinski (Athens: University of Georgia Press, 1995), 314–15. To cite Smolinski's introduction to this text: "While Cotton Mather had originally subscribed to his father's orthodox position on the natural conversion of the Jews (Romans 11) as the most significant event to occur before the Second Coming, he abandoned this literalist mainstay of prophetic exegesis a few years before his death and joined the allegorical camp of Henry Hammond, John Lightfoot, and Richard Baxter, who insisted on a preterite reading of Paul's Epistle to the Romans" (5).

91. Increase Mather, *A Dissertation Concerning the Future Conversion of the Jewish Nation,* 18.

92. Ibid., 5.

93. Ibid., 26.

94. Bozeman, *To Live Ancient Lives,* 206–7, on Brightman's biblical eschatology.

95. Samuel Mather (Increase's eldest brother) agrees: Jews despise "the grosser sort of *Idolatry:* such an indelible Conviction as hath never been blotted out to this day. Insomuch, that their great stumbling Block at this day against the Christian Religion is, the Idolatry of the Popish Christians: For the poor blind Jews consider the Christian Religion no otherwise, but as corrupted with those Antichristian Abominations and Idolatries: And therefore their Conversion and Return is not to be expected till Antichrist, that great stumbling Block, be removed out of the way": *The Figures or Types of the Old Testament* (Dublin, 1683, 2d ed. London, 1705; reprint, New York: Johnson Reprint Corporation, 1969), 41.

96. Increase Mather, preface, *Some Important Truths About Conversion, Delivered in Sundry Sermons,* "To the Second Church and Congregation at Boston in New England" (London, 1674). "Do you consider what is here said concerning the absolute necessity of a true Conversion unto God in Christ, and the exceeding danger of living unprofitably under means of Grace, and that God's Spirit may soon give you over and then you are undone."

97. Arthur Hertzberg, "The New England Puritans and the Jews," in *Hebrew and the Bible in America,* ed. Goldman, 107. The same essay appears in *Israel and the Nations: Essays Presented in Honour of Shmuel Ettinger* (Jerusalem: The Historical Society of Israel and the Zalman Shazar Center for Jewish History, 1987).

98. The Church's opposition to chiliasm was also wrong: as Perry Miller wrote years

ago, Increase Mather was "further confirmed" in his chiliasm "by discovering the doctrine of the millennium to be that for which Satan has a particular spite, and 'that but few Papists have been Chiliasts'": *The New England Mind: From Colony to Province* (Cambridge, Mass.: Harvard University Press, 1953), 187.

99. To follow up connections between the Jesuits' missions in the New World and the Puritans' sense of urgency about converting the Jews, one might start with Marjorie Reeves, *Prophecy in the Later Middle Ages*, 274. See also Firth, *The Apocalyptic Tradition*, 64. A pamphlet that circulated among leaders of the Puritan migration to America, *General Observations for the Plantation of New England* (1629), includes: "To carrye the Gospel into those partes of the world, and to rayse a bullwarke against the kingdom of Antichrist which the Jesuites labour to rear up in all places of the worlde would obviously be a service to the Church of great Consequence" (cited in Zakai, *Theocracy in Massachusetts*, 62). Cotton Mather makes the equation between French Canada and Babylon: see Bercovitch, *The American Jeremiad*, 115n. Anti-Catholic rhetoric intensified in the eighteenth century: the Quebec Act, which guaranteed Roman Catholic inhabitants of Quebec the right to their religion, could be nothing more than a plot to place the Scarlet Whore in America: see James West Davidson, *The Logic of Millennial Thought: Eighteenth-Century New England* (New Haven: Yale University Press, 1977), especially chapter 6, "Revelation and Revolution." See also Richard Baxter's widely read *A Key for Catholicks, To open the Jugling of the Jesuits, and satisfie all that are but truly willing to understand whether the cause of the Roman or Reformed Churches be of God; and to leave the Reader unexcusable that after this will be a Papist* (London, 1659).

100. Increase Mather, *A Dissertation Concerning the Future Conversion of the Jewish Nation*, 13.

101. Scholem, "Toward an Understanding of the Messianic Idea," 11. Compare the *parousia* parables in Luke 12:35–40.

102. Robert M. Healey, "The Jew in Seventeenth-Century Protestant Thought," *Church History*, vol. 46, no. 1 (March 1977): 73.

103. As every student of Puritanism knows, Christopher Hill has written a book called *The World Turned Upside Down: Radical Ideas During the English Revolution* (Harmondsworth: Penguin, 1991); one of the epigraphs is taken from Isaiah 24:1: "Behold, the Lord maketh the earth empty, and maketh it waste, and turneth it upside down."

104. Compare Mather's *The Mystery of Israel's Salvation*: "Observe the Scripture and you will find, that when God hath brought desolating and astonishing plagues upon the earth it hath been chiefly for the sin of persecution. Hence come *overturnings, overturnings, overturnings*, hence come Wars, Plagues, Famines, Fires, and eternal desolations" (67).

105. See John Davenport's "An Epistle to the Reader," which introduces Mather's *The Mystery of Israel's Salvation*: "The kingdom of Christ hath indeed been set up by his effectual operation of the spirit in the Ministry of the Gospel, from the first publishing of the Gospel, according to *Psal.* 24.7, 9. & 110.2, 3. But there is another, a *Political Kingdom of Christ* to be set up in the last times, foretold by *Dan.* in chap. 2 . . .

and by the Angel *Gabriel* unto the Virgin *Mary* . . . and by the Apostle *John*, in *Rev* 19. and 20."

106. Scholem, "Toward an Understanding of the Messianic Idea," 30.

Chapter Four

1. *The Complete ArtScroll Machzor, Succos*, trans. and commentary by Rabbi Avie Gold, in collaboration with Rabbi Meir Zlotowitz and Rabbi Nosson Scherman (Brooklyn, N.Y.: Mesorah Publications, 1989), 93.

2. Mason I. Lowance, introduction, Samuel Mather, *The Figures or Types of the Old Testament* (London, 1705; reprint, New York: Johnson Reprint Corporation, 1969), v–vi.

3. Samuel Mather, *The Figures or Types of the Old Testament*, 10; 8. Mather's discussion of the Feast of Tabernacles can be found on pages 424–34 of this edition, hereafter cited in the notes as *Figure or Types*.

4. Mather, *Figure or Types*, 324.

5. Gerald Bray, ed., *Documents of the English Reformation* (Cambridge: James Clarke, 1994), 501. The passage cited appears in chapter 19 of the Westminster Confession.

6. Mather, *Figures or Types*, 277–78.

7. Ibid., 41.

8. See *Jewish Encyclopedia*, ed. I. Singer, 12 vols. (New York, 1901–1906) s.v. "Tabernacles, feast of."

9. C. H. Dodd, *The Interpretation of the Fourth Gospel* (Cambridge: Cambridge University Press, 1953; reprint, 1988), 350–51.

10. Mather, *Figures or Types*, 425.

11. Ibid., 426–27.

12. Ibid., 432, 427. Compare Joseph Mede's *Discourse* on the Feast of Tabernacles, which Samuel Mather has more or less plagiarized: "At the Birth of Christ every man, woman and child was to goe to be taxed at the City whereto they belonged, whither some had long journeys: But the middle of Winter was not fitting for such a business, especially for women with child and children to travel in: Therefore Christ could not be born in the depth of Winter.

"Again, At the time of Christ's Birth the Shepherds lay abroad watching with their flocks in the night-time; but this was not likely to be in the middle of Winter. And if any shall think the Winter-wind was not so extreme in those parts, let him remember the words of Christ in the Gospel, *Pray that your flight be not in the Winter* [Matt 24:20]. If the Winter was so bad a time to flee in, it seems no fit time for Shepherds to lye in the Fields in, and Women and Children to travel in.

"They [Chronologers and some early Fathers] conclude therefore, That the Birth of Christ was in September." Joseph Mede, *Discourse* XLV (on Deut. 16:16–17), in *The Works of the Pious and Profoundly Learned Joseph Mede*, ed. John Worthington (London, 1664), vol. 1 of 2 vols., 350–51.

13. Edward Taylor, *Upon the Types of the Old Testament*, 2 vols., ed. Charles W. Mignon (Lincoln: University of Nebraska Press, 1989); cited in the body of the chap-

ter as *Types* followed by volume and page number, or simply by volume and page number.

14. See Harald Riesenfeld, *Jésus Transfiguré* (Copenhagen: Ejnar Munksgaard, 1947). Citing a seminal essay by Israël Lévi on the sacrifice of Isaac, published in 1912, Riesenfeld notes "l'association faite entre les cornes du bélier qui, dans le récit, intervient comme substitut d'Isaac et le *sophar* du rituel du jour de l'An" (88). On the eschatological significance of the sacrifice of Isaac, he also mentions "la croyance qu'on sonnera de la corne de bélier au commencement du siècle à venir" (94). Perhaps the most important and accessible essay on the relation between the sacrifice of Isaac and the crucifixion is one by Geza Vermes, "Redemption and Genesis XXII: The Binding of Isaac and the Sacrifice of Jesus," in *Scripture and Tradition in Judaism: Haggadic Studies* (Leiden: E. J. Brill, 1961), 193–227; on the *shofar*, see 213–14.

15. With reference to Gregory of Nyssa's sermon on the Nativity, Jean Daniélou writes, "The Gradual of the Second Mass of Christmas contains three verses from Psalm CXVII [118 AV]—and precisely those which our author [Gregory] applies to the nativity": *The Bible and the Liturgy* (Notre Dame, Ind.: University of Notre Dame Press, 1956), 347.

16. PG 46, 1128–49. For the English version of Gregory's nativity sermon I am wholly indebted to Robert (C. T. R.) Hayward of the University of Durham, without whom the present chapter could not have been written. Infelicities of phrasing are mine, not his: Dr. Hayward, sight-reading from the Greek text, dictated his translation while I wrote it down. The authenticity of Gregory's nativity sermon has been defended by patristic scholars. See Johannes Quasten, *Patrology* (Westminster, Md.: Christian Classics, 1990), vol. 3, 277: "The Christmas sermon *In natalem Christi* (MG 46, 1128–49), highly important for the history of the feast of the Nativity, was delivered on the 25th of December, 386. H. Usener denies its authenticity (*Weihnachtsfest*, p. 247); K. Holl (*Amphilochius v. Ikon.*, p. 231) defended it and has found approval." On the authenticity of the Christmas sermon, see G. Soell, "Die Mariologie der Kappadozier im Lichte der Dogmengeschichte," *Theologische Quartalschrift* (Stuttgart), vol. 131 (1951): 178–88. For a French translation of one small section of Gregory's nativity sermon, and for valuable notes defending its authenticity, see Jean Daniélou, "Le Tabernacle Restauré," in "Notes sur Trois Textes Eschatologiques de Saint Grégoire de Nysse," *Recherches de Sciences Religieuse*, vol. 30, no. 3 (July 1940): 353–56.

17. Jean Daniélou, *The Bible and the Liturgy*, 347.

18. Henry Ainsworth, *Annotations upon the Five Bookes of Moses, the Booke of the Psalmes, and the Song of Songs, or Canticles* (London, 1627), on Leviticus 23:34. In the writing of this and the foregoing chapters I have used with pleasure at least five different copies of Ainsworth's *Annotations* (held at Palace Green Library at the University of Durham, at the Fisher Library at the University of Toronto, and at Oxford's Bodleian Library). Sometimes annotations on the Psalms and on Canticles are bound in with commentaries on the Pentateuch; sometimes the Psalms appear alone; sometimes only one or two books of the Pentateuch are printed with the commentary on Psalms; sometimes Ainsworth's metrical Psalms are added at the end of the book. But apart from the odd corruption, I have not discovered a significant variant in the text.

Therefore, when citing Ainsworth, I simply refer to the biblical text under discussion; there is no point referring the reader to page numbers.

19. See Joseph Klausner, *The Messianic Idea in Israel: From Its Beginnings to the Completion of the Mishnah*, trans. from the third Hebrew edition by W. F. Stinespring (London: Allen and Unwin, 1956), 425. See also Riesenfeld, *Jésus Transfiguré*, who cites Israël Lévi's discussion of the Book of Jubilees: "la création du monde et l'avènement du Messie [sont] dans le mois de Tisri" (89).

20. Riesenfeld, *Jésus Transfiguré*, 52.

21. Robert E. Lerner, "Refreshment of the Saints: The Time after Antichrist as a Station for Earthly Progress in Medieval Thought," *Traditio* 32 (1976), 97–144, 101.

22. PL 25, 1536 A; *In Zach* III, 14; cited by Daniélou, *The Bible and the Liturgy*, 338. See Daniélou's essay, "Le symbolisme eschatologique de la Fête des Tabernacles," *Irénikon* XXXI (1958): 19–40, 22: "Cette interprétation messianique de la fête s'est continuée dans le judaïsme jusque dans les premiers siècles chrétiens. Saint Jérôme . . . expose que les Juifs voient dans la Fête des Tabernacles, «par une fallacieuse espérance, la figure des chose qui arriveront dans le règne millénaire»."

23. Lerner, "Refreshment of the Saints," 102; see also John P. O'Connell, *The Eschatology of St. Jerome* (Mundelein, Ill.: Apud aedes Seminarii Sanctae Mariae ad Lacum, 1948), 64–72.

24. Cited in Lerner, "Refreshment of the Saints," 97.

25. C. T. R. Hayward, *Saint Jerome's Hebrew Questions on Genesis*, trans. and with an introduction and commentary by C. T. R. Hayward (Oxford: Clarendon Press, 1995), 1. According to Geza Vermes, Jerome "even complains that one of his Hebrew masters, a rabbi from Lydda, was charging an exhorbitant fee for his lessons on Job": *Jesus and the World of Judaism* (London: SCM Press, 1983), 59.

26. Jean Daniélou, *The Theology of Jewish Christianity*, trans. and ed. John A. Baker (London: Darton, Longman & Todd, 1964), 382. See also Geza Vermes, "Redemption and Genesis XXII," 214.

27. Methodius, *Banquet* IX, 5:120; cited in Daniélou, *The Bible and the Liturgy*, 337.

28. Increase Mather, *The Mystery of Christ Opened and Applyed* (Boston, 1686), 84–85. Edward Taylor knew the Mathers intimately. When in 1723 Increase Mather died, Taylor wrote a commemorative poem, whose opening lines allude to the death of Richard Mather in 1669: "Nigh Sixty years ago I wept in verse / When on my shoulder lay thy Father's hearse." Edward Johnson, ed., *The Poetical Works of Edward Taylor* (Princeton, N.J.: Princeton University Press, 1971), 223.

29. Jonathan Edwards, *Some Thoughts Concerning the Revival*, in *The Great Awakening*, ed. C. C. Goen, vol. 4 of *The Works of Jonathan Edwards* (New Haven: Yale University Press, 1972), 359–62.

30. Vermes, "Redemption and Genesis XXII," 214.

31. This may be the place to insert a note about Revelation and its interpreters. "Revelation's continuity with the Old Testament . . . is precisely what offends some modern critics," writes Richard Bauckham. "Rudolf Bultmann, in a famous phrase, condemned it as 'weakly Christianized Judaism'. But the phrase betrays the influence of the tendency of nineteenth- and early-twentieth-century Christianity to deny its

Jewish roots. It makes the extraordinary suggestion that only what is not Jewish is really Christian and that Christianity somehow came into being by negating Judaism": Richard Bauckham, *The Theology of the Book of Revelation* (Cambridge: Cambridge Univerity Press, 1993), 147–48. Readers may overlook allusions to the Jewish Feast of Tabernacles in Revelation: the plentiful water supply, the perpetual light, the tabernacle of God, the redeemed with their palm branches, and so on. As Daniélou confirms, "l'Apocalypse est remplie d'allusions à la Fête des Tabernacles" ("Le Symbolisme eschatologique de la Fête des Tabernacles," 26). See Bauckham's meticulous readings of Revelation and its relation to Jewish writings, biblical and extrabiblical: *The Climax of Prophecy: Studies on the Book of Revelation* (Edinburgh: T & T Clark, 1993).

32. Another *Discourse* by Mede is acknowledged by Mather at one point: *Figures or Types*, 163–64.

33. Joseph Mede, *Discourse* XLV (on Deut. 16:16–17), in *The Works of the Pious and Profoundly Learned Joseph Mede*, 350. Mede's "Works" were first collected in 1648; apparently that edition was part of Edward Taylor's library. I cite the enlarged edition of 1663–1664.

34. Needless to say, Edward Taylor despised Nestorianism: see Taylor's *Christographia*, ed. Norman S. Grabo (New Haven: Yale University Press, 1962), 86, passim.

35. Calvin, *Institutes of the Christian Religion*, ed. John T. McNeill, trans. Ford Lewis Battles, vols. 20, 21 of the Library of Christian Classics (London: SCM Press, 1961), II.xiv.4. To explore Calvin's christology is very much beyond my competence. The main focus of this chapter is Taylor's *sukkah* christology, but even this brief allusion to Calvin's writings may clear some ground.

36. E. David Willis, *Calvin's Catholic Christology: The Function of the So-called Extra Calvinisticum in Calvin's Theology* (Leiden: E. J. Brill, 1966), 64: "Even when Calvin says the Son 'indwelt' the flesh or 'clothed' himself with the flesh, he explicitly wishes to avoid Nestorianism. He obviously considers that what makes one Nestorian is not the use of such language in itself, but the misuse of this terminology to suggest something less than the unity of the two natures into One Person. To put on, or to clothe oneself in, human nature is uniquely descriptive of the Incarnation, for Calvin."

37. François Wendel, *Calvin: Origins and Development of His Religious Thought*, trans. Philip Mairet (Durham, N.C.: Labyrinth, 1987), 218, 219, 222.

38. See the extended entry for *skene* in the *Theologicical Dictionary of the New Testament*, ed. Gerhard Kittel and Gerhard Friedrich, 9 vols. (Grand Rapids, Mich.: Eerdmans, 1974).

39. *The Poems of Edward Taylor*, ed. Donald E. Stanford (Chapel Hill: University of North Carolina Press, 1963, reprint 1989), 125–27.

40. The Babylonian Talmud tractate *Sukkah* prescribes the size of the booth: its walls cannot be more than twenty cubits high; otherwise a man does "not 'know' that he is dwelling in a booth, since his eye does not descry it" (the covering, that is). How do we know that a *sukkah* cannot be higher that twenty cubits? Rabbi Zera cites Isaiah: "And there shall be a booth [*sukkah*] for a shadow in the daytime from the heat" (4:6;

the AV reads "tabernacle"). "With a booth up to twenty cubits high, a man sits in the shade of the booth," the rabbi says, referring to the roof covering; "but with one higher than twenty cubits, he sits not in the shade of the booth, but in the shade of its walls" (*Sukkah* 2b).

41. See the entry for "Tabernacles, Feast of" in *The Jewish Encyclopedia*, ed. I. Singer, 12 vols. (New York: Ktav, 1901–1906), whence information about the *sukkah* is taken; see also *Encyclopedia Judaica*, ed. C. Roth, 16 vols. (Jerusalem: Macmillan, 1971) s.v. "Sukkot."

42. Daniélou, *The Bible and the Liturgy*, 334; Riesenfeld, *Jésus Transfiguré*, 189. See also Arthur Michael Ramsey, *The Glory of God and the Transfiguration of Christ* (London: Longmans, Green, 1949), 103.

43. Jean Daniélou, *From Shadows to Reality: Studies in Biblical Typology of the Fathers*, trans. Dom Wolstan Hibberd (London: Burns & Oates, 1960), 155.

44. Elucidating the "eternal tabernacles" of Luke 16:9, Daniélou connects them to the eschatological booths of the Feast of Tabernacles, noting that the same expression (*aionai scenai*) appears frequently in Revelation "pour désigner l'habitation des justes dans le ciel. . . . Or l'*Apocalypse* est remplie d'allusions à la Fête des Tabernacles" ("Le Symbolisme eschatologique de la Fête des Tabernacles," 26).

45. H. St. John Thackeray, *The Septuagint and Jewish Worship: A Study in Origins*, The Schweich Lectures, 1920, 2d ed. (London: Oxford University Press, for the British Academy, 1923), 65.

46. Vermes, "Redemption and Genesis XXII," 214. See Klausner, *The Messianic Idea in Israel*, 470–71.

47. On the subject of the water libations of the Feast of Tabernacles, and citing John 7:37, Taylor writes: "They had a Custom on this day to fetch much Water out of the River Shilo, a type of Christ, & the Priests poured it on the Altar, & they then Sung Isa.12.3. With joy ye shall draw water out of the Wells of Salvation. It is thought, that Christ in respect unto that Custom presents himselfe to them now on this day as the true Shilo to draw the Waters of Life out of, & presents himselfe also, as the thing designd in the feast of Tabernacles . . ." (*Types* 2, 533).

48. Daniélou, *The Bible and the Liturgy*, 342–43.

49. Ibid., 336.

50. Ibid., 345.

51. In passing, Karl Keller says about Taylor's Meditation 24, second series: "The Tabernacle becomes the body of Christ; it is a structure made of '[in]Carnation leafes,' a cross of pine boughs, staples for crucifying nails, and repentance for rent"; "'The World Slickt Up in Types': Edward Taylor as a Version of Emerson," in *Typology and Early American Literature*, ed. Sacvan Bercovitch ([Amherst]: University of Massachusetts Press, 1972), 177.

52. Taylor supposes that "the Myrtle is an Emblem of the Church in a flourishing State . . . as opposed to her enemies & adversities, & the Angell or rather Christ himselfe was seen among the Myrtle Trees Zech.1.8. to import Christs presence with his Church" (*Types* 2, 529). On Christ as an angel, see chapter 2 of the present study (on Jonathan Edwards).

53. Henry Ainsworth, *Annotations upon the Five Bookes of Moses, the Booke of the Psalmes, and the Song of Songs, or, Canticles* (London, 1627), on Leviticus 23:40.

54. See Daniélou, "Le symbolisme eschatolique," 29. To follow the *Encyclopedia Judaica*, containers for the *etrog* "most frequently take the form of a rectangular box ranging in style from the simple to the baroque. . . . In Eastern Europe the etrog was very often kept in a silver box." I have seen such a box, about four inches square, made of hammered silver, with a sort of peaked cover, like a tent. There are also palm-leaf holders—elongated receptacles for the *lulab*—which are "traditionally made of knotted palm leaves."

55. Like Riesenfeld in *Jésus Transfiguré*, Daniélou hears in the transfiguration scene "an explicit allusion to the Feast of Tabernacles" (*The Bible and the Liturgy*, 339).

56. Riesenfeld, *Jésus Transfiguré*, 189.

57. Samson H. Levey, *The Messiah: An Aramaic Interpretation*, The Messianic Exegesis of the Targum (Cincinnati: Hebrew Union College, 1974), 131. See *1 Enoch* 60; see also *Sanhedrin* 99a.

58. Karen Rowe gives a close reading of Taylor's Meditation 24, second series: "By blending secular and scriptural images, such words as 'tabernacle,' 'house,' 'buttond,' 'Cabbin'd,' and 'Tent,' recreate the mystery of Christ's incarnation, an emwombing and embodying within mortal flesh. And the pun on 'Carnation leafe' and 'Incarnation' succinctly links Christ's assumed humanity to the motivating cause, for when Adam and Eve fell into shameful disgrace, they clothed themselves with leaves." *Saint and Sinner: Edward Taylor's Typology and the Poetics of Meditation* (Cambridge: Cambridge University Press, 1986), 123.

59. Gold et al., ed., *The Complete ArtScroll Machzor, Succos*, 259.

60. Cited in Thackeray, *The Septuagint and Jewish Worship*, 69.

61. Ibid., 69.

62. Prayers in the daily services for the Feast of Tabernacles allude to the verse from Amos 9. Sometimes the fallen Sukkah is compared with the ruined Temple at Jerusalem.

63. I suspect that Puritan commentators have conflated the *lulab* (palm, willow, and myrtle) and the so-called *hoshana*-bundle of willow twigs, which on the seventh day of the Feast is either waved or beaten on the ground. See Mishnah *Sukkah* 4.3.

64. So far as I can make out, Ainsworth's annotations of the Psalms do not vary from printing to printing or format to format. *Annotations upon the Book of Psalmes, where the Hebrew words and sentences are compared with, and explained by the Greek and Chaldee versions: but chiefly by conference with the holy Scriptures*, 2d ed. [Amsterdam] 1617).

65. Ainsworth, annotations on Psalm 45.

66. Taylor follows Joseph Mede closely: Mede writes, "For while they gathered and carried *the Boughs* whereof they made their *Tabernacles*, there used a kind of Litanie to be sung, in which the people continually cried *Hosanna, Hosanna*, that is, *Save now*; which was so usual, that in time the Feast, and Boughs, and all came to be called Hosanna's: whence came the cry of the people in the Gospel, when they cut down boughs to honour our Saviour's riding upon an *Asse, Hosanna to the Son of David, Hosanna in the Highest*. For though it were at another time of the year than the *Feast of Tabernacles*, yet the *carrying of Boughs* put them in minde of the accustomed acclama-

tion at that Feast. All which seems of purpose so to be ordered by the providence of the Almighty, to shew, First, what this ceremony of *Tabernacles* aimed at, namely the mysterie of our Redemption by God in the *Tabernacle* of our flesh; or the *Incarnation* of Christ, which is that which made him *Jesus*, a Saviour, and us to cry unto him by Faith, *Hosanna, Save now*" (Mede, *Discourse*, 351).

67. Augustine, *Homilies on The Gospel According to St. John*, vol. 1 (Oxford, 1848), 434.

68. As cited earlier; Mather, *Figure or Types*, 425. In January, 1668, when Mather wrote that sermon, thousands of Jews were indeed passing through Europe toward Palestine to greet Sabbatai Zevi, the false Messiah.

69. Franz Rosenzweig, *The Star of Redemption*, trans. from the second edition of 1930 by William W. Hallo (1921; reprint, Notre Dame, Ind.: University of Notre Dame Press, 1985), 367. The link made between the stable and the *sukkah* deserves close attention.

Afterword

1. R. A. Markus, "Presuppositions of the Typological Approach to Scripture," *Church Quarterly Review* 158 (1957): 444.

2. Gerald Bray, ed., *Documents of the English Reformation* (Cambridge: James Clarke, 1994), 501. (Chapter 19 of the Westminster Confession.)

3. Oscar Cullmann, *Christ and Time: The Primitive Christian Conception of Time and History*, trans. Floyd V. Filson (1951; reprint, London: SCM Press, 1957), 134.

4. Markus, "Presuppositions," 447.

5. Of course I am alluding to Erich Auerbach's "'Figura,'" trans. Ralph Manheim, *Scenes from the Drama of European Literature* (Minneapolis: University of Minnesota Press, 1984), 29.

6. Markus, "Presuppositions," 446.

7. Augustine, PL 34, col. 625; cited in J. N. D. Kelly, *Early Christian Doctrines*, 2d ed. (London: Adam and Charles Black, 1960), 69.

8. Cited in Mason I. Lowance, Jr., *The Language of Canaan: Metaphor and Symbol in New England from the Puritans to the Transcendentalists* (Cambridge, Mass.: Harvard University Press, 1980), 162–63. See also Mason I. Lowance, Jr., "Cotton Mather's *Magnalia* and the Metaphors of Biblical History," in *Typology and Early American Literature*, ed. Sacvan Bercovitch ([Amherst]: University of Massachusetts Press, 1972), 139. Appended to the collected of essays is an annotated bibliography.

9. Samuel Mather, *The Figures or Types of the Old Testament* (1705; reprint, New York: Johnson Reprint Corporation, 1969), 10, 8.

10. Origen, *Hom. in Lev.* 1.1; cited in Beryl Smalley, *The Study of the Bible in the Middle Ages*, 2d rev. ed. (Oxford: Basil Blackwell, 1952), 1.

11. K. J. Woollcombe, "The Biblical Origins and Patristic Development of Typology," in G. W. H. Lampe and K. J. Woollcombe, *Essays on Typology* (London: SCM Press, 1957), 24, 72.

12. Cullmann, *Christ and Time*, 24.

13. Cullmann, *Christ and Time*, 25.

14. Edward Taylor, *Upon the Types of the Old Testament*, 2 vols., ed. Charles W. Mignon (Lincoln: University of Nebraska Press, 1989), 2, 529.

15. Taylor, *Upon the Types of the Old Testament*, 2, 707.

16. Increase Mather, *Some Important Truths About Conversion, Delivered in Sundry Sermons* (London, 1674), 151. To bring the model up to date: in Walter Lewis Wilson's popular, helter-skelter *Dictionary of Biblical Types*, published in 1957 and reprinted in 1990 (Grand Rapids: Eerdmans), Psalm 69:22 is glossed from the same christocentric point of view: "The Lord Jesus Christ is speaking here [Wilson claims] and asking His Father to change the plans of the enemies," 420.

17. Samuel Mather, *Figures or Types*, 15.

18. R. P. C. Hanson, *Allegory and Event: A Study of the Sources and Significance of Origen's Interpretation of Scripture* (London: SCM Press, 1959), 77.

19. Elsewhere, making reference to Paul de Man and other literary theorists, I discuss the paradigm in more detail; Linda Munk, "Giving Umbrage: The Song of Songs which is Whitman's," *The Trivial Sublime: Theology and American Poetics* (London: Macmillan; New York: St. Martin's, 1992), 66–67, esp. 72–74.

20. C. T. R. Hayward, *Saint Jerome's Hebrew Questions on Genesis*, trans. and with an introduction and commentary by C. T. R. Hayward (Oxford: Clarendon Press, 1995), 100–101.

21. Justin Martyr, *Dialogue with Trypho, a Jew*, chap. 61; in *The Ante-Nicene Fathers*, vol. 1, ed. Alexander Roberts and James Donaldson (New York: Scribner's, 1913); reprint of the Edinburgh edition.

22. Origen, *Contra Celsum* v. 37; cited in *The Early Christian Fathers*, ed. and trans. Henry Bettenson (Oxford: Oxford University Press, 1956), 241.

23. R. P. C. Hanson, "Biblical Exegesis in the Early Church," *The Cambridge History of the Bible*, vol. 1, *From the Beginnings to Jerome*, ed. P. R. Ackroyd and C. F. Evans (Cambridge: Cambridge University Press, 1970), 416.

24. The term "typological allegory" appears in John MacQueen, *Allegory* (London: Methuen, 1970), 18 (The Critical Idiom). Charles W. Mignon uses "allegorical typology"; introduction, Edward Taylor, *Upon the Types of the Old Testament*, vol. 1, xli. The other terms are cited by Morton Bloomfield, "Allegory as Interpretation," *New Literary History* 3 (1972): 301–17, 307.

25. W. H. Auden, "The Meditation of Simeon," *For the Time Being* (London: Faber and Faber, 1945), 108.

26. Jean Daniélou, ever concerned to reconcile Judaism and Christianity, or to acknowledge Christianity's debt to Judaism, describes "the eschatological typology of Judaism," but that phrase too confounds models of thought. Christian "eschatological typology" must refer to the incarnation (the Parousia is the second, not the first, advent of Christ). Daniélou writes: "Judaism knew an eschatological typology . . . it freely acknowledges that events in Jewish history are types of the end of time. What it will not accept is that they have been fulfilled in Jesus Christ": *From Shadows to Reality*, 234–35. In the end, I think, nothing is accomplished by discussing Jewish messianism in Christian terms.

27. David Daube, *The New Testament and Rabbinic Judaism* (London: Athlone

Press, 1956), 290. See *Sanhedrin* 97b–98a; see also Gershom Scholem, "Toward an Understanding of the Messianic Idea," in *The Messianic Idea in Judaism* (New York: Schocken, 1971).

28. Joseph Klausner, *The Messianic Idea in Israel: From Its Beginning to the Completion of the Mishnah*, trans. from the third Hebrew edition by W. F. Stinespring (London: Allen and Unwin, 1956), 427.

29. Thomas Brightman, "To the friendly reader," in "A Most Comfortable Exposition of the last and most difficult part of the Prophecy of Daniel." This is included in Brightman's *The revelation of Saint Iohn Illustrated with Analysis and Scholions. Wherein the sense is opened by Scripture: and the Events of things foretold, shewed by Histories Together with A most Comfortable Exposition of the last and most difficult part of the Prophecy of Daniel Wherein the restoring of the Jewes, and their calling to the faith of Christ, after the overthrow of their three last enemies, is set forth in lively colours* (Amsterdam, 1644), 298.

30. Cotton Mather, *The Threefold Paradise of Cotton Mather* (an edition of "Triparadisus"), ed. Reiner Smolinski (Athens: University of Georgia Press, 1995), 29.

31. In a short piece about "Conversion Wars," *The New York Times Magazine* remarks that "the Southern Baptist Convention has re-upped its efforts to reel in Jews": Sunday, July 21, 1996, 9.

32. David S. Katz, *Philo-Semitism and the Readmission of the Jews to England 1603–1655* (Oxford: Clarendon Press, 1982). As I remark in a note to chapter 3, I am not the first to identify the term "philo-semitism" as doublespeak. See Norma Perry: "Anglo-Jewry, the Law, Religious Conviction, and Self-interest (1655–1753)," *Journal of European Studies*, vol. 14 (1984): 18.

33. Frances A. Yates, "Science, Salvation, and the Cabala," in *Ideas and Ideals in the North European Renaissance*, vol. 3 (London: Routledge & Kegan Paul, 1984), 247–55, 251. (Review first published in *New York Review of Books*, May 27, 1976.)

34. Taylor, *Upon the Types of the Old Testament*, 2, 596, 601.

35. Cullmann, *Christ and Time*, 145.

36. Cited in Leonhard Goppelt, *Typos: The Typological Interpretation of the Old Testament in the New*, trans. Donald H. Madvig (Grand Rapids: Eerdmans, 1982), 7. This important study of the typological method was first published in German in 1939.

37. Markus, "Presuppositions," 450.

38. Erich Auerbach, *Mimesis: The Representation of Reality in Western Literature*, trans. Willard Trask (1953; reprint, Princeton, N.J.: Princeton University Press,1974), 158.

39. *The Threefold Paradise of Cotton Mather* (an edition of "Triparadisus"), ed. Reiner Smolinski, 26; citing Mather's "Problema Theologicum," MS American Antiquarian Society, 1703. "Until late in his life [until 1726], Cotton Mather held fast to the premillennialist tenets of the literal restoration of the Jewish nation, whose return to the Holy Land was foretold in Paul's Epistle to the Romans. Virtually all seventeenth- and early eighteenth-century millennialists on both sides of the Atlantic agreed that even though the Jews were still languishing in their Diaspora, Jehovah had not forgotten his chosen people and would, in due time, restore them to their once-elevated position among the nations": Reiner Smolinski, introduction, *The Threefold Paradise*, 21.

Index